Das Internationale Design Jahrbuch 2001/2002

Das Internationale Design Jahrbuch

© deutschsprachige Ausgabe:
bangert verlag
Verlagsbüro Schopfheim
Blütenweg 10,
D-79650 Schopfheim
fon 07622.67080 fax 07622.64618
e-mail: hello@bangertverlag.com
www.bangertverlag.com

© 2001 Calmann & King Ltd
71 Great Russell Street
London WC1B 3BP
fon +44 20 7430 8850
fax: +44 20 7430 8880
e-mail: enquiries@calmann-king.co.uk
www.laurence-king.com

Nach einer Idee von Stuart Durant
Kommentare und Einleitungen:
Jennifer Hudson
Redaktion: Paul Harron
Assistenz: Helen McFarland
Übersetzung:
Dr. Jeremy Gaines
Petra Soukup

All rights reserved. No part of this publication may be reproduced or transmitted in any form or by any means, electronic or mechanical, including photocopy, recording or any information storage and retrieval system, without permission in writing from the publisher.

ISBN 3-925560-39-4

Das Internationale Design Jahrbuch 2001/2002

Herausgeber: Michele De Lucchi

Einleitung: Jeremy Myerson

Redaktion: Jennifer Hudson

Design: Lovegrove Associates

bangert verlag

Inhalt

EINLEITUNG	6
MÖBEL	14
LICHT	86
TISCHDEKOR	126
TEXTILIEN	158
PRODUKTE	178
DESIGNERBIOGRAFIEN und Register	226
HERSTELLERADRESSEN und Register	234

Michele De Lucchi
Leuchtenfeld
Prototyp, 1994

Einleitung
Jeremy Myerson

Im Pantheon des modernen italienischen Designs gehört Michele De Lucchi sicherlich zu den ganz Grossen. Oft wird er als die kreative Brücke zwischen den Pionieren der Nachkriegszeit und der zeitgenössischen Designszene gesehen. Der Bogen lässt sich immerhin von Ettore Sottsass und Achille Castiglioni über Andrea Branzi, Alessandro Mendini bis De Lucchi spannen. Er begreift seine Rolle als Wegbereiter aus einer eher transnationalen Perspektive. In einer Pause – während seiner mühseligen Auswahlarbeit für das Internationale Design Jahrbuch 2001 in London – schaute De Lucchi vom Lichtkasten auf, strich sich durch seinen auffälligen, lehrmeisterhaft wirkenden Bart, schaute mich über den Rand seiner Brille an und verkündete: „Meine Berufung ist es nicht, primär Architekt oder Designer zu sein, vielmehr geht es darum, eine Brücke zwischen Industrie und Humanität zu schlagen."

Schon sehr lange interessiert sich De Lucchi für die Vermittlung zwischen der zynischen Logik des Unternehmertums, wie er es nennt, und einer Welt, die eine grössere Sinnhaftigkeit in der Materialität der Objekte sucht. In der Auswahl für die jetzige Ausgabe des Design Jahrbuchs spielte das sicherlich eine Rolle. Jede Idee, die sich als gut durchdacht und funktionell erwies, wurde positiv bewertet. Alles, was in irgendeiner Form dem menschlichen Bedürfnis entgegenzustehen schien, landete im Papierkorb, ganz gleich, wie gut es sich vermarkten lassen würde.

Alessandro Mendini wurde einmal gebeten, seine Bewunderung für Michele de Lucchi in fünf Punkten zusammenzufassen. Seine lakonische Antwort reflektierte De Lucchis Philosophie und Leistung auf signifikante Art und Weise. Mendini nannte an erster Stelle die Klarheit, die den Ideen De Lucchis von Anfang an innewohnt, zweitens die Unabhängigkeit seiner Formensprache in der Zeit nach Memphis und der Bewegung in den achtziger Jahren, die seinen internationalen Status festigte. An dritter Stelle erwähnte Mendini De Lucchis Organisationstalent, wie es sich in seiner erfolgreichen Designstudie äussert und in seiner Bereitschaft, jungen Designern immer einen Platz in seinem Team einzuräumen. Viertens bewunderte er De Lucchis Fähigkeit, Formen zu entwerfen, die sich auch in der Übertragung auf grosse Formate bewährten und somit die Grenzen zwischen Design und Architektur überschreiten. An fünfter und letzter Stelle hob er De Lucchis Sinn für Poesie hervor, was er vor allem in den gelungenen Gestaltungen zum Thema Wohnumfeld dokumentiert.

Klarheit, Unabhängigkeit, Organisation, Maßstab und Poesie sind tatsächlich die Merkmale von De Lucchis Arbeit. In vielen Aspekten seines professionellen Schaffens kommen diese Vorzüge zum Tragen. Sie sind auch erkennbar in der Auswahl der Arbeiten in den Bereichen Möbel, Leuchten, Tischdekor, Textilien und Produkte, die De Lucchi für diesen Band so sorgfältig getroffen hat. So ist die Auswahl De Lucchis von feiner Toleranz und einem Sinn für Verschiedenartigkeit geprägt, die zugleich Ausdruck seiner Bewunderung für eine grenzüberschreitende Kultur und Interdisziplinarität in den Arbeiten anderer ist und sich auch in der eigenen Arbeit, in der Form des offenen Denkens, wie er es beschreibt, niederschlägt (S. 8). Tatsächlich entsprang seine Teilnahme an der Radical Design-Bewegung in den frühen siebziger Jahren, als er in Florenz Architektur studierte, seiner Ungeduld und Ablehnung des damaligen Status Quo des Designs in Italien.

Radical Design war zu dieser Zeit Teil der radikalen Studentenbewegung in ganz Europa und hatte es sich zur Aufgabe gemacht, die gängigen kapitalistischen Ideologien, vor allem in Bezug auf Stadtplanung, kritisch zu hinterfragen. Die Absichten waren ernst, die Techniken, so wie die Popkultur, der sie entlehnt waren, experimentell und oft surrealistisch. Mit drei Kommilitonen gründete Michele De Lucchi 1973 in Padua seine eigene Radical Design-Gruppe, die Gruppa Cavart. In den folgenden drei Jahren produzierten sie Manifeste und Filme, veranstalteten Seminare über die Zukunft der Architektur – allesamt Impulse für das neue italienische Design der achtziger Jahre.

1977, nachdem er als Assistent an der Florenzer Universität gearbeitet und seine ersten Ausflüge ins Industriedesign unternommen hatte, zog De Lucchi nach Mailand. Es sollte ein entscheidender Schritt in seiner Karriere sein. Durch seine Tätigkeit für Ettore Sottsass, Andrea Branzi und Gaetano Pesce wechselte er von der Architektur zum Design. Auf der Grundlage seiner Studien über italienisches Design der 50er Jahre entwarf er Leuchten für die Designergruppe Studio Alchimia. Das helle, lebendige, von der Op-Art inspirierte Design, das er für Hifi-Anlagen entwickelte, wurde schon bald in der wichtigen Architekturzeitschrift Domus vorgestellt.

Gegen Ende der 70er Jahre griff eine Gruppe radikaler Designer und Architekten aus Mailand konsequent jedes glatte, konformistische, moderne Design an. Es galt, im Vergleich zu dem demokratischeren Ansatz der 50er Jahre in Italien, als überheblich und damit elitär. Als sich mit dem neuen Jahrzehnt auch eine neue Bewegung formierte, fand De Lucchi ein ihm entsprechendes Milieu. Sottsass, der seit den 50er Jahren Berater von Olivetti war, hat eine grosse Bedeutung für den nun folgenden Karrieresprung De Lucchis. 1979 begann De Lucchi ebenfalls für Olivetti zu arbeiten, aber auch an anderen Projekten mit Sottsass. Seine intuitive Fähigkeit, abstrakte architektonische Formen auf elektronische Produkte zu übertragen, war genau das Prinzip, für das sich De Lucchi mit seinem eigenen Ansatz der Versöhnung in Bezug auf die Bedürfnisse von Herstellern und Konsumenten interessierte.

Als Sottsass 1981 Memphis ins Leben rief, war es nur logisch, dass dem gerade dreissigjährigen De Lucchi eine Schlüsselrolle zufallen musste. De Lucchi war nicht nur kreativer Funke innerhalb der Gruppe, er organisierte und koordinierte unermüdlich die Arbeit der Mitglieder und suchte nach Geldgebern. Während Memphis in den frühen Achtzigern die Designwelt schockierte und in Aufregung versetzte, zeichneten sich De Lucchis Entwürfe durch zunehmende Reife und Qualität aus. Persönliche Aufträge von Firmen wie Artemide, Fontana Arte und Bieffeplast bewiesen, wie sehr Memphis – und auch De Lucchi in seiner Rolle innerhalb der Bewegung – das öffentliche Interesse auf sich gezogen hatte. De Lucchi selbst wollte es aber nicht bei seiner Entwurfsarbeit belassen. 1986 rief er Solid, eine eigene provokative und radikale Mailänder Gruppe ins Leben, um seiner Idee des Geometrischen im Design nachzugehen.

Nachdem De Lucchi aus der Sichtweise eines Architekten an das Design herangegangen war, widmete er sich nun erneut der Architektur und der Innenarchitektur – diesmal aus der Sicht des Produktdesigners und der entsprechenden Betonung des Metaphorischen. Auf der Basis seiner seit 1988 erworbenen praktischen Erfahrungen gestaltete er nun mehr als 50 Fiorucci-Läden, sowie eine Reihe von Produkten und Systemen für Olivetti und entwickelte, indem er theoretische und praktische Aspekte von Architektur und Design miteinander verwob, eine spielerische und poetische Formensprache, die für ihn charakteristisch wurde.

Neben kommerziellen Aufträgen und öffentlichen Manifesten initiierte De Lucchi 1990 seine eigene Produzione Privata, die ihm die Möglichkeit gab, Objekte in limitierten Editionen aufzulegen, um eine Debatte jenseits aller Marktinteressen zu entfachen und dabei neuen Ideen Gültigkeit zu verleihen. Mittlerweile ist er bekannt für sein Interesse an einer nonkonformistischen kulturellen Produktion, die in Opposition zum Mainstream steht. Daraus erklärt sich wohl auch, dass viele der Objekte von Hidden (S. 34-35) bis Droog Design (S. 84-85) für das Internationale Design Jahrbuch 2001 von kulturellen Veranstaltungen oder Kollektivprojekten stammen. Produzione Privata sollte exemplarisch vorführen wie sich das Handwerkliche durch die Definition neuer taktiler und formaler Eigenschaften und Materialien positiv auf die Serienproduktion auswirken kann. Durch den rasanten technologischen Fortschritt sah De Lucchi die Würde und Bedeutung des einzelnen Gestaltungsobjektes oder -raumes, wie sie erst durch die Erfahrung des Benutzers entstehen, in Frage gestellt, und gerade diese wollte er unterstützen und bewahren.

Für diesen humanistischen Ansatz begannen sich in den frühen neunziger Jahren manche grossen Unternehmen, deren Glaube an den ungebremsten technologischen Fortschritt zunehmend schwand, zu interessieren. 1991 erhielt Michele De Lucchi den Zuschlag bei einem internationalen Wettbewerb, in dem es um die Gestaltung der Filialen für die Deutsche Bank ging. In der darauffolgenden Zeit konnte De Lucchi seine organisatorischen Fähigkeiten und sein Ambition, junge Designer zu fördern, unter Beweis stellen. Obwohl De Lucchi sein Team mittlerweile auf 35 Leute heruntergeschraubt hat, ist er gerade dabei, eine neue Generation italienischer Postämter zu gestalten. Zudem ist er bekannt als jemand, der grosse Design-Projekte sicher umsetzt und leitet.

Ungewöhnlich für einen Designer diesen Ranges legt De Lucchi grossen Wert auf die Dynamik innerhalb des Design-Teams. Seine Erfahrung mit Olivetti hat ihn gelehrt, das In-House-Design von Unternehmen zu schätzen, wobei die Star-Berater in dieser Branche oftmals genau das übersehen. In der Kategorie Produkte des Internationalen Design Jahrbuchs 2001 – die Auswahl, die De Lucchi als die stärkste im Buch ansieht – erfahren insbesondere die Arbeiten der Design-Teams von Siemens (S.191), Philips (S.185) und Sharp (S.182) seine Hochschätzung. Die Leistung von Sharp sieht er in diesem Sinne als besonders konsequent an. Auch die Arbeit von Jonathan Ive, Design-Direktor bei Apple-Computer, fand sein Lob. „Nur Apple konnte das erreichen, was bei der Firma jetzt geleistet wurde", kommentiert er. Der Verdienst von Apple ist eine neue Formensprache für Computer-Produkte, die schon jetzt oftmals kopiert worden ist und die Farbe und Transparenz mit ausserordentlicher technischer Präzision und Qualität verbindet. Das riesige, einer Staffelei ähnelnde Cinema-Display (S.188) oder die Leichtigkeit des Gehäuses für den G4-Cube (S.189) erfüllen für De Lucchi auf nahezu vollkommene Weise die Verbindung von Industrie und Humanität. Sie sind technologische Objekte, die geradezu dazu auffordern, sich mit ihnen zu beschäftigen und sie zu besitzen.

Als Architekt hat De Lucchi vielleicht seine grössten Leistungen im Bereich Produktdesign vollbracht: Die legendäre Tolomeo-Leuchtenserie für Artemide, zum Beispiel, verbindet technische Präzision mit poetischer Subtilität und findet eine zeitgemäße Form für die Anglepoise- und Tizio-Tischleuchte. So ist es naheliegend, dass De Lucchi andere Architekten, die sich im Bereich Möbel oder Leuchten versuchen wollen, unterstützt. Foster, Chipperfield, Moneo und Hadid sind allesamt mit ihren Arbeiten in dieser Publikation vertreten. Norman Fosters Leuchten wurden sogar von De Lucchi für die neue Gestaltung der italienischen Postämter ausgewählt. De Lucchi wechselt mit verblüffender Leichtigkeit von der Grösse architektonischer Projekte zum kleineren Format des Produktdesigns, vom kleinen tragbaren Objekt zum ausgedehnten öffentlichen Innenraum.

Zu den Architekturaufträgen der frühen neunziger Jahre gehört auch die Aussengestaltung und die Inneneinrichtung einer Abteilung des Museums von Groningen, das selbst eine verrückte und spektakuläre architektonische Verschmelzung aus der Hand Alessandro Mendinis ist, zu der neben De Lucchis quadratischem Ziegelsteinbau, der der Stadtgeschichte und ihrer Archäologie gewidmet ist, auch Philippe Starck und Coop Himmelblau Beiträge geleistet haben. Bei diesem Projekt, das den Stand der Architektur- und Designavantgarde Europas verkörpern sollte, offenbart sich in De Lucchis Beitrag ein radikaler Zugang, der aber auch Zurückhaltung mit Interesse für Tradition verbindet. Vittorio Magnago Lampugnani, der frühere Herausgeber von Domus, schrieb über De Lucchi: „Einst ein Revolutionär des Designs wandelt er sich nun zum sanften Fürsprecher von Schlichtheit und Diskretion und nähert sich unerschrocken auch der Vergangenheit. Ich finde diese Entwicklung sehr interessant, da in seinem Fall nichts revisionistisches oder reaktionäres mit hineinspielt."

In welchem Ausmaß De Lucchi bereit war, sich historischen Bezügen zu öffnen, zeigte sich 1990 in einem Design-Projekt – einer Möbelserie namens Sangirolama für Vorstandsetagen von Olivetti – bei dem er mit Achille Castiglioni zusammenarbeitete. Inspirationsgrundlage für diese Arbeit war Antonellis berühmtes Gemälde 'San Gerolamo nello Studio' (Der Heilige Jeremias in seinem Arbeitszimmer) aus dem Jahre 1418. De Lucchi und Castiglione antizipierten die Übertragung der behaglichen Stimmung des häuslichen Interiors auf die streng organisierte Büroausstattung. Ein Jahrzehnt später ist diese Idee weit verbreitet. Heute setzt De Lucchi ausschließlich Home Office-Möbel bei der Gestaltung der Armani-Büros ein. Die Trennung von Wohn- und Arbeitsplatz, was für die letzten 150 Jahre galt, ist obsolet geworden. Durch neue Technologien und Methoden hält der Arbeitsplatz wieder Einzug im häuslichen Bereich. De Lucchis Auswahl an Möbeln und Leuchten in diesem Buch reflektiert diese neue Entwicklung. So kommentiert er seine Auswahl: „Ich erwarte noch einiges mehr an Innovation für den häuslichen Bereich".

Sicherlich sind komplexe hochmaschinelle Bürosysteme und -produkte im Home Office-Bereich nicht angemessen. De Lucchi ist der Überzeugung, dass das schlichte Wiederentdecken bewährter traditioneller Objekte – beispielhaft sind die kürzlich entwickelten Sitzbänke aus Buchenholz und Leder für Poltrona Frau (S.8) – ein wirksames Korrektiv zur Unruhe des beständigen technologischen Wechsels sind. In der Versöhnung des menschlichen Umgangs mit den Ansprüchen der Serienproduktion kommt dem Zeitlos-Klassischen oder Allgemeingültigen im Design, speziell in der Beziehung zum Benutzer, eine Schlüsselrolle zu. Diese Idee findet in der Auswahl De Lucchis ihren Ausdruck in Starcks Aluminiumstuhl für Emeco (S.32), Emanuel Bableds Murano-Glas (S.153) oder Christopher Deams Airstream-Trailer (S.225).

Die neuen technologischen Ideen finden gebührende Anerkennung in diesem Buch: Von intelligenten Textilien über Leuchten, die auf Leuchtdioden basieren, bis zu Ron Arads computer-animierten Vasen, die mittels Stereolithografie hergestellt wurden. Treu bleibt De Lucchi auch seiner Bewunderung für die einfachen altbewährten Dinge, die ihre Funktion unter einem praktischen und emotionalen Gesichtspunkt für den Menschen unter Beweis stellen. 1986 beschrieb De Lucchi seine Solid Design Collection als einen Akt des Glaubens an die Zukunft; sie veranschauliche die Tatsache, dass Design, anders als in der Beschränkung auf das Produzieren schöner Dinge, pragmatisch und greifbar den Fortschritt bewirken könne. Ähnliches kann man zur Auswahl des Internationalen Design Jahrbuchs 2001 sagen.

Michele De Lucchi
Bank Piazza di Spagna
Poltrona Frau, Italien
1999/2000

Einleitung
Michele De Lucchi

Den Verlegern und Jennifer Hudson möchte ich herzlich dafür danken, dass sie mich als Gastherausgeber für das Internationale Design Jahrbuch 2001 auserkoren haben. Es ist nicht nur eine gute Gelegenheit, mich mit den neuesten Entwicklungen weltweit im Bereich Design und Produktion vertraut zu machen, ich kann auch meine persönliche Sicht als Designer und Architekt im Zusammenhang unserer Gesellschaft und Umwelt neu überdenken.

Die Auswahlarbeit für das Internationale Design Jahrbuch 2001 umfasst ein sehr breites Spektrum an Entwurfsarbeiten. Ich habe das erwartet und wurde nicht enttäuscht. Ich glaube sogar, dass eine solche Vielfalt, Energie und Enthusiasmus berechtigt und auch nützlich sind. Ungefähr 2000 Gegenstände habe ich angeschaut, und sie lassen sich bis auf eine grobe Unterscheidung nach Produkttypen unmöglich in Kategorien von Stil, Eigenschaften, figurativem Ursprung oder ikonografischem Bezugspunkt unterteilen. Es wird immer schwieriger, sprachliche Grenzen und formale Referenzen zu unterscheiden. Ich glaube, dass wir, so wie Herbert Schulte es am Ende seiner Tätigkeit als Leiter der Designabteilung bei Siemens formulierte, uns nun in einem neuen Zeitalter des ‚offenen Denkens' befinden. Alles muss ungehindert ineinander überfliessen können, von einer Kultur zur anderen, von einer Disziplin zur nächsten, von Rolle zu Rolle, von einer Fähigkeit zur anderen. Wir befinden uns an der Schwelle zur Ära der Informations- und Telekommunikationstechnologie, und wir sind sozusagen die Ersten, die diese weltumspannende Orgie mit all den Verbindungsmöglichkeiten, dem verfügbaren Wissen, dem Überfluss an Information und Bildern und dem Reichtum an Auswahlmöglichkeiten, die sie uns bietet, feiern dürfen. Als das Team des Internationalen Design Jahrbuchs 2001 haben wir angesichts all der eingesandten CD-ROMs und der kaum zu bewältigenden Menge an digitalen Bildern die Erfahrung gemacht, dass unser menschliches Vermögen kaum genügte, dieser Flut an Auswahlmöglichkeiten gerecht zu werden, jedes Objekt genau anzuschauen und zu analysieren. Und wer weiss, wie es in den nächsten Jahren aussehen wird?

Experten meinen, eine der gefragtesten Eigenschaften jetzt und in Zukunft wird die Fähigkeit zur Toleranz sein, und dies nicht nur im gesellschaftlichen und politischen Sinne. Ich kann dem nur beipflichten, denn besonders im Bereich des Designs ist Toleranz von grosser Bedeutung, weniger, indem man Dinge akzeptiert, die einem nicht gefallen oder die unsere Zustimmung nicht finden, als vielmehr im Sinne von Offenheit in der Zusammenführung von Dingen, Stilrichtungen, Visionen und verschiedenen Technologien gegensätzlichen Ursprungs. Die Prämisse für das Design im Jahr 2001 lautet: Offenheit, Toleranz und Kreativität. Letztere darf natürlich am wenigsten fehlen. Aber wie kann man die unterschiedlichsten Konzepte und Aspekte zusammenführen, ohne ein entsprechend ausgeprägtes Interesse für Studien, Innovation, neue Produkte, Phantasie und Träume? Meine Interpretation in der Rolle des Designers heutzutage setzt genau an diesem Punkt an: Er sollte die Freiheit des Ausdrucks für alle, die mit Design, Kreationen, Geschichten und Metaphern arbeiten, unterstützen. Der Designer und der Architekt sind Geschichtenerzähler, so pflegte sich Ettore Sottsass in den siebziger Jahren während des Höhepunktes des Radikalen Designs und erst kürzlich Jean Nouvel in seinen faszinierenden Vorträgen zu äussern. Ein Design verbirgt auch eine Geschichte. Durch das Objekt – oder Produkt – werden die Aspekte des Erzählerischen visualisiert, sei es in direkter oder lediglich symbolischer Form. Design ist Kommunikation, es vermittelt den Geist des Zeitgenössischen, des Engagements und wirkt als Anreiz für kreative Freiheit. Dies unterscheidet sich nicht so sehr von dem, was ich gemeinsam mit Ettore Sottsass vor über 30 Jahren festgestellt habe, dass nämlich der Architekt Metaphern entwickeln muss, um die schöpferische Begabung, die in jeder Persönlichkeit verborgen liegt, anzuregen. Der Unterschied ist nur, dass diese Theorie damals in Opposition zum traditionellen Design stand und es provokativ-kritisch ablehnte. Heute ist es ein Konzept, das uns hilft, die uns umgebenden Dinge in der Welt besser zu verstehen und zu akzeptieren.

In meiner Auswahl habe ich, wie es bislang im Internationalen Design Jahrbuch immer der Fall war, Kategorien ähnlicher Produkte getrennt aufgeführt. Auch im Zeitalter des ‚vernetzten Denkens' bleibt die Entwicklung von spezifischen individuellen Produktsphären voneinander unabhängig. Möbel, Leuchten, Accessoires, Stoffe, elektronische Produkte, Fahrzeuge etc. durchlaufen unterschiedliche Entwicklungsprozesse, die sich nicht gut miteinander vergleichen lassen. Produktionstechnologien und die Merkmale von Vertriebssystemen und Marktanforderungen stellen immer noch eine kaum zu überwindende Barriere zur Durchsetzung innovativer Bewegungen dar. Ich habe, wenn möglich, ähnliche sprachliche Kategorien unterstrichen, um neue figurative Trends sichtbar zu machen. Es ist sicherlich nach wie vor interessant, einen Stuhl mit einem Stuhl, einen Tisch mit einem Tisch und eine Leuchte mit einer Leuchte zu vergleichen. Zweifellos ist dies einer der wichtigsten Beiträge, die das Internationale Design Jahrbuch in seiner jährlichen Erscheinungsweise leistet.

Dennoch möchte ich einige Aspekte besonders hervorheben. Der erste bezieht sich auf unternehmerische Initiativen: Es scheint tatsächlich viele Events zu geben, die durch individuelle, öffentliche oder private Investoren getragen werden und wo das kulturelle Interesse nur vorgeblich im Vordergrund steht, denn gerade der Designbereich wird als reiche Fundgrube betrachtet.

Michele De Lucchi
Lampe Rumi
Ausstellung 'Thinking of Sufi Poets'
2000

Im Beispiel von Hidden hat Leon van Gerwen das Unternehmen sdb Aluminium Display gekauft und zwölf Designer verpflichtet, die frei von irgendwelchen Vermarktungsbedingungen Produkte für das häusliche Umfeld gestalten sollten. Die Designer konnten Möbel und Objekte als Gestaltungsvorschläge einbringen ohne die Vorgabe, dass ihre Produkte möglichst funktional oder marktorientiert ausgerichtet sein sollten. Das Ergebnis waren Produkte mit einer starken Ausstrahlung, manchmal fast provokativ, ganz so wie die Philosophie dieses neugegründeten Unternehmens.

Dieser provokative Ansatz zeichnet auch Droog als das weitaus bekanntere Beispiel aus. Ebenfalls holländischen Ursprungs handelt es sich hierbei um eine freie nonkonformistische Gruppe, deren Leitidee es ist, die Bedeutung von Design neu zu überdenken. Droog wurde 1993 in Amsterdam gegründet und definiert sich weniger über einen bestimmten Produktkatalog als über eine bestimmte Weltanschauung. In den letzen Jahren wurden von Droog mehrere experimentelle Projekte zusammen mit jungen Designern entwickelt. Der internationale Vertrieb der Droog-Produkte wurde bislang durch die Firma DMD in Vaarburg durchgeführt. Über die Produktentwicklung hinaus konzentriert sich Droog vor allem auf produktbegleitende Präsentationen, Ausstellungen und Events. Aus der Überzeugung heraus, dass eine rasante Entwicklung in der Grenzverschiebung zwischen den einzelnen Disziplinen stattfindet, verkündet man bei Droog, dass Architekten, Innenarchitekten, Werbe- und Grafikagenturen nun einen Beitrag dazu leisten, den Erfolg Droogs (droog = trocken) zu verbreiten. Unverwechselbar, unterhaltend, authentisch, originell und subversiv sind Begriffe, die den do-Katalog sicherlich am besten beschreiben. Nicht weniger als 10 Designer bzw. Studios, einschließlich Marti Guixé

Michele De Lucchi
Lampe Nizami
Ausstellung 'Thinking of Sufi Poets'
2000

aus Spanien, Thomas Bernstrand aus Schweden, Radi aus Frankreich und Dawn Finley aus den Vereinigten Staaten haben für eine experimentelle Marke Produkte gestaltet, die von der Amsterdamer Werbeagentur KesselsKramer ins Leben gerufen wurde. Der Titel des Projekts 'do create' spielt sowohl auf den Designer als auch auf den Konsumenten an: Der Designer gestaltet die Produkte, mit denen der Konsument interagieren muss. Er entwickelt ein Produkt, das nicht seine eigene Signatur trägt und erst durch den Konsumenten, der ihm seinen persönlichen Touch verleiht, vollendet wird. Der Benutzer ist somit aufgefordert, an den Produkten aktiv teilzuhaben und mit verschiedenen Möglichkeiten zu spielen. Er kann das Design beeinflussen, und über das Produkt kann wiederum die Persönlichkeit des Konsumenten identifiziert werden. Man kauft nicht länger eine Form, einen Stil oder eine Funktion, sondern man kauft eine Erfahrung.

Ich bin ein grosser Bewunderer der Arbeit von Gijs Bakker und Renny Ramakers, die durch ihre Publikationen eine bemerkenswerte Kommunikationsstärke offenbaren. Sie haben meiner Meinung nach eines der innovativsten und lebendigsten Konzepte in der Design-Szene der letzten Jahre entwickelt. Ausserdem haben sie in der Art und Weise, wie sie die typischen Hindernisse, die ihren Projekten im Wege standen, überwunden haben, ein ausserordentliches Talent bewiesen und eine unabhängige und originelle Designkultur verbreitet.

Cappellini, obgleich etwas weniger experimentierfreudig, überrascht uns auch jedes Jahr neu. Er bringt eine beachtliche Anzahl exzellenter Designer aus aller Welt zusammen, die immer originelle, faszinierende, niemals banale Produkte und Projekte präsentieren. Auch dieses Jahr ist keine Ausnahme.

Die öffentliche Initiative des Kunstindustrimuseet und die Ausstellung 'Walk the plank' 1999, die von Louise Campbell, Cecilia Enevoldsen und Sebastian Holmbaeck initiiert wurde, sind bemerkenswert. Es handelt sich hierbei um einen freundschaftlichen und zwanglosen Wettbewerb, die Suche nach Ideen, Fantasie und Fertigkeiten zwischen Designern und Kunsttischlern, zwischen Design- und Produktionstalenten. Ungefähr 20 Designer wurden eingeladen, paarweise mit ebenso vielen Kunsttischlern, aus einer Holzbohle ein Möbelstück herzustellen. Die Arbeiten, die entstanden, wurden in einer Ausstellung im Museum für Dekorative Kunst in Gronnengarden gezeigt und anschliessend in einer Auktion versteigert. Der Erlös kam einem Fond zugute, der Designer in der experimentellen Arbeit mit Prototypen unterstützt.

Es gibt viele private Initiativen einzelner Designer, die im industriellen Bereich keine ausreichende Unterstützung für ihre persönliche Forschungsarbeit fanden und die daraufhin kleine, beachtenswerte, innovative Unternehmen gegründet haben, und zwar mit grossem Erfolg, der oftmals die ursprüngliche Zielvorstellung übertraf.

Ingo Maurer, Ron Arad und Philippe Starck haben mit einer spannenden Geschäftsidee experimentiert, die nicht etwa auf einem bestimmten Unternehmensplan, sondern allein auf dem Prinzip poetischer Logik beruht. So etwas ging schon oft gut, ganz besonders in Ingos Fall, denn er hat seine Geschäftsidee erfolgreich in eine poetische Haltung umgemünzt. Mit meiner 'Produzione Privata' stehe ich dem sehr nahe, denn ich versuche, im kleinen Rahmen etwas zu simulieren, was ich gerne im industriellen Zusammenhang umgesetzt sähe und was der industriellen Logik jedoch bislang entgegenzustehen schien. Die Erfahrung, die ich mit meiner 'Produzione Privata' gemacht habe, hat mir geholfen, dieses Phänomen zu verstehen, weshalb ich es auch an dieser Stelle erwähne. Ich möchte noch einmal die besondere Bedeutung betonen, die ich dem Handwerk beimesse und dem Wert der Dinge, die von einem Einzelnen per Hand in einer kleinen Auflage oder als Unikat hergestellt werden. Industrie und Handwerk unterscheiden sich nicht voneinander, wenn man sie unter dem Aspekt ihres Beitrages zur Kultur des Designs betrachtet.

Ich habe die Rolle des Handwerks als ideales Forschungsforum für die Industrie immer besonders unterstützt, da es durch die Höhe der Investition bedingte Zwänge, Entwicklungsrisiko und die mit ihm einhergehenden positiven oder negativen Konsequenzen nicht gibt. Die Zusammenarbeit mit dem Handwerk schafft ein ideales Experimentierfeld, dessen Potential oftmals nicht erkannt und genutzt wird. Ideal deshalb, weil das Handwerk Technologie und Talent, Wissen, Sensitivität, Know-How und Geschicklichkeit des Menschen miteinander verbindet.

Eine der positiven Errungenschaften des italienischen Designs ist, dass es sich trotz der wenigen neuen Namen, die es bietet, eines ungetrübten Erfolges freuen und seinen Ruf als internationales Designzentrum bewahren kann. In Italien ist es einer begrenzten Anzahl von Unternehmern, weder Industrie und noch Politik, zu verdanken, dass einige der wichtigen Handwerkstraditionen intakt bleiben konnten und dass es möglich ist, jedes Jahr auf der Möbelmesse, dem Salone del Mobile in Mailand, eine unendliche Fülle neuer Ideen, Produkte und Visionen zu präsentieren.

Diese Handwerkstraditionen sind es auch, die die Welt des Designs und der Mode einander näher bringen – ein Vorteil für das Design, da es von dem ausserordentlichen Erfindungsreichtum der Modewelt, ihrer Produktivität, der unaufhörlichen Fähigkeit, Interesse zu wecken und immer wieder neue Visionen zu entwickeln, profitieren kann. Darüber hinaus führt die Mode auf exemplarische Art und Weise den spannenden kontinuierlichen Wechsel von Entscheidungen, Formen, Ambitionen und Hoffnungen vor, wie es auch für den Designbereich wünschenswert wäre.

Bemerkenswert sind auch die von Architekten entwickelten Design-Projekte. Oftmals muss für eine bestimmte Architektur auch der dazugehörige Innenraum und seine Ausstattung mitgestaltet werden. Dies setzt ein gewisses Verständnis für die Objekte, die für ein häusliches Umfeld kreiert werden, voraus. Da ich ebenfalls Architekt bin, ist mir auch dieser Aspekt unmittelbar vertraut.

Dank der Auswahlarbeit konnte ich überprüfen, inwieweit Architektur die industrielle Kultur beeinflusst und wie meine eigene Arbeit als Designer meinen Ursprung als Architekt ahnen lässt. Design und Architektur verbinden sich hauptsächlich dort, wo es Innenräume und Möbel gibt. Es sind funktionale und ästhetische Orte und Umgebungen, die von Menschen mit Hilfe von Objekten, eingebauten oder mobilen Gebrauchsgegenständen bewohnt werden.

Es ist schwierig, Konzepte zu erklären, die sich der Beschreibung durch Worte entziehen. So ist es auch schwer zu verstehen, warum die Welt des Raumes und der Objekte hinsichtlich ihrer Zugehörigkeit zu einer Disziplin auf so unterschiedlich begrifflichen Ebenen stattfinden. Selten wird die Distanz dazwischen überwunden. Beide Welten treten miteinander in Verbindung, um sich wechselseitig zu befruchten. Der Architekt gestaltet Möbel und Ausstattungen intuitiv, Stein auf Stein, Form auf Form, hinzufügend und wegnehmend. Dabei arbeitet er immer frenetisch an seiner Komposition, angelehnt an sein Metier, eines das so alt ist wie die Menschheit selbst. Ausstattungen, Möbel, Objekte und Gebrauchsgegenstände entspringen heutzutage einer industriellen Kultur, der in Bezug auf Produktionslogik, technologische Vorteile, Marktforschung und Geschmack andere Wertvorstellungen zugrunde liegen. Es ist schwierig, unterschiedlichste, weit voneinander entfernte Parameter zusammenzufügen. Nur in wenigen Fällen von Erfolg gesegnet, konnte dies unerwarteterweise dank eines dritten Protagonisten – nämlich der Kunst – erst möglich werden. Manchmal sind die Ergebnisse besser als vermutet – ein Konzept wird erweitert, es kommen andere hinzu und schließlich werden alle in einer Formsprache vereinigt. Das ist vielleicht das, was wir als Kunst bezeichnen. Ich ziehe es jedoch vor, von Zeitgeist zu sprechen, dem Geist aller Formen, Ideen, Stimmungen, den spezifischen Bildern eines präzisen, historischen Augenblicks. Es ist dieser ideale Ort, an dem sich Architekten und Designer mit ihrer Fähigkeit zu konstruieren und zu produzieren treffen sollten. Eine vielversprechende Idee des ‚offenen Denkens' ist die Kombination von Architektur und industrieller Kultur, die Durchdringung der erst etwas mehr als ein Jahrhundert alten Industriekultur mit der jahrtausendealten Tradition der Architektur.

Für diese Ausgabe des Internationalen Design Jahrbuchs hatte ich das Glück, die Arbeit von grossen Architekten wie Foster, Sejima, Moneo und Chipperfield zusammentragen zu können, die mit jeweils geringerer oder grösserer Nachsicht gegenüber der industriellen Logik bezeichnende Möbelprojekte entwickelt haben. Sicherlich machen sie der Verlockung der Massenprodukte keine Zugeständnisse und keinen Gebrauch von den neuen Ausdrucksmöglichkeiten, wie sie durch Computerprogramme ermöglicht werden. Die derzeitige Vorliebe für abgerundete Ecken, geschwungene Oberflächen, Griffe und quasi-organische Vorsprünge scheinen jedoch bislang die figurative Quellensuche des Architekten nicht zu beeinträchtigen. Die Tendenz, Formen weicher zu gestalten, Oberflächen abzupolstern und stark geometrisch wirkende Formen aufzubrechen, ist überall sichtbar und kaum zu verleugnen. Sie ist zweifellos die Hauptströmung, die das figurative Experiment unserer Zeit bestimmt.

Der Minimalismus scheint mittlerweile wieder neuen Schwung zu bekommen – noch reduzierter und abstrakter, hat er neue Ausdrucksmöglichkeiten eröffnet, verbindet Formales mit einer subtilen Auswahl an Materialien, Texturen und Tönen. Diese neue Richtung entsteht aus dem Bedürfnis, die Dinge unserer Zeit weniger gewöhnlich zu gestalten, sie möglichst aus dem Kontext zu reissen, und sie mit einem authentischen Hauch von Ironie und Desillusionierung auszustatten. Es mag manchmal banal und anspruchslos erscheinen, sich lustig zu machen, mitunter kann es jedoch auch schwierig sein, zwischen etwas Bedeutungsvollem und einem abgenutzten Gag zu unterscheiden.

Auf der diesjährigen Liste ausgewählter Designer fehlt keiner der grossen Namen: Sottsass, Starck, Citterio, Cibic und viele andere, die wichtige Beiträge in Form experimenteller Projekte und kommerzieller Produkte geleistet haben. Gleichbedeutend ist die Präsenz von Philips, Siemens und Sharp, deren Designstudios in den letzten Jahren ausserordentliche Arbeit geleistet haben, indem sie Produkte auf den Markt gebracht haben, die sich durch eine besondere figurative Qualität auszeichnen und Konsumenten Objekte und Umgebungen bieten, die bezüglich ihres Images und Stils auf den neuesten Stand gebracht worden sind.

Zum Schluss möchte ich allen, deren Arbeiten nicht aufgenommen wurden, sagen, dass der Raum, den wir zur Verfügung hatten, natürlich begrenzt war. Niemand soll sich betroffen fühlen, denn mein Urteil ist nicht eigentlich maßgebend und das, was kulturell verbreitet wird, verdient es nicht immer wirklich, auch wenn es fundiert und kommerziell erfolgreich ist. Ich hoffe, dass auch dieses Jahrbuch die Qualität der bislang erschienenen Internationalen Design Jahrbücher erfüllt und es im gleichen Maße zur Inspirationsquelle wird, wie es die vorangegangenen für mich waren, denn alles, was die Kreativität anregt, verdient es, publiziert zu werden.

Michele De Lucchi
Klemmleuchte Tolomeo
Pinza
Artemide, Italien
1996

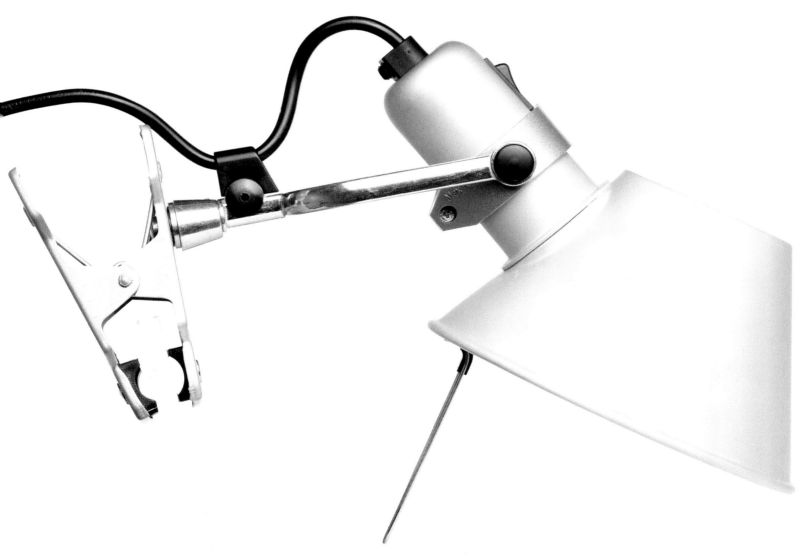

möbel

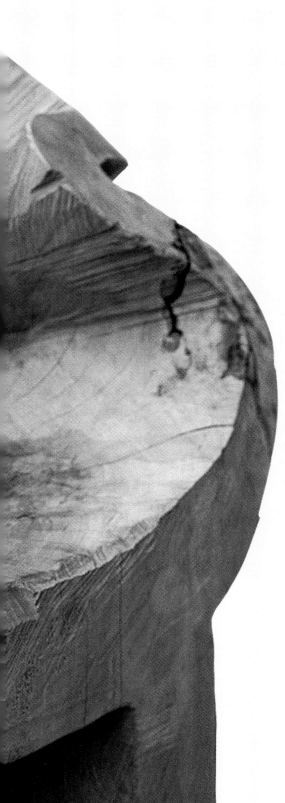

Die Mailänder Möbelmesse ging auch im Jahr 2000 kein Risiko ein. Ein Grossteil der zur Schau gestellten Entwürfe unterliegt nach wie vor dem Gebot des Kommerziellen. Vordergründig schien es mehr Farbe zu geben als im letzten Jahr, bei näherer Betrachtung entpuppte sich das meiste jedoch als Wiederauflage oder Neuinterpretation der Pop-Kultur. Kein Wunder, dass so bei der Presse die Anlehnung an die 70er Jahre im Vordergrund standen: Pesces Wiederauflage der roten monolithischen 'Up'-Serie für B&B Italia, die nostalgische 70er-Reminiszenz mit Ross Lovegroves 'Air One', einem stapelbaren Stuhl in Biba-Farben, Philippe Starcks neue Version des 'Emeco'-Aluminiumstuhls. Im gleichen Geist muss man auch die Eröffnung des Kartell-Museums sehen, das die Geschichte des Unternehmens von seinen Pionierleistungen in Sachen Plastikverarbeitung bis heute darlegt.

Wie immer boten die Ausstellungen der Nebenschauplätze und der 'Salone Satellite' eine breitere Vielfalt als das Hauptereignis. Hier waren Sammlungen zu sehen, die von risikofreudigen Unternehmern getragen und organisiert wurden. Auch wenn die Schau Capellinis mit der Titelmelodie von 'Clockwork Orange' – als Erinnerung an die futuristischen Pop-Kultur-Konnotationen des Films – unterlegt war, wirkten die ausgestellten Arbeiten von Barber Osgerby, den Bouroullec Brüdern, Mauro Mori, Jasper Morrison, Alfredo Häberli und anderen, frisch und innovativ. Leon van Gerwen präsentierte Hidden, die Inneneinrichtungen einer individuellen Designergruppe, die für dieses Projekt ohne kommerziellen Druck arbeiten konnten. Mit einer neuen Objektserie, der der Benutzer spielerisch seinen persönlichen Touch verleihen kann, hat Droog unsere Sicht aufs Design sozusagen wieder neu erfunden. Sputnik von Teruo Kurasaki für die japanische Edition von Idee entwickelt, bot Design für das Internet. Es wurde eine Objekt-Sammlung von Michael Young, Marc Newson, Tim Power, Emmanuel Babled und anderen, die normalerweise nur über das Internet verfügbar wären, gezeigt. Totem, von David Shearer gegründet, finanzierte die G7-Show. Shearer geht es vor allem darum, das amerikanische Design und insbesondere das der jungen aufstrebenden Designergeneration zu unterstützen. Nachdem er die Designer ausgewählt hatte, brachte er sie mit Herstellern zusammen, vermarktete ihre Produkte oder ließ diese durch das In-House-Produktionsteam von Totem produzieren. Die Ausstellung reflektierte die Verbindung von Kunst und Kommerz, wie es für das amerikanische Design so bezeichnend ist. Die Auswahl, die Michele De Lucchi für dieses Buch getroffen hat, spiegelt sein Interesse an diesen neuen Hersteller- und Vermarktungsinitiativen.

Darüberhinaus war es für De Lucchi wichtig, die Verbreitung der Home-Office-Möbel auf dem Markt hervorzuheben. Er nahm Gegenstände auf, denen seines Erachtens ein neuer ästhetischer Wert innewohnt und die sich im Zusammenhang unseres Lebens- und Arbeitsumfeldes als vorteilhaft erwiesen: wie 'Plano' von Defne Koz, N2s 'Ajax' für ClassiCon, sowie Dante Donegani und das Design von Givanni Lauda für Radice. Vorgestellt werden auch junge Designer mit experimentellen Ideen, die ihre eigenen Firmen oder Studios gegründet haben. Insbesondere die Arbeit von Pascal Tarabay mit ihrer Kombination von Ironie und Funktionalität ist interessant. Der 'Frog Chair' ähnelt einem Gartenstuhl aus Plastik, ist aber tatsächlich aus Holz und die Bank 'Beirut' untersucht die archetypisch-formellen Merkmale der Bank und dennoch lädt sie zum Zurücklehnen und Verweilen ein. Nicht zuletzt kommt das Handwerkliche in der Auswahl zum Tragen. Hier sieht De Lucchi den kreativen Impuls nicht durch Anforderungen des Marktes oder die Konsequenzen kommerziellen Erfolgs beeinträchtigt. Er betrachtet den experimentellen Freiraum, wie er hier gegeben ist, als eine gute Möglichkeit, neue Konzepte für industrielle Prototypen zu entwickeln.

Und was wird die Zukunft bringen? Zwei voneinander nicht unabhängige Trends zeichnen sich ab. Erstens scheint der Normalbürger mehr als je zuvor über Design zu reden – es gibt ein bislang beispielloses Interesse an Innenarchitektur und eine Flut von Lifestyle-Magazinen. Design ist zur populären Bewegung geworden. Jede Einkaufstrasse hat mittlerweile einen Designladen, und es gibt eine verstärkte Nachfrage nach erschwinglichem zeitgenössischem Design. Viele Designer begrüssen diese Entwicklung: Alessi und Authentics machten den Anfang mit preiswerteren Objekten und Jasper Morrison, Mario Bellini, Matthew Hilton, Ron Arad und Philippe Starck haben alle Möbel entwickelt, die man zu einem passablen Preis erstehen kann. In diesem Sinne verkündet Starck: "Meine Aufgabe ist es, für die Utopie zu kämpfen: Populäres Design und demokratische Designer. Ich möchte, dass gutes Design für viele Leute erschwinglich wird. Meine grösste Herausforderung ist, die Preise um zwei Nullen zu kürzen".

Zweitens entstehen mit dem Fortschritt in der digitalen Technologie neue Formen und Materialien. Mit CAD-Programmen können komplizierte und geschwungene Formen kreiert und Prototypen mit einer computergesteuerten Fräsmaschine direkt hergestellt werden. Diese runden, organischen Formen führen zu einer verstärkten Nachfrage nach geschmeidigeren Materialien wie Schaumstoff, Plastik, Filz, Aluminiumguss und Polypropylen, was wiederum auch in der Farbgebung neue Möglichkeiten bietet. Solche Materialien können billig und ohne grossen Aufwand produziert werden. Das sind Vorteile, die dem Konsumenten zugute kommen. Schließlich werden die neuen Technologien jedermann eine Chance geben, sich an Design aus erster Hand erfreuen zu können.

Roderick Vos
Sitz Merak
Edelstahl, Rattan
h. 110cm b. 81cm l. 52cm
Espaces et Lignes, Belgien
Kleinserie

Roderick Vos
Sitz Sari
Edelstahl, Rattan
h. 63.5cm b. 82cm l. 69.5cm
Driade SpA, Italien
Kleinserie

Roderick Vos
Sessel Kraton
Edelstahl, Rattan
h. 76cm b. 81cm l. 74cm
Driade SpA, Italien
Kleinserie

Rechte Seite:
Roderick Vos
Sessel Agung
Edelstahl, Rattan
h. 75cmb. 90.5cm l. 115cm
Driade SpA, Italien
Kleinserie

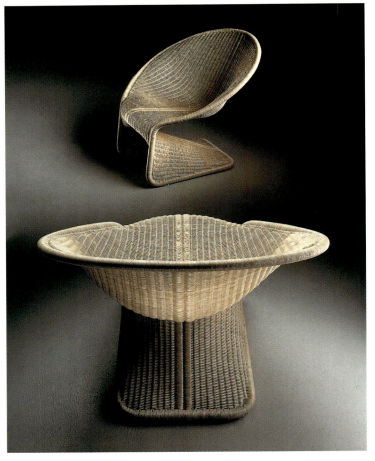

Karim Rashid
Korbstuhl
h. 101cm Ø. 56cm
Idee, Japan

Caroline Casey
Liege Zella
Seegras, Rohr
h. 58cm b. 95cm l. 202cm
Kleinserie

Ross Lovegrove
Chaiselongue
Loom Gewebe, Aluminium, Stahl/Inox
h. 25cm b. 80cm l. 185cm
Loom, Deutschland

Ross Lovegrove
Tisch
Aluminium, Glas, Stahl/Inox
h. 72cm Ø. 110cm
Loom, Deutschland

MÖBEL

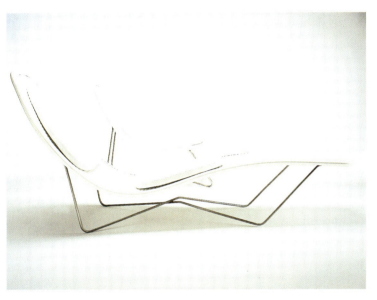

Godobert Reisenthel von Loom ist der deutsche Importeur von Lusty Lloyd Loom. Loom produziert auch eigene Entwürfe, wobei die Ross Lovegrove-Kollektion ein Beispiel für die erfolgreiche Zusammenarbeit eines traditionellen Herstellers mit zeitgenössischen Designern ist. Lovegroves Kombination aus archaischen menschlichen Formen und einem modernen technischen Ausdruck hatte Reisenthel beeindruckt. Das Design wurde auf dem Computer entworfen, und dem traditionellen Papier und Drahtgewebe wurde Strangaluminium hinzugefügt.

Gitta Gschwendtner
Sessel
Lloyd Loom-Gewebe, Metall
Lusty Lloyd Loom, Grossbritanniens

Jane Dillon und Tom Grieves
Sessel
Lloyd Loom-Gewebe, Plastik
h. 79.2cm b. 71cm t. 54cm
Lusty Lloyd Loom, Grossbritannien
Prototyp

Die Lloyd Loom-Objekte, die von Engländern für alle Ewigkeit mit den Sommerhäusern eines verblichenen Empires assoziiert werden, sind traditionellerweise aus gezwirntem und verwebtem Papier hergestellt, mit Stahldraht verstärkt und auf einen Rattan- oder Buchenrahmen aufgespannt oder befestigt. Hier haben sie ein neues Gesicht bekommen. Nach einer erfolgreichen Zusammenarbeit mit Nigel Coates hat Lusty Lloyd Loom neue Gestaltungsvorschläge bei Mitgliedern des Royal College of Art in London in Auftrag gegeben: Ron Arad, Professor für Produktdesign, Jane Dillon, Dozentin für Produktdesign, und die ehemalige Studentin Gitta Gschwendtner. Ausgangspunkt war der technologische Fortschritt, den das Unternehmen ursprünglich gemacht hatte, um mit dem Material arbeiten zu können. Darauf aufbauend hat auch die neue Kollektion zur Entwicklung neuer innovativer Techniken geführt. Jane Dillon hat mit ihrem Design einen wichtigen Durchbruch bewirkt: Der Stoff erhält durch speziell entwickelte Gussformen seine Form und kann auf einem einfachen Rahmen befestigt werden. Diese Rahmen werden aus Kunststoff hergestellt, das in seiner äusseren Beschaffenheit Holz oder Metall gleicht und gegenüber Rattan den Vorteil hat, geschmeidiger und wasserfest zu sein.

Paola Navone
Raumteiler Black 90
Bambus
h. 190cm l. 189cm
Gervasoni SpA, Italien

Paola Navone
Sofa Black 02
Geflecht, Teakholz
h. 110cm l. 175cm t. 85cm
Gervasoni SpA, Italien

Paola Navone
Paravent Black 99
Schwarzer Bambus
Nussbaumholz
b. 150cm h. 180cm
Gervasoni SpA, Italien

Mauro Mori
Stuhl Round
Massivholz
h. 40–60cm Ø. 60cm
Unikat

Paola Navone
Sofa Malaka 02
Rattan
h. 62cm b. 126cm Ø. 88cm
Gervasoni SpA, Italien

Natanel Gluska
Sessel
Buche
Unikat

Um seinen Glauben an die Bedeutung des Handwerklichen zu betonen, hat De Lucchi Objekte nebeneinander gestellt, die sich durch einen besonderen volkskundlichen Touch auszeichnen – entweder bezüglich des verwendeten Materials (Holz, Rattan etc.) oder durch ihre Form. Die Stuhlgebilde von Gluska sind alle Unikate. Er bearbeitet einen unberührten Baumstamm mit einer Kettensäge und fertigt aus diesem Stück eine Art Skulptur und zugleich funktionalen Gegenstand. De Lucchi erklärte in seinem Vorwort, dass das Handwerk Technologie und menschliche Begabung, Wissen und Sensibilität, Know-How und Geschicklichkeit miteinander verbindet. Hier gibt es keine Einschränkungen, weder kreative noch durch den Markt bedingte. Der Designer hat somit grosse expressive Freiheit bei der Gestaltung des Objekts.

MÖBEL

Cecilia Enevoldsen und Mark Burer
Hocker
Ahornholz
h. 45cm b. 30cm t. 30cm
Prototyp

Louise Campbell
Sitzschale Ho'nesty
Eschenholz
t. 65cm Ø. 130cm
Unikat

Komplot Design
Liegestuhl Clinker
Eschenholz
h. 100cm b. 80cm l. 140cm
Komplot Design, Dänemark
Unikat

Hans Sandgren Jakobsen
Hocker The Rockable
Eschenholz
h. 48.4cm b. 76cm t. 38cm
Andre Skriver, Dänemark
Unikat

Die Ausstellung 'Walk the plank' des Kunstindustrimuseet dokumentiert auf sehr schöne Weise die Synergie, die die Verbindung von Tradition und Modernität freisetzt. Zwanzig Designer wurden gebeten, gemeinsam mit ebenso vielen Kunsttischlern, eine Möbelserie aus Massivholz zu fertigen. Nach der Ausstellung wurden die Stücke versteigert und der Erlös soll zukünftigen Prototypentwicklungen zugute kommen. Michele De Lucchi war von dem Projekt besonders angetan, denn es unterstrich den kulturellen Wert des Designs und förderte gleichzeitig Entwicklungen in der Möbelindustrie.

Hans Sandgren Jakobsen
Hocker The Unrockable
Eschenholz
h. 48.4cm b. 76cm t. 38cm
Andre Skriver, Dänemark
Unikat

MÖBEL

Henrik Schulz
Sitz Rubber Chair
Gummi
h. 55cm b. 73cm l. 62cm
-ing, Dänemark, Prototyp

Henrik Schulz
Schaukelstuhl Modern Rocker
Stahlrohr, Leder
h. 58cm b. 65cm l. 82cm
-ing, Dänemark, Prototyp

Todd Bracher
Café Environ Open Privacy
Eschensperrholz furniert
h. 180cm b. 180cm l. 180cm
-ing, Dänemark

Hanspeter Steiger
Stuhl Loi
Sperrholz
h. 78cm b. 41cm l. 45cm
-ing, Dänemark, Prototyp

Dögg Gudmundsdóttir
Stuhl/Liege Wing
Sperrholz
h. 125cm b. 47cm l. 59cm
-ing, Dänemark, Prototyp

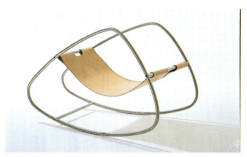

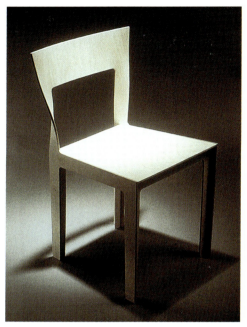

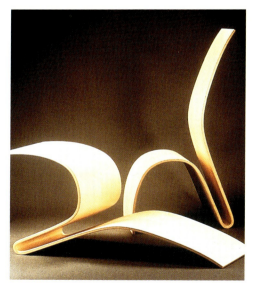

'-ing' ist ein von jungen Designern gemeinsam gegründetes Projekt, für das eine Serie inspirierend gewagter und zugleich funktionaler Objekte entworfen wurden. Die Beteiligten, Dögg Gudmansdottir/Island, Todd Bracher/USA, Hanspeter Steiger/Schweiz und Henrik Schulz/Schweden kommen aus unterschiedlichen Bereichen, angefangen von Architektur und Zimmerhandwerk bis zu Industrie-, Möbel- und Grafikdesign. Die sich daraus ergebende Fülle von Einflüssen bereicherte die erste Ausstellung, die im 'Salone Satellite' in 2000 gezeigt wurde. Mit 'Open Privacy' wurde eine architektonische Form entwickelt, die einen Raum im Raum zeigt, während 'Wing' und 'Loi' das ganze Potential des Materials für sich sprechen zu lassen – Sperrholz wird zu einem 'geraden' Stuhl mit einer dennoch ungewöhnlichen Drehung, und ein weiterer Stuhl wird ergonomisch an den Körper angepasst.

Ely Rozenberg
Liege Moby
Federstahl, Reissverschluss
h. 63cm b. 60cm l. 160cm
oz, Italien
Kleinserie

Ely Rozenberg
Sessel Poltronalampo
Federstahl, Reissverschluss
h. 90cm b. 60cm l. 65cm
oz, Italien
Kleinserie

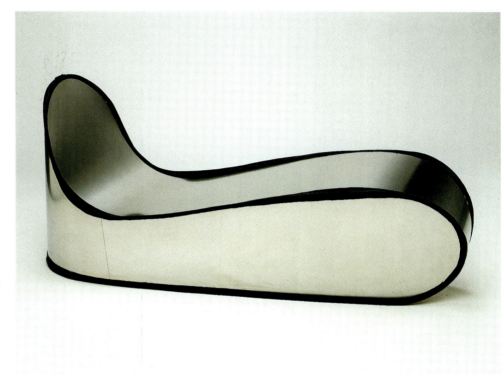

In seiner Einführung zum Internationalen Design Jahrbuch 1999 hat Jasper Morrison seine Vorstellung von experimenteller Designarbeit formuliert: „….die besten Entwürfe enthalten ein konzeptuelles Element, das Formen verschiedenen Anwendungen entleiht und entsprechend anpasst, wodurch neue interessante Ergebnisse dank eines subtilen Zusammenspiels der Materialien mit der richtigen Betonung entstehen". Diese Aussage passt sehr gut zu den Stühlen 'Zipper' von Ely Rozenberg. Rozenberg hat mit einem Laser 0,6 mm dünnen Stahl geschnitten – wie er in der Produktion von Sprungfedern benutzt wird – um eine Schablone anzufertigen. Ein starker Kleber wurde dann auf die Ecken des Musters aufgetragen, der Reissverschluss hinzugefügt und das Ganze sauber zusammengesetzt. Dank dieser neuen Technik können die Objekte geöffnet, auseinandergenommen und leicht verstaut werden. Stahl, normalerweise unnachgiebig und verlötet oder vernietet, wird hier so bearbeitet als wäre es ein maßgeschneiderter Stoff. Diese phantasievolle Verbindung eines industriellen Materials mit einer Erfindung des 20. Jahrhunderts ist eine Provokation angesichts der konventionellen Methoden in der Materialkombination.

Riccardo Blumer
Stuhl Laleggera
Holz, Polyurethan, Nylon
h. 79cm b. 44cm t. 53cm
Alias srl, Italien

Riccardo Blumer
Stapelstuhl Laleggera
Tische Ilvolo
Ahorn/Esche, Polyurethan, Nylon
h. 73cm l. 90–220cm b. 90cm
Alias srl, Italien

Riccardo Blumer
Hocker Laleggera
Holz, Polyurethan, Nylon
h. 44cm b. 36cm t. 35cm
Alias srl, Italien

Hannes Wettstein
Stuhl Alfa
Aluminium
h. 80cm l. 49cm t. 50cm
Molteni & C SpA, Italien

Pascal Mourgue
Stuhl Smala
Stahl, Aluminium
h. 82cm b. 65cm t. 62cm
Ligne Roset, Frankreich

Konstantin Grcic
Hocker Allievo
Buche, Sperrholz
h. 97cm l. 54cm t. 87cm
Montina International srl, Italien

Konstantin Grcic
Hocker Scolaro
Buche, Sperrholz
h. 75cm l. 54cm t. 87cm
Montina International srl, Italien

Michele De Lucchi wollte einige der minimalistischen Entwürfe, die er ausgewählt hatte, nebeneinander stellen. Auch wenn nicht alle minimalistischen Objekte in einer Gruppe zusammengefasst werden konnten, kann man hier deutlich sehen: Der Minimalismus bleibt. Er war eine bezeichnende Bewegung des zwanzigsten Jahrhunderts und bleibt für das einundzwanzigste bestehen. Durch die Reduktion des Dekorativen können Material und Form in den Vordergrund treten, und der Designer erhält die Möglichkeit, sich in der Kategorie des Puristischen auszudrücken.

Perry King und Santiago Miranda
Stapelstuhl Lisa
Thermoplastisches Technopolymer
Aluminium, Stahl, Gummi
h. 85cm b. 44cm t.44cm
Baleri Italia SpA, Italien

Peter Wheeler und Mary Little
Gartensitz Lulu
Terracotta
h. 22cm Ø. 60cm
Bius, Grossbritannien
Prototyp

Gabriela Nahlikova und Leona Matejkova
Stuhl Airchair
Aufblasbare Kissen, Edelstahl
h. 85cm b. 38cm t. 39cm
Prototyp

**Shin Azumi und
Tomoko Azumi
Barhocker LEM**
Stahl, Sperrholz
h. 65–75cm b. 39cm t. 42cm
Lapalma, Italien

**Gabriela Nahlikova und
Leona Matejkova
Stuhl Sesle**
Buchenholz, Seidenbezug
h. 82cm b. 42cm t. 39cm
Prototyp

MÖBEL

Nachdem sie am Royal College of Art in London ihren Abschluss gemacht hatten, gründeten Shin und Tomoko Azumi 1995 ihr eigenes Studio. Sie sind beide Mitte der sechziger Jahre in Japan geboren und haben Produkt- bzw. Umweltdesign studiert. Ihre Entwürfe sind zeitlos und praktisch. Die frühen Arbeiten lassen ihren Glauben erkennen, dass Design jedem zur Verfügung stehen und ausserdem die Probleme des Alltagslebens lösen sollte. Die verwandelbaren Objekte der späten Neunziger versagten sich eingrenzenden Definitionen und vereinigten als Gebrauchsgegenstände für den kleinen Raum gleich zwei oder drei Verwendungsmöglichkeiten in sich. Die 'Wire Frame'-Serie bedient sich der Technologie von Einkaufswagen, um einen preiswerten Stuhl und eine Bank zu schaffen. Wie den Stühlen ist den späteren Serienprodukten stets die gleiche Schlichtheit und Aufmerksamkeit für das Detail zu eigen. „Wir wollen uns auf die funktionalen, nicht auf die dekorativen Aspekte des Designs konzentrieren," kommentiert Tomoko.

Emilio Ambasz
Stapelstuhl Vox
Stahlrahmen, Aluminium
h. 79cm b. 53cm t. 47cm
Vitra, Deutschland

Vardit Laor
Stuhlvitrine
Sperrholz, Glas
h. 285cm b. 80cm t. 40cm
Kleinserie

François Azambourg
Sessel mit Fussteil
Birkensperrholz, Schaumgummi
h. 71cm b. 70cm l. 97cm
VIA, Paris
Prototyp

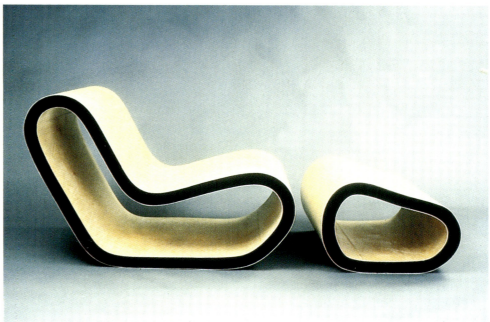

Eine der aufregendsten Ausstellungen anlässlich der Mailänder Messe im Jahr 2000 war die 'Design France – Generation 2001'-Show von VIA, mit der das 20-jährige Bestehen der französischen Möbel-Fördervereinigung VIA gefeiert wurde. VIA wurde 1979 von CODIFA (das Komitee zur Förderung der französischen Möbelindustrie) und dem französischen Ministerium für Industrielle Produktion gegründet. Heute spielt VIA ohne Zweifel eine wichtige Rolle für die französische Möbelproduktion. VIA hat verschiedene Funktionen: Es soll neue Trends, die sich aus der Veränderung von Lebensstilen ergeben, aufspüren, mit den verschiedenen Kunstakademien in Frankreich zusammenarbeiten, das französische Design fördern, als Forum für kreative Köpfe in Frankreich agieren (Agora des Createurs) und Hersteller in Sachen Strategie und Produktentwicklung beraten. Für die junge Generation aufstrebender Designer ist die VIA 'Appels Permanents'-Kommission von grosser Wichtigkeit, da sie jährlich über 1.000 Mappen sichtet und die Produktion von Prototypen der besten unter ihnen finanziert. Die Kommission vergibt auch ein Forschungsstipendium, die Carte Blanche, an Designer, die sowohl Originalität als auch eine reife kreative Vorgehensweise zeigen. Kaum ein anderes Land hat bislang eine solche Organisation wie die VIA, die den innovativen Charakter ihrer Inneneinrichtungsindustrie fördert.

Ross Lovegrove
Stapelstuhl Air One
Polypropylenschaum
h. 53cm t. 115cm
Edra, Italien

Danny Lane
Tisch Laughing Water
Glas, Edelstahl
h. 72cm b. 170cm l.193cm
Unikat

One Foot Taller
Stuhl Chasm
Kunststoff
h. 75cm b. 70cm t. 75cm
Nicehouse, Grossbritannien
Kleinserie

One Foot Taller
Stuhl Ravine
Kunststoff, Edelstahl
h. 80cm b. 50cm t. 55cm
Nicehouse, Grossbritannien
Kleinserie

Aus einem Polypropylenschaum hergestellt, der normalerweise für Verpackungen verwendet wird, verströmt der Stapelstuhl 'Air One' von Ross Lovegrove in Disco-Blau und Silber den Zeitgeist der 70er Jahre. Er ist sehr leicht und kann leicht transportiert und gestapelt werden.

Ron Arad
Sofa Victoria and Albert Collection
Polyester, S tahl, Polyurethanschaum
h. 85–145cm b. 180–290cm
Moroso SpA, Italien

Ron Arad
Sessel Victoria and Albert Collection
Polyester, S tahl, Polyurethanschaum
h. 75cm b. 74cm
Morosa SpA, Italien

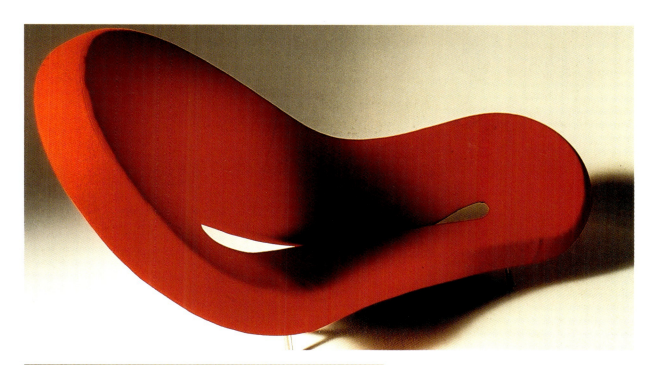

Ron Arads Sofa 'Victoria und Albert' für Moros ist nach einer Ausstellung zu Arads Werk benannt, die im gleichnamigen Museum in London von Juni bis Oktober 2000 gezeigt wurde. Es besteht aus einem einzelnen gehärteten Stahlband, das mit Schaum verkleidet ist, und einem Polster aus waschbarem, aber nicht abnehmbaren Material, das in Primärfarben gehalten ist. Jede Grösse ist lieferbar, dennoch gilt: je grösser, umso besser. Nachdem er das Sofa auf der Moroso-Ausstellung in Mailand gesehen hatte, bemerkte Javier Mariscal, dass die Grösse, die Opulenz und die sinnlichen Kurven dem Sofa einen fast anzüglichen Touch verleihen würden, ein Liebessofa, auf dem man sich vergnügen und spielen sollte.

MÖBEL

Philippe Starck
Stuhl Hudson
Poliertes Aluminium
h. 84cm b. 42cm t. 46cm
Emeco, USA

Pascal Tarabay
Stuhl Frog
Holz, Aluminium, Kunststoff
h. 84cm b. 50cm l. 50cm
KLeinserie

Mario Bellini
Stuhl Arco
Fiberglas, Polymer
h. 85cm b. 63.5cm t. 54.5cm
Heller Inc., USA

Karim Rashid
Stuhl Oh Chair
Polypropylen, Stahl
h. 86.3cm b. 61cm t. 56cm
Umbra, Kanada

Philippe Starck war seit jeher von dem Aluminium-Stuhl 'Emeco' überzeugt und – entgegen seiner üblichen Arbeitsweise – fragte er sogar bei dem Hersteller nach, ob er die Verantwortung für die Neuinterpretation des Stuhles übernehmen könne. Er bemerkte in diesem Zusammenhang: „Der 'Emeco'-Stuhl hat ein zeitloses Design, trotzdem kann man sehen, dass es aus den 40ern oder 50ern stammt. Ich wollte den Stuhl sozusagen in einen Klassiker der Zukunft verwandeln, jedoch das Erbe bewahren." Er behielt die Silhouette des Originals größtenteils bei, passte aber den Stuhl den heutigen Bedürfnissen an, indem er ihn leichter und stapelbar machte.

Karim Rashid ist zweifellos der bekannteste heute in den USA arbeitende zeitgenössische Designer. Seine international anerkannten gestalterischen Fähigkeiten schließen sowohl Möbeldesign als auch Leuchten und Geschirr ein. Seine Beherrschung des Materials, die fließenden und sinnlichen Kurven – sei es Meran-Glas oder das neueste recyclebare Polypropylen – münden in ein eklektisches Spektrum von Objekten. Der Stuhl 'Oh' ist ein ergonomischer und stapelbarer Mehrzweckstuhl. Die Idee war die Entwicklung eines eleganten, aber nicht teuren Designs. Die Verwendung flexiblen Polypropylens bedeutet in der Konsequenz, dass sich auch der Normalbürger einen solchen Plastikstuhl, der zudem sehr bequem ist, leisten kann.

Gunilla Allard
Stuhl Cosmos
Stahl, Holz
h. 80cm b. 36cm t. 50cm
Lammhults Mobel AB, Schweden

Kasper Salto
Stapelstuhl Blade
Birkenholz
h. 79cm b. 49cm l. 50cm
Botium, Dänemark

Emilio Ambasz
Stapelstuhl Vox
Stahlrahmen, Aluminium
h. 79cm b. 53cm t. 47cm
Vitra, Deutschland

Alberto Meda
Bürostuhl Meda 2
Kunststoff, Netzbespannung
h. 96–101cm b. 67cm t. 67cm
Vitra, Deutschland

MÖBEL

Richard Hutten
Stuhl One of a Kind
Aluminiumblech
h. 45–82cm b. 40cm
sdb Industries, Niederlande

Jörg Boner
Schrank Hoover
Aluminium, Stoff
h. 199cm b. 67cm t. 57.5cm
sdb Industries, Niederlande

Richard Hutten
Sessel One of a Kind
Aluminiumblech
h. 69cm b. 67cm t. 50cm
sdb Industries, Niederlande

Group Kombinat
Regal High in the Sky
MDF, Furnier, Aluminium
h. 42cm b. 40 cm t. 40cm
sdb Industries, Niederlande

Group Kombinat
Sessel Missy
Aluminium, Polyurethan
h. 104cm b. 60cm t. 60cm
sdb Industries, Niederlande

Geert Koster
Regal Reflex
Multiplex, Plexi, Aluminium
h. 160cm b. 215cm t. 70cm
sdb Industries, Niederlande

Group Kombinat
Beleuchtete Sitzbank Zebra
MDF, Furnier, Stoff
h. 48cm b. 140cm t. 49cm
sdb Industries, Niederlande

Ron Arad
Tisch No Waste
Aluminium
h. 75cm b. 220cm t.130cm
sdb Industries, Niederlande

Richard Hutten
Schrank Wheels
MDF, Stahl, Aluminium
h. 150cm b. 100cm t. 70cm
sdb Industries, Niederlande

Geert Koster
Beistelltisch 3 Headed Table
Aluminium, Stahl
h. 60cm Ø. 35cm
sdb Industries, Niederlande

Leon van Gerwen ist ein verständnisvoller Unternehmer und sehr enthusiastisch, was die Unterstützung des zeitgenössischen Designs angeht. Als Marketing Manager kam er 1996 zu sdb, einem Unternehmen, das vor allem im mittleren Segment der Vitrinenherstellung vertreten war, dessen Wirtschaftlichkeit aber schon abnahm. Zu diesem Zeitpunkt wurde auch Hidden ins Leben gerufen. Die grundlegende Idee war eine Sammlung origineller Produkte, die von einer Gruppe junger Designer mit ähnlichen Ideen und Visionen entworfen wurden. Es wurden neun individuelle Designer bzw. Studios beauftragt: N2, Kombinat, Ron Arad, Richard Huten, Geert Koster, Dumoffice, El Ultimo Grito, Atelier Oi und Christophe Pillet.

Warum der Name Hidden? Van Gerwen möchte, dass die Kollektion dem, was die Designer als markttauglich empfinden, entspricht. Allzu oft werden bestimmte Entwürfe, die man nicht für kommerziell genug hält, von den Herstellern einfach versteckt (=to hide).

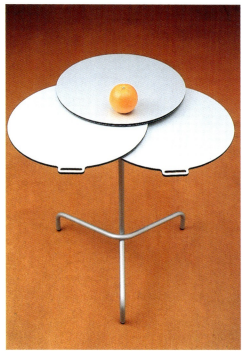

Giancarlo Piretti
Klappstuhl Torsion
(mit schwingender Rückenlehne)
Aluminium, Polypropylen
h. 81cm b. 47cm t. 58.5cm
Prototyp

Alberto Meda
Sitzsystem Floating Frame
Aluminium, Kunststoffnetz
Diverse Grössen
Alias srl, Italien

MÖBEL

Verner Panton
Stuhl Pantostack
Aluminiumguss, Polypropylen
h. 84cm b. 65cm t. 55cm
VS Vereinigte Spezialmöbelfabriken
GmbH & Co, Deutschland

Der 'Pantostack' war Verner Panton's letztes Möbeldesign. Obwohl er im September 1998 starb, verzögerten Produktionstests die Herstellung bis Ende 1999.

MÖBEL

Erwan Bouroullec
Sessel/Liege Spring
Stahl, Fiberglas, Polyurethan, Gummi
h. 36–68cm b. 72cm t. 80cm
Cappellini SpA, Italien

Mauro Mori
Marmortische M2544
Ø. 33cm
Cappellini SpA, Italien

Barber Osgerby
Hocker/Tisch Hula
Teakholz
h. 34cm b. 40cm l. 75cm
Cappellini SpA, Italien

Mauro Mori
Beistelltisch M2546
Massivholz
h. 40cm b. 61cm l. 38cm
Cappellini SpA, Italien

Alfredo Häberli
Hocker PO/0028
Polyurethanschaum
h. 42cm Ø. 43cm
Cappellini SpA, Italien

Cappellini SpA erstaunt uns immer wieder mit neuen und aufregenden Entwürfen von Designern aus der ganzen Welt. Ein Team von fünf Leuten sichtet Hunderte von Produkten, die dem Unternehmen jedes Jahr angeboten werden. Alle ausgewählten Stücke passen zur CI des Unternehmens, und jedes einzelne findet die persönliche Zustimmung von Cappellini persönlich. Seiner Meinung nach muss sich jedes Design durch eine innovative Form bzw. eine besondere Verwendung des Materials auszeichnen, um in seine Kollektion aufgenommen zu werden. Cappellini: „Jedes neue Produkt muss immer besser sein als das vorhergehende". Auf die Frage, ob die Mischung aus grossen Namen und relativen Newcomern eine bewusste Vermarktungsstrategie sei und ob die garantierten Erfolge durch Lissoni oder Morrison es ihm erlaubten, experimentelleres Design zu unterstützen, antwortete er: „Kein Produkt hat für mich Priorität. Sie sind alle gleichwertig. Ich kann Objekte von berühmten Designern genau so gut verkaufen wie die von jungen begabten Anfängern. Jeder Prototyp bedarf jahrelanger Entwicklung, bevor er in eine Kollektion aufgenommen wird und dann durchlaufen die Produkte einen sehr langsamen Prozess der Marktreifung; das macht aber nichts, da wir bei Cappellini ohnehin lieber mit Long-Sellern als mit Bestsellern arbeiten." Ihm ist klar, dass es nur wenige Unternehmen gibt, die mit bahnbrechendem Design arbeiten wollen und führt dies als Grund dafür an, dass der Markt so wenig Auswahl bietet. „Der Designer der Zukunft befasst sich nicht ausschließlich mit guten Produkten, sondern ist auch darum bemüht, eine gute Atmosphäre zu schaffen. Sie werden menschliche Projekte entwickeln, die den Benutzer träumen lassen. Ich habe das Gefühl, dass einige der Designer, die mit Cappellini zusammenarbeiten, in dieser Richtung denken." Das Unternehmen Cappellini exportiert in mehr als 50 Länder, beschäftigt Hunderte von Leuten und der Umsatz steigt jedes Jahr. Das gestalterische Auge Cappellinis und seine Fähigkeit zu erkennen, was neu und zeitgemäß ist, sowie sein Bemühen, neuen Designern eine Chance zu geben, garantiert seinen Kollektionen nicht nur kommerziellen Erfolg, sie sind darüberhinaus immer variationsreich und formschön.

Jasper Morrison
Stapelstuhl Tate
Buchensperrholz, Eiche
Polypropylen
h. 45–81cm b. 53cm t. 47.5cm
Cappellini SpA, Italien

Alfredo Häberli
Ausziehtisch Easy Long
Nickel, Eiche, Buche
h. 73cm b. 130cm l. 130cm
Cappellini SpA, Italien

Piero Lissoni
Regal Uni
Lackiertes Metall
h. 64cm l. 270cm b. 61.2cm
Cappellini SpA, Italien

Claudio Silvestrin
Tisch/Bank Millennium Hope
Walnussholz
Tisch: h. 72cm l. 315cm t. 80cm
Bank: h. 45cm l. 157.5cm t. 40cm
Cappellini SpA, Italien

Erwan Bouroullec
Schrankbett Lit Clos
Stahl, Birkensperrholz, Aluminium
Verschiedene Materialien
h. 75–324cm b. 240cm t. 200cm
Cappellini SpA, Italien

Carlo Colombo
Regalsystem Archi
Edelstahl, Glas, Holz
Diverse Grössen
Cappellini SpA, Italien

Kasper Salto
Kinderliege Leaf
Birkenholz
h. 15cm b. 35cm l. 85cm
Prototyp

Pascal Tarabay
Bank Beirut
Metall, Holz oder
recycelter Kunststoff
h. 75cm b. 180cm l. 120cm
Kleinserie

Pascal Tarabay
Liege Lazy Lounge
Metall, Holz, EVA-Schaum
h. 50cm b. 65cm l. 180cm
Kleinserie

MÖBEL

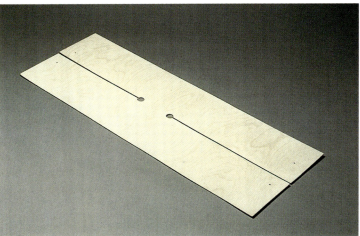

Kasper Salto hat das Design für sein Tageskinderbett auf Papier erarbeitet. Er ging davon aus, dass etwas, was auf Papier gelingt, auch aus Sperrholz funktionieren müsste. Er schnitt zuerst ein Rechteck und dann an beiden Enden einen Schlitz, wodurch zwei Laschen entstanden. Diese Enden wurden zusammengepresst und miteinander vernietet, so dass eines die Rückenlehne, das andere eine Beinstütze für das Kind formte.

Werner Aisslinger
Liege Soft
Stahl, Aluminiumlegierung
Technogel®
h. 85cm b. 60cm l. 180cm
Zanotta, Italien

Christian Ghion
Liege Blue Lagoon
Aluminium, Polyurethangel
h. 45cm b. 60cm l. 160cm
Everstyl, Frankreich
Kleinserie

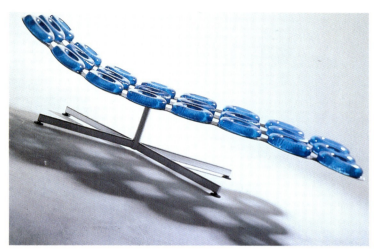

Werner Aisslinger war der Mittelpunkt in Köln und Mailand im Jahr 2000. Ungeheuer produktiv und sozusagen allgegenwärtig hat er allein im Möbelbereich etliche neue Produkte vorgestellt, z.B. Tisch, Stuhl und Bank 'Linn' für Jonas and Jonas, den Tisch 'Lid' für denselben Hersteller, den 'x'-Tisch für Böwer (S. 64), die 'Plus'-Elemente für Magis, das Tischsystem 'Juli' für Cappellini, weitere Teile für seine 'Soft Cell'-Möbel, das 'Cell'-System für Zeritalia (S. 48), den Stuhl 'Pat' für Arflex und 'Soft', eine Chaiselongue, für Zanotta (oben). Aisslinger interessiert sich für Technologie und neue Materialien, da er der Ansicht ist, dass dieser Bereich neue Typologien eher hervorbringen wird als die künstliche Entwicklung innovativer Formen. Sein Ziel ist es, mit 3D-Formen zu arbeiten, die nicht wie Objekte der neunziger Jahre minimalistisch und glatt sind.

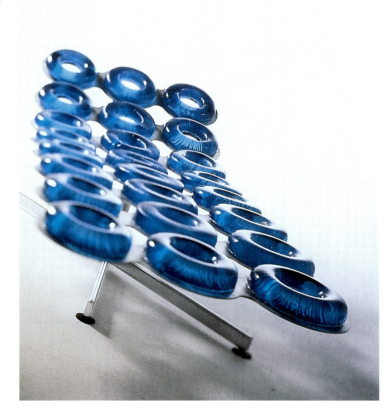

Khodi Feiz
Sofa Chaise-bas
Schaumgepolsterter Stoff, Stahl
h. 50cm B. 100cm t. 100cm
Prototyp

Maarten Van Severen
Sitz Low chair
Aluminium
h. 63cm b. 50cm t. 92cm
Maarten Van Severen Meubelen
Belgien

Pascal Tarabay
Sitzregal w+all
Metall, Holz, Filz
h. 105cm b. 65cm l. 75cm
Kleinserie

Paolo Piva
Sofa Ronda
Metall, Leder
b. 120/150/180/210cm
Wittman GmbH, Österreich

Hannes Wettstein
Sofa Master
Metall, Holz, Polyurethan
Polyester, Gänsefedern
h. 75cm l. 232cm t. 95cm
Arflex International SpA, Italien

Paolo Rizzatto
Sofa Flexus
Polyurethan, Stahl, Naturstoff
h. 91/106cm l. 240cm t. 78cm
Alias srl, Italien

Erwan Bouroullec
Sofa 1 and a Half
Fiberglas, Eisen, Schaum, Wollstoff
h. 85cm l. 140cm b. 70cm
Domeau & Peres, Frankreich

Francesco Binfaré
Sofa Flap
Stahl, Polyurethan
h. 84cm l. 355cm t. 166cm
Edra, Italien

Claudio Bellini
Ledersessel DS-460
h. 92cm b. 119–137cm
de Sede, Schweiz

Claudio Bellini
Ledercouch DS-460
h. 92cm b. 232cm
t. 90–106cm
de Sede, Schweiz

Patricia Urquiola
Couch Lowland
Holz, Leder, Polyester
Stahl, Polyurethanschaum
b. 180–260cm
Moroso SpA, Italien

Piero Lissoni
Sofa Metro 2
Holz, Metall, Stoff weiss/orange
h. 71cm b. 160–210cm t. 100cm
Living Divani, Italien

Antonio Citterio
Sofa Freetime
Verchromtes Metallgestell, Polsterung
h. 62cm t. 107cm
b. 174.5cm/259.5cm
B&B Italia, Italien

MÖBEL

Werner Aisslinger
Regalsystem Cell System
Glas, Aluminium
h. 80cm b. 36cm t. 50cm
Zeritalia, Italien

Cini Boeri
Sofa Meter
Polyurethanschaum
Daunen, Metall
h. 76cm b. 220/260cm t. 97cm
Molteni & C SpA, Italien

Emaf Progetti
Sofa Alfa
Stahl, Stretch, Polyurethan
Nylon, Daunen
h. 65cm l. 230cm t. 92cm
Zanotta, Italien

Alfredo Häberli
Sideboard Florence
MDF, Aluminiumlegierung, Stahl
Diverse Grössen
Zanotta SpA, Italien

Lodovico Acerbis
Medienwand The Jolly Units
Wenge, Kirschbaum oder lackiert
h. 161cm b. 120cm t. 41cm
Acerbis International SpA, Italien

Lodovico Acerbis
Regalwand The Shelvings
Wenge, Kirschbaum, Lack
h. 220cm b. 80–120cm t. 35cm
Acerbis International SpA, Italien

Lodovico Acerbis
Regal Wall Shelves
Wenge, Kirschbaum, Lack
h. 6cm t. 30cm
Acerbis International SpA, Italien

Chiara Cantono
Faltmobiliar Mat
Holz, Teppich
h. 350cm b. 360cm t. 2cm
Prototyp

MÖBEL

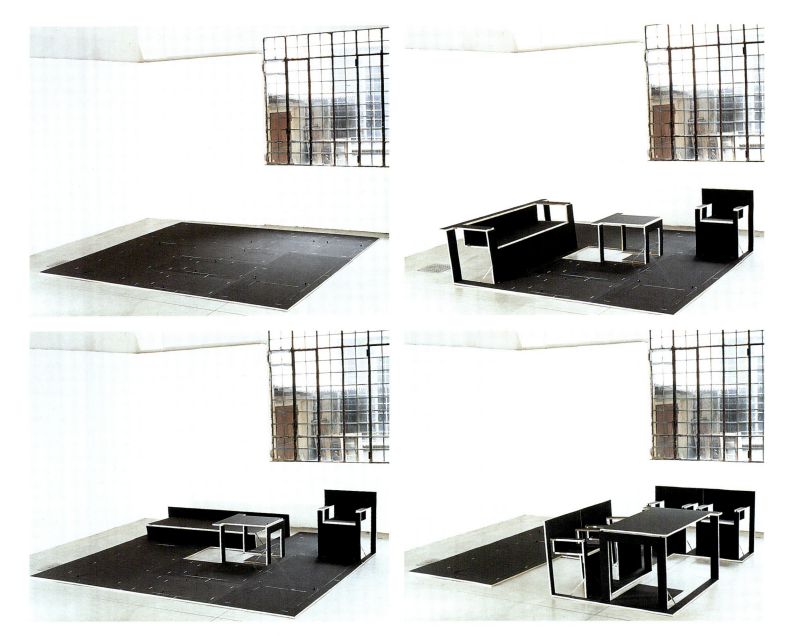

Die junge italienische Möbeldesignerin Chiara Cantono hat einen neuen Begriff der Innenarchitektur entwickelt. Wenn sie gerade nicht benötigt werden, können die von ihr entworfenen Elemente in einen 10 qm grossen 'Sperrholzteppich' verwandelt werden, der innerhalb weniger Sekunden in eine Reihe verschiedener Interieurs zurückverwandelt werden kann. Diese Elemente sind durch einen eigenständig funktionierenden Arretierungsmechanismus gesichert.

Kazuyo Sejima
Interieur Una Stanza Tutta Per Sé
Driade SpA, Italien

Stuhl Atsuatsu
Holz, Polyurethan
Wolle, Stretch, Aluminium
h. 19cm b. 230cm t. 105cm

Tischchen Picapica
Edelstahl, Nylon
h. 36cm Ø. 30cm

Blumenständer Hanahana
Edelstahl
h. 160cm b. 92cm t. 25cm

Sitz Maramuru
Stahl, Polyurethan
Edelstahl, Nylon
h. 56.8cm Ø. 73ccm

Zaha Hadid
Sofa Z. Scape
Gummi, Holz, Metall
Diverse Grössen
Sawaya & Moroni, Italien

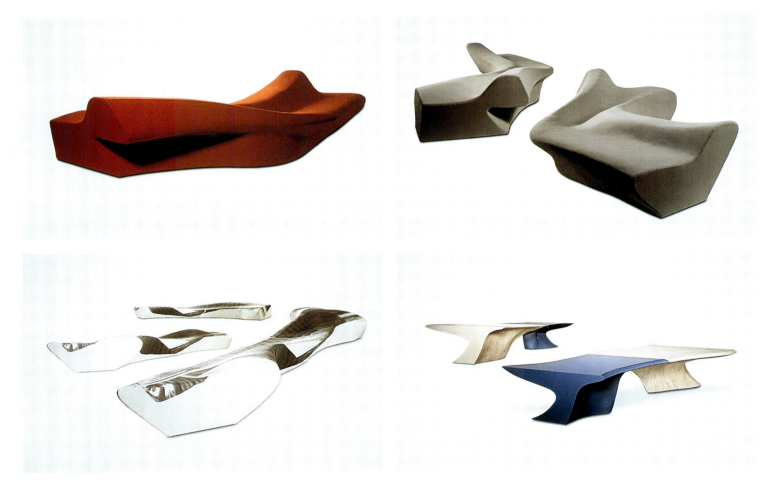

Michele De Lucchi war erstaunt über die grosse Anzahl Architekten, die im Jahr 2000 für führende Hersteller Produkte entwarfen. Unter anderem haben Zaha Hadid 'Z.Scape' für Sawaya & Moroni, das Büro von Norman Foster die 'A900'-Serie, bestehend aus Tischen und Stühlen, für Thonet, David Chipperfield 'Home Office'-Möbel, Kazuo Seijma 'Una Stanza Tutta per Sé' für Driade, Claudio Silvestrin die 'Millenium Hope'-Bank für Cappellini, Rafael Moneo die 'Estocolmo'-Bank für Casas, Steven Holl und Perault Leuchten für FontanaArte und Uchida farbige horizontale Schränke für Buil entworfen. Paolo Moroni von Sawaya & Moroni, dem diese Tendenz auch auffiel, bemerkte dazu: „Irgendwie gab es im Jahr 2000 in Mailand besonders viele Architekten. Auch Unternehmen, die normalerweise mit Produktdesignern zusammenarbeiten, haben sich jetzt vermehrt etablierten Architekten zugewandt". De Lucchi ist der Auffassung, dass es trotz der unterschiedlichen Herangehensweisen an das Produkt (räumliche Definition versus Produktidentität) zwischen Architektur und Design eine starke interdisziplinäre symbiotische Verbindung gibt.

Im Design hat der Architekt Gelegenheit, expressiver zu arbeiten. Jean Nouvel sagte einmal: „Hier gibt es nicht die Zeitverzögerung, wie sie beim Errichten eines Gebäudes entsteht. Design kann experimentell sein, es gibt dem Designer die Freiheit zur Innovation. Er kann seine Ideen wie ein Künstler direkt umsetzen" (Internationales Design Jahrbuch 1995). Hadid's 'Z.Scape' illustriert dies sehr gut. Es bietet ein umfassendes neues Konzept zur Gestaltung des Lebensraumes. Die Formgebung ist durch Landschaftsformationen beeinflusst und spiegelt die erosive Kraft von Gletschern wider. 'Glacier' und 'Moraine' sind zwei Sofas, die monolithisch konstruiert sind und aus Schaum bestehen, der mit einem Polsterstoff überzogen ist. Sie wurden mit zwei komplementären Tischen präsentiert: 'Stalactite' und 'Stalagmite', die beide aus lackiertem Naturholz bestehen. Das Ganze kann als grosse Gruppe zusammengestellt oder in seine konstitutiven Einzelteile verstreut werden. Dieser Prozess verleiht traditionellen Raumformen und konventionellen Ideen eine neue Dynamik und einen kritischen Impuls.

Foster-Programme A 900:
Tisch A 1910
Holz, Glas, Aluminium
h. 74cm l. 250cm b. 90cm
Gebrüder Thonet GmbH
Deutschland

Bank
Aluminium, Leder
Stoff, Sperrholz
h. 73cm l. 127cm t. 63cm
Gebrüder Thonet GmbH
Deutschland

Stuhl A 900
Aluminium, Sperrholz
Kunststoff, Stoff
h. 68cm b. 59cm t. 53cm
Gebrüder Thonet GmbH
Deutschland

Stuhl A 902PF
Aluminium, Sperrholz
Kunststoff, Stoff
h. 68cm b. 59cm t. 53cm
Gebrüder Thonet GmbH
Deutschland

Die Vision eines Architekten wirkt vielleicht manchmal weniger verführerisch oder modisch als die des Designers, aber sie wurzelt immer in einem tiefen Verständnis für den Innenraum. Das Interesse des Architekten an Möbeln und Lebensräumen ist zweifelsohne neu (vgl. das Totale Design des Bauhaus oder der Arts and Crafts-Bewegung). 1994 gründete John Small die Produktdesigngruppe bei Foster and Associates. Er erklärte: „Das Foster-Büro gestaltet Gebäude immer nach einer ganzheitlichen Methode. Aus diesem Grund sind die Elemente innerhalb des Gebäudes immer Teil des Ganzen und stehen nicht isoliert für sich". Foster erklärte bezüglich der neuen 'A900'-Serie für Thonet: „Für mich sind Möbel eine mikrokosmische Form von Architektur mit dem entscheidenden Unterschied, dass die Zeitspanne zwischen Entwurf und Effekt drastisch verringert werden kann". Foster bewunderte den ursprünglichen Bugholz-Stuhl von Thonet und auch die nachfolgende Generation von Sitzmöbeln, die dann aus gebogenen Stahlrohren hergestellt wurde. Seine 'A900'-Serie versucht die Thonet-Tradition aufzugreifen, bedient sich dabei jedoch heutiger Produktionsmöglichkeiten. Von der Schlichtheit der frühen Produkte beeindruckt, besteht seine Kollektion konsequenterweise nur aus einer begrenzten Anzahl an Komponenten, die mit alle einem Elektroschraubenzieher zusammengesetzt werden können.

David Chipperfield
Home Office
Driade, Italien

Arbeitstisch
Mahogani, Aluminium
l. 80cm t. 80cm h. 73cm

Bücherregal
Mahogani, Aluminium
l. 180cm t. 40cm h. 172cm

Aktenschrank
Mahogani, Aluminium
l. 180cm t. 40cm h. 150cm

Rafael Moneo
Bank Estocolmo
UDF, Ahornfurnier
h. 79.5cm b.66cm
l. 200–250cm t. 66cm
Casas, Spanien

Shigeru Uchida
Wandschränke Horizontal
Eiche, Aluminium
h. 91cm b. 90cm l. 18cm
Build, Japan
Prototyp

Rodolfo Dordoni
Bett Favignana
Ahorn
h. 158cm l. 200cm
b. 171/181/191cm
Flou SpA, Italien

Patrizia Scarzella
Bett Meridiana Testata Alta
Aluminium, Holz
l. 200cm/210 cm
b. 160cm/170cm/180cm
Flou SpA, Italien

MÖBEL

Hans Sandgren Jakobsen
Bett Grandlit
Buche, Stahl
h. 78cm b. 220cm l. 200cm
Fredericia Furniture A/S, Dänemark

'Grandlit' von Hans Jakobsen beruht auf einem neuen Bettkonzept. Tisch und Rückenlehnen können rund um das Bett beliebig am Rand befestigt und entsprechend genutzt werden.

MÖBEL

Boum Design:
Liege Air Lounge
Vinyl
5 x h. 20.3cm b. 61cm l. 61cm
Boum Design, USA

Sitzkissen Air Cushion
Vinyl
h. 20.3cm b. 61cm l. 61cm
Boum Design, USA

Paravent Air Wall
Plexiglas, Vinyl
9 x h. 203cm l. 182.8cm t. 25.4cm
Boum Design, USA

Während der Mailänder Messe 2000 war der Aufschrei überall zu hören: „Die Amerikaner kommen". Auf der G7-Show, die auf einem Nebenschauplatz stattfand, stand Pierre Bouguennec (Boum Design) mit seinen beeindruckenden aufblasbaren Objekten im Zentrum des aufgeregten Interesses. Die anderen Mitglieder der G7-Gruppe sind Once (Marre Moerel, Harry Paul van Iersel und Camilla Vega), CCD (Christopher Deam), Prototype and Production (Chris Bundy und Ross Menuez), Worx (Michael Solis), Comma (David Khouri und Robert Guzman) und Dinersan Inc. (Nick Dine). Insgesamt bietet die Gruppe ein neue und farbenfröhliche Produkte. Sie repräsentieren mit ihrem Design in seiner ausgeprägten Taktilität, der leichten Zugänglichkeit und hohen Funktionalität den Aufbruch zu einer neuen Bewegung in den Vereinigten Staaten. Paola Antonella vom MoMA sagte: „Eine neue Generation amerikanischer Designer ist in den Vordergrund getreten und wird vielleicht bald dafür sorgen, dass die Kreativität eine Gewichtsverlagerung zugunsten dieser Seite des Atlantiks erfährt... Es ist ein grosser Augenblick in der Geschichte des nordamerikanischen Designs". Entsprechend wurde auf der Uburbia-Show in New York, zeitgleich mit der Internationalen Möbelmesse 2000 in Mailand, die Arbeit einer Gruppe junger Amerikaner – es gab teilweise Überschneidungen mit G7 Designern – gefeiert:
Nick Dine, Jeffrey Bernett, Richard Shemtov, Michael Solis, David Khouri und Harry

Sitz Air Chair
Plexiglas
2 x h. 61cm b. 81cm l. 81cm

MÖBEL

Allen, die Möbeln für das urbane Leben entworfen haben. Shemtov, dessen Firma Dune das Projekt initiierte, bat jeden der Beteiligten um einen Entwurf, „der Grösse und Brauchbarkeit mit einer geschliffenen modernen Ästhetik verbindet." Das Ergebnis hiess 'Uburbia', eine in ihrem inneren Zusammenhang sehr überzeugend wirkende Alternative zum üblichen Möbelmischmasch des durchschnittlichen New Yorkers.

Jacob Timpe
Tischuntergestell Tischbocktisch
Unbehandelte Esche, Gummiauflagen
h. 73cm l. 190cm t. 85cm
Moormann Möbel Produktion
Deutschland

Pascal Mourgue
Ecktisch Smala
Eiche, Aluminium
h. 46cm l. 100cm b. 100cm
Ligne Roset, Frankreich

Piero Lissoni
Tisch M.P
Lack/Aluminium, Wenge/Buche
h. 24cm b. 90cm l. 130cm
Artelano, Frankreich

Paolo Ulian
Couchtisch/Bank Bench 2000
Sperrholz, Aluminium
h. 30cm b. 75cm t. 150cm
Prototyp

MÖBEL

Im Jahr 2000 wurde ein neuer Preis, der Design Report Award, unterstützt durch die gleichnamige deutsche Zeitschrift, ins Leben gerufen. Die Juroren, Matali Crasset, Konstantin Grcic, Ross Lovegrove und Nasir Kassamali, wählten aus Hunderten von Entwürfen der 'Salone Satellite' eine Bank, die 'Bench 2000' von Paolo Ulian, aus. Der Couchtisch ist aus flexiblem Sperrholz hergestellt, das Oberteil kann mit einem Handgriff angehoben werden, und so entsteht eine Bank mit Rückenlehne und integriertem Stauraum.

Jeffrey Bernett
Stuhl Beta
Birkensperrholz, Laminat, Velourleder
49cm/51.5cm t. 82.5cm
Dune, USA

Michael Solis
Couchtisch Four Forty
Dune, USA

Interieur aus der Urburbia Show New York:
Michael Solis
Beistelltische Fuse+ und Fuse-
Walnussfurnier, Aluminium
Matte MDF-Lackierung
b. 41cm t. 41cm h. 60cm
Dune, USA

Harry Allen
Bed, La La Salama
Walnussfurnier, Chrom satiniert
Matte MDF-Lackierung
b. 223.5cm t. 51.5cm h. 228.5cm
Dune, USA

'La La Salama', das bedeutet auf Suaheli 'friedlicher Schlaf'. Harry Allens Bett 'Murphy' sieht nicht nur gut aus, sondern ist auch bequem. Das Requisit unzähliger amerikanischer Schwarzweiss-Kommödien (wo eine heimliche Zusammenkunft zweier Liebender durch einen unerwarteten Gast gestört wird und alles, einschließlich der abgelegten Strumpfhosen, in der Wand verschwindet) hat Allen in diesem Möbelstück wieder aufleben lassen. Im Gehäuse aus Nussholz sind ein ausklappbares grosses Bett, verborgene Fächer mit Türen, Regale mit Spiegeln und ein Nachttisch eingebaut. Da das Bett an der Decke befestigt wird, eignet es sich als Raumteiler.

Antonio Citerio
Workstation Vademecum
Stahl, Aluminium, MDF
h. 180cm b. 120cm t. 105cm
Vitra, Deutschland

Peter Maly
Bürosystem Modul 5000
Stahl, Lack, Glas
Ahorn, Buche, Walnuss
Diverse Grössen
Mauser Office, Deutschland

Das Home-Office-Konzept liegt Michele De Lucchi sehr am Herzen. Seine Auswahl liefert viele Beispiele für Möbel, die zwar für das Arbeiten entworfen wurden, aber visuell und manchmal auch von ihrer Funktionalität so angepasst wurden, dass sie sich in ein Wohnumfeld einfügen. 'N2', die Tische von Defne Koz und 'Go-Car' von Power (S.66) sind somit Neuinterpretationen des Büromöbels. Power hat die Grösse des Computerarbeitsplatzes auf ein Minimum reduziert und für die Konstruktion leuchtendes farbiges Glas verwendet, wodurch eine neue Ästhetik der Home Office-Typologie entsteht. Bei der Firma Radice (S.68-69) hingegen wird das Büro nach dem Arbeitstag weggepackt. De Lucchi empfindet Büromöbel oftmals als zu kompliziert, Home Office-Produkte hingegen schaffen ein anderes Umfeld. Gegenwärtig arbeitet er an der Gestaltung eines Büroraumes und möchte nur Möbel einsetzen, die für Wohnzwecke entworfen wurden. Auch wenn er aufeinander abgestimmte Teile verwendet, kann er sich vorstellen, dass eines Tages die unterschiedlichen Bestandteile jeweils die Arbeitspersönlichkeit des Einzelnen reflektieren.

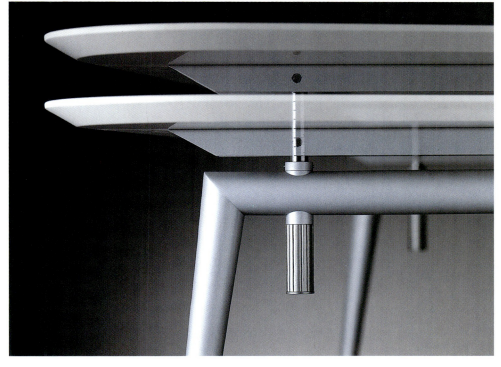

**Christian Deuber und
Jörg Boner (N2)
Tisch Ajax
Holz, Stahl
h. 77cm b. 110cm t. 93cm
ClassiCon, Deutschland**

**Defne Koz
Sekretär Plano
Edelstahl, Sperrholz
h. 92cm b. 105cm t. 90cm
Mobileffe, Italien**

**Werner Aisslinger
x-tisch
Holz, Stahl, Aluminium
h. 70–78cm b. 90cm l. 220cm
Böwer GmbH, Deutschland**

Werner Aisslinger's 'x-tisch' ist ein multifunktionaler Tisch, der sowohl im Büro als auch im Wohnbereich eingesetzt werden kann. Er ist zusammenklappbar und höhenverstellbar. Die Stabilität wird durch die x-förmigen Beine, die sich bei der Anpassung der Höhe verschieben, gewährleistet.

Benjamin Thut
Falttisch Alu 1
Kunstharz, Edelstahl
b. 80cm l. 160cm
Sele 2, Schweiz

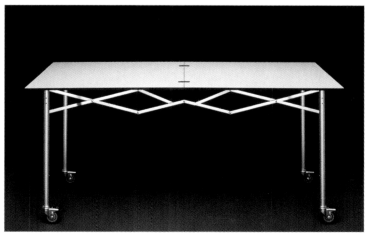

Pekka Tiovola
Elektronisch verstellbarer Tisch Promo
Laminat, Furnier, Stahl
h. 70–120cm
Martela OYJ, Finnland

L. Carniatto
Workstation Navigator
Aluminium, Laminat
h. 132cm l. 102cm t. 44cm
Bellato, Italien

Tim Power
Computertisch Go-Car
Glas, Metall
h. 81cm b. 52cm t. 72cm
Zeritalia, Italien

Geoff Hollington
Home Office VuTable
Polyester, Kunstharz, Stahl
h. 130cm b. 100cm t. 68cm
Herman Miller, Grossbritannien (Sponsor)
Prototyp

Mit dem Tisch 'Vu' wurde die Idee des Home Office auf die Spitze getrieben. Vu ist ein interaktiver Tisch für die Familie der Zukunft, an dem jegliche Kommunikation, ob geschäftlich, privat oder schulisch per E-mail, Sprachsteuerung, Mouse-Click und Video möglich ist. Sogar soziale Kontakte können geknüpft werden, ohne den Arbeitsplatz verlassen zu müssen. Eine eingebaute Kamera schickt ein Bild zu Freunden oder Verwandten. So entsteht ein virtueller Treffpunkt auf dem Weitwinkelbildschirm.

Dante Donegani und Giovanni Lauda
Home Office Big Foot
Metall, Holz
h. 72cm b. 75cm l. 125–325cm
Radice SNC, Italien

Alberto Meda und Paolo Rizzatto
Bürosystem Partner Office
Buche, Aluminium
h. 125cm b. 70cm l. 100cm
Kartell SpA, Italien

Dante Donegani und Giovanni Lauda
Home Office Midi
Metall, Holz
h. 80cm b. 60cm l. 135cm
Radice SNC, Italien
Kleinserie

Home Office Compact
Metall, Holz
h. 80cm b. 60cm l. 110cm
Radice SNC, Italien

Pepe Tanzi
Bürosystem Popoffice
Aluminium, Laminat, Kunstharz
Album srl, Italien

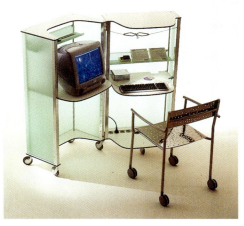

Teppo Asikainen
Schallwand Soundwave
Formgegossenes Polyester
l. 60cm h. 60cm
Snowcrash, Schweden

Annette Egholm und Jacob Agger
Paravent Shade
Aluminium, Textilgewebe
Grösse 1: h. 188cm b. 89cm
Grösse 2: h. 153cm b. 89cm
Bent Krogh A/S, Dänemark

MÖBEL

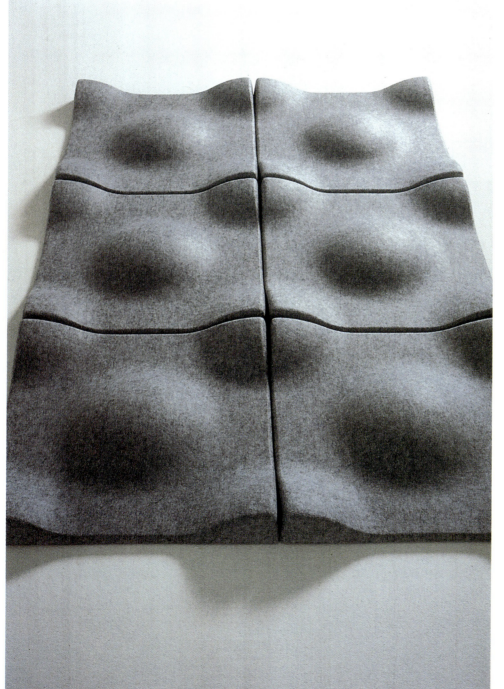

'Snowcrash', eine innovative Gruppe junger finnischer Designer, wurde in den späten neunziger Jahren gegründet. In ihrer ersten Ausstellung in Mailand 1997, die die Aufmerksamkeit der internationalen Presse erregte, boten sie eine Bandbreite von Produkten, die sich durch ein aufregend experimentelles Design auszeichneten. Im Anschluss an diesen Erfolg wurden sie von einem schwedischen Unternehmen, Proventus Design, aufgekauft, dem auch Artekand, die Textilfirma Kinnasand angehört. Im Jahr 2000 hat die Gruppe wiederum einen entscheidenden Schritt in ihrer Entwicklung getan. Obwohl 'Snow-crash' in letzter Zeit am Markt nicht so präsent war, hat die Proventus-Gruppe nun stark in seine Entwicklung investiert und die Weichen sind gestellt, um auf der ursprünglichen Vision aufzubauen. Die Trennwand 'Soundwave' von Teppo Asikainen wurde in Köln als früher Prototyp gezeigt. Mittlerweile ist sie in Produktion gegangen. Sie besteht aus geformten Polyesterfasern, ein Material, das vor allem für Innenwandverkleidungen von Flugzeugen, Autos und Zügen verwendet wird. Dieses filzartige Polyestermaterial wird aus recycleten Plastikflaschen gewonnen und kann mit unterschiedlichen Stoffen und entsprechenden Farbkombinationen überzogen werden. Die handgemachten Platten werden untereinander mit Klettverschlüssen verbunden.

Antonio Citerio
Schranksystem Cross
Stahl, Eiche, Wenge
Glas, Aluminium, Marmor
Diverse Grössen
B&B Italia, Italien

Hannes Wettstein
Regalsystem Items
Holz, Aluminium
h. 15/62/76cm
l. 180/270cm
t. 64cm
Cassina SpA, Italien

Peter Maly
Regalsystem Duo-Medienbank
Ahornholz, Aluminium
Diverse Grössen
Interlübke GmbH, Deutschland

Lorenzo Damiani
Wandhalterung Flex
für Stereoanlage und CDs
Holz, Stahl
h. 100cm b. 150cm t. 50cm
Prototyp

Gabriela Nahlikova und
Leona Matejkova
Schrank Cube
PUR
h. 40cm b. 40cm l. 40cm
Modell

Louise Campbell
Regal und Kommode
Furnier, Esche, Velcro
h. 180cm b. 40cm t. 30cm
Bahnsen Collection, Dänemark

Benny Mosimann
Containersystem Wogg 20
PET, Buchenfurnier, Aluminium
h. 96/184cm b. 76cm t. 57cm
Wogg AG, Schweiz

Mit 'Wogg 20' erweitert jetzt der Schweizer Designer Benny Mosimann seine sehr erfolgreiche Reihe von Behältermöbeln. Ein speziell für 'Wogg 20' entwickeltes halbtransparentes Folienmaterial gleitet um den Korpus. Die runden Ecken und die metallische Oberfläche des Kunststoffs schaffen Container für den Wohnbereich, hinter denen Fernsehgeräte, Musikanlagen und sogar Kühlschränke elegant verschwinden können. Glastablare erweitern die Einsatzmöglichkeiten der ein- und zweistöckigen Behälter.

Hannes Rohringer
Wagen und Schränke
Holz, Lack, weisses Aluminium
h. 171cm b. 39cm l. 156cm
Streitner GmbH, Österreich

Stephan Titz
Regalsystem Homebase
Zwetschgen-/Buchenholz
h. 130cm b. 130cm l. 130cm
Team 7, Österreich
Kleinserie (Zwetschgenholz)
Massenproduktion (Buchenholz)

'Homebase' von Stephan Titz, 'Flow' von Rihl/Proctor und 'Pebble' und 'Erratic' von Jiri Pelcl (S.80) sind allesamt Herausforderungen für das traditionelle, zweidimensionale Bücherregal. 'Homebase' ist eine Serie quadratischer, schiefwinkeliger Kuben, die nach Belieben verdreht und verstellt werden können. Auch 'Flow' ist vollkommen flexibel. Den Designern zufolge beruhen beide auf einem Zufallsprinzip, denn der Benutzer kann die Konfiguration selbst bestimmen.

Fernando Rihl und Christopher Procter
Regalwand Flow
Birkensperrholz
h. 227.5cm b. 227.5cm t. 37.5cm
Spatial Interference, London
Kleinserie

Shigeru Uchida
Regal Kaja
Laminat
h. 350cm l. 210cm t. 22cm
Abet Laminati SpA, Italien

Ettore Sottsass
Regalsystem Kampa
Lack, Stahl
h. 211cm b. 66cm l. 112cm
Memphis srl, Italien

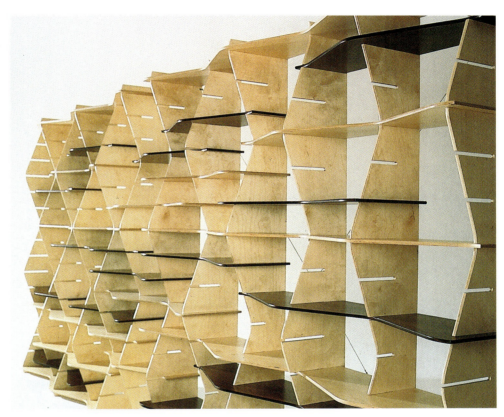

Jiri Pelcl
Sitz + Bücherregal Pebble
Holz, Acryl
h. 50cm l. 118cm t. 48cm
Atelier Pelcl, Tschechien

Martine Bedin
Bücherregal Slate
Laminat
h. 180cm b. 50cm l. 140cm
Abet Laminati SpA, Italien

Jiri Pelcl
Bücherregal Erratic Block
Holz, Acryl
h. 130cm b. 110cm t. 50cm
Atelier Pelcl, Tschechien

Maarten Van Severen
Sideboard Castors 94
Aluminium
h. 40cm b. 240cm t. 40cm
Maarten Van Severen Meubelen, Belgiem

Alfredo Haberli und Christophe Marchand
Modularsystem SEC
Aluminium, Stahl, Glas, Methacryl
Diverse Grössen
Alias srl, Italien

Dakota Jackson
Glasregal Mainframe
Lack, Glas, Acryl
h. 219.7cm b. 115cm t. 38cm
Dakota Jackson, USA

Carlo Cumini
Schrank Cut-al
Aluminium
h. 34–194cm l. 64–328cm t. 49cm
Horm srl, Italien

Studio Technico Horm
Vitrine Expò
Aluminium, Glas
h. 194cm l. 32–64cm t. 34cm
Horm srl, Italien

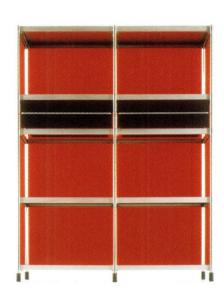

Piero Lissoni
Schrank One
Metall, Lack, Kunststoff
h. 64cm l. 270cm b. 61.2cm
Cappellini SpA, Italien

Carlo Tamborini
Möbelsystem
Edelstahl, Lack/Eiche
h. 115cm b. 254cm t. 66cm
Pallucco Italia, Italien

Petra Runge
Spiegel Book
Aluminium
h. 127cm l. 47/90cm
De Padova srl, Italien

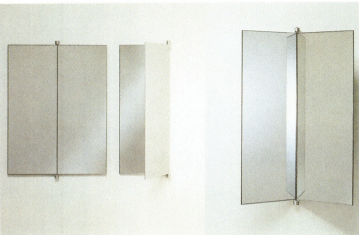
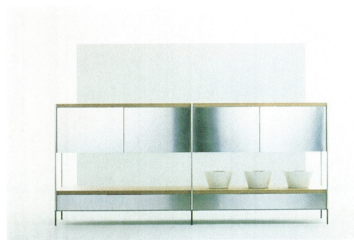

Marco Giunta
Aktenschrank L4RU
Karton
h. 188cm b. 36cm l. 30cm
Disegni, Italien

Martin Szekely
Schrank Armoire
Aluminium, Kunststoff
h. 107cm b. 64cm t. 41cm
Galerie Kreo, Frankreich
Kleinserie

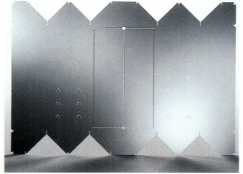

MÖBEL

Jurgen Bey
do add #1
Laminat, verchromter Stahl
h. 83cm b. 40cmt. 45cm
do + Droog Design

Marti Guixé
do reincarnate
Nylonschnur, Leuchte
do + Droog Design

Marti Guixé
Lampe do scratch
Lichtbox, Aussenseite schwarz
h. 9cm b. 65cm t. 9cm
do + Droog Design

Droog Design wurde 1993 gegründet mit Sitz in Amsterdam. Man initiiert und entwickelt zusammen mit jungen Designern experimentelle Projekte, wobei jedes eine bestimmte Ideologie widerspiegelt. 1999 hat Droog mit 'Couleur Locale' für die Stadt Oranienbaum ein schlüssiges Projekt zur regionalen Identität einer in Ostdeutschland zur Zeit noch relativ verarmten Gegend erarbeitet. Im Jahr 2000 hat 'do Create' Entwürfe von zehn Designern und Studios zusammengetragen: unter anderem von Radi Design/Frankreich), Mari Guixé/Spanien, Thomas Bernstrand/Schweden und Jurgen Bey/ Niederlande. Von ihnen wurde für die experimentelle Marke 'do', die von dem holländischen PR-Unternehmen KesselsKramer ins Leben gerufen wurde, Entwürfe gemacht. Die klare Aufgabenstellung durch Kesselskramer – es sollten Produkte entwickelt werden, die zu einer bereits existierenden Marke passten – bot genügend Raum für Erfindungsgeist und Innovation. Wie der Name schon suggeriert, ist 'do' eine sich kontinuierlich verändernde Marke, die sich in Abhängigkeit von dem, was man 'tut', entsprechend anpasst. Eine Idee, die für alles und jeden offen ist. So wurden durch Droog Objekte entworfen, mit denen der Benutzer emotional und körperlich interagiert. Dieses Konzept ist jedoch für Droog nichts Neues. Die Tapete 'Peep' von Gijs Bakker funktioniert nur, wenn damit alte Tapeten oder Poster überklebt werden, und die Vorhänge Dyoke de Jongs können mit ihrem Jackenschnittmuster in ein Kleidungsstück verwandelt werden, wenn sie nicht mehr gebraucht werden. Die 'do'-Kollektionen fügen der Idee der persönlichen Produktion auf jeden Fall einen neuen Aspekt hinzu. Der Benutzer beeinflusst das Design, und dieses wiederum weist auf dessen Charakter hin.

'do add #1'
Um arbeiten zu können, muß man dem Stuhl etwas hinzufügen. Was zunächst wie ein kaputter Stuhl aussieht, entpuppt sich als brandneu, wenn man nur etwas nachdenkt und tut – so der Katalog.

'do reincarnate'
Jeder Gegenstand, der einem zu vertraut oder den man bereits leid ist, kann zu neuem Leben erweckt werden. Man kann die durchsichtige Nylonschnur an jeder alten Lampe oder an jedem alten Bild festbinden, an der Decke befestigen und herunterhängen lassen – das Ergebnis ist ein sehr aufregendes neues Beleuchtungsobjekt.

'do scratch'
Diese Lampe gibt zunächst kein Licht, bis man etwas mit ihr anstellt. Indem man eine Nachricht oder ein Graffiti hineinkratzt, beginnt sie dann als eine sehr persönliche Lampe zu leuchten.

Dinie Besems und Thomas Widdershoven
Allzweckkette do connect
Silber, Metall, Kunststoff
l. 13cm
do + Droog Design

Frank Tjepkema und Peter v.d Jagt
Vase do break
Porzellan, Gummi, Silikon
h. 34cm Ø. 15cm
do + Droog Design

Jurgen Bey
Bank do add #2
Laminat, verchromter Stahl
h. 83cm b. 110cm t. 45cm
do + Droog Design

Marijn Van der Poll
Sessel do hit
1.25mm Stahl
h. 75cm b. 100cm t. 70cm
do + Droog Design

Thomas Bernstrand
Leuchte do swing
Edelstahl, Lampenschirm
do + Droog Design

Marti Guixé
Rahmen do frame
Klebeband
b. 5cm l. 100m
do + Droog Design

'do connect'
Das Potential dieses Stranges aus 13 Ketten ist unerschöpflich – man könnte Schmuck damit kreieren, Waschbeckenstöpsel daran befestigen oder sie als Hundeleine benutzen.

'do break'
Der schlimmste Streit kann die Schönheit dieser Vase nicht zerstören. Dank ihrer klebrigen Innenbeschichtung aus Gummi bleibt die Vase, ganz gleich wie fest man sie aufschlägt, intakt, auch wenn sich auf ihrer Aussenseite die Spuren der Aggression ablesen lassen.

'do add #2'
Man muss mit dieser Bank spielen, um ihre absurde Funktionalität zu entdecken. Nur durch Hinzufügen von etwas am jeweils anderen Ende kann die Bank ausbalanciert werden. Man kann so ziemlich alles einsetzen, einen Freund, dem man vertraut, einen Schäferhund oder – ein bisschen gewagter – etwas Heisses oder Zerbrechliches.

'do hit'
Beteilige dich am Design dieses Sessels. Nimm den Hammer und das Stahlrohr und schlage auf ihn ein, bis er die Form hat, die du dir wünschst.

'do swing'
Im Wohnzimmer kann man spielen oder turnen. An der von der Decke hängenden Leuchte, die mit zwei Glühbirnen und Lampenschirmen ausgestattet ist, kann man den ganzen Tag schaukeln.

'do frame'
Eine einfache Rolle reichverzierten Klebebands verwandelt jedes noch so banale Bild in ein spektakuläres Kunstwerk.

licht

In diesem Jahr wurde erstmals die Lichtgeschwindigkeit überschritten. Dr. Lijun Wang vom NEC Forschungsinstitut der Princeton Universität ließ einen Lichtimpuls gleichzeitig an zwei Orten erscheinen – ausgestrahlt wurde er mit einer Geschwindigkeit, die 300 mal höher war als die des Lichtes. Nicht nur, dass dies eine Herausforderung zumindest für einen Teil der Einsteinschen Relativitätstheorie bedeutet, es ergibt sich nun vor allem die Möglichkeit, die Natur des Lichtes besser zu ergründen. Auch im Bereich des Leuchtendesigns, wenn auch nicht ganz so weltbewegend, zeichnet sich eine Revolution ab.

Die Verwendung von Leuchtdioden für Raumbeleuchtungen beginnt sich auf dem Markt durchzusetzen. Der kommerzielle Einsatz von Leuchtdioden in der Beleuchtungsindustrie steckt noch in den Kinderschuhen. Früher für die Rücklichter von Autos oder Kontrollampen elektronischer Geräte benutzt, verändert nun ihre zunehmende Verwendung bei Leuchten unsere herkömmliche Vorstellung. Da sehr viele Leuchtdioden benötigt werden, um einen Raum zu erhellen, sind sie im Moment noch sehr teuer, aber ihre niedrige Temperatur, ihr gebündeltes Licht, der geringe Wartungsaufwand und nicht zuletzt ihre Lebensdauer von 15 Jahren garantieren ihre Weiterentwicklung. Leuchtdioden haben ungefähr die Grösse von Stecknadelköpfen und basieren auf halbleitenden Materialien, die Elektrizität direkt in Licht umwandeln.

Siemens war mit der Beleuchtung eines Raumes durch Leuchtdioden erfolgreich. Obwohl rote, grüne und orangefarbene Leuchtdioden seit einiger Zeit erhältlich sind, wurde kürzlich eine blaue Version entwickelt. Siemens hat dieses neue blaue Licht mit den schon existierenden Farben gemischt, um ein Licht zu erzeugen, das dem der konventionellen Glühbirne gleicht. Für eine Installation des Tiroler Architekturforums hat Siemens 14.000 dieser Leuchtdioden in eine Decke integriert. Zusätzlich wurde von dem Unternehmen die O.L.E.D. (Organic Light Emitting Diode=Organische Leuchtdiode), eine nur 1 mm-dünne High-Tech-Folie entwickelt. Man stellte eine 16 qcm grosse Tafel vor, die nicht nur extrem helles Licht erzeugen, sondern auch Videosignale wiedergeben kann, was die Idee einer Tapete, die plötzlich die Farbe verändert und zum Bildschirm mutiert, in greifbare Nähe rücken und nicht länger wissenschaftliche Fiktion bleiben lässt.

Michele De Lucchi hat vier Beispiele dieser Leuchtdioden-Technologie ausgewählt: die Entwicklung der 'Globlow'-Leuchte von Snowcrash, Zumtobels 'Phaos' und 'Ledos' sowie Ingo Maurers Prototyp 'Bellissima Bruta'. Es gab keine allzu grosse Auswahl, aber wir erwarten mehr im nächsten Jahr.

Eine weitere wichtige Entwicklung gibt es in der Beleuchtung von Büroräumen. Eine neue Norm schreibt vor, dass die Lichtstärke 200 cd pro Quadratmeter in einem Winkel von 60 Grad aus der Vertikalen nicht übersteigen darf, um optimale visuelle Bedingungen am Arbeitsplatz sicherzustellen. Unter den ausgewählten Beispielen befinden sich: Gecchelins 'Light Air System', Hosoes Leuchten 'Onda', 'Arca' und 'Vola' sowie das 'Megan System' von Gismondi. De Lucchi ging auch auf die Leuchten ein, die sowohl direkte als auch indirekte Lichtquellen darstellen, was sie für den häuslichen Bereich wie auch für das Büro qualifiziert. Bemerkenswerte Beispiele kamen von Tobias Grau, King und Miranda sowie Claudio Bellini.

Ausserdem wurden Leuchtenversionen aus Plastikflaschen, 'Alpha' von Siggi Bussinger und Iwan Seiko, aus Plastiktassen, Mo-billy 'Cuplight', aus Glühbirnen, 'Follow your bliss' von Ralph Ball, und aus einem Plastikhut, 'Palombella' von Paolo Ulian, ausgewählt. Nicht zuletzt wurde die poetische Form von Out Designs 'Flow' entsprechend gewürdigt. Witzige Spielereien mit Form und Funktion kamen vom Büro für Form mit 'Flapflap', einer Leuchte, die auf ihrem eigenen Kabel steht. Auch die 'Wallpaper'-Leuchte von Droogs Jaap van Arkel und 'Whoosh' von Dumoffice gehört in diese Kategorie.

Licht beeinflusst unsere Emotionen und durch neue Technologien wird das Lichtdesign kontinuierlich weiterentwickelt. Von Jahr zu Jahr gibt es mehr Designer, die, eigentlich in anderen Bereichen tätig, sich dem Thema Licht widmen und mit diesem Medium experimentieren.

Claudio Bellini
Hängeleuchte ITI
Kristallglas
100w Halogen
h. 100–200cm Ø. 40cm
Artemide, Italien

Architettura Laboratorio
Hängeleuchte Saturno
Aluminium
55w Leuchtstoff
h. 100–160cm Ø. 58cm
Artemide, Italien

Artemide hat eine Leuchten-Kollektion entwickelt, die sowohl für das häusliche Umfeld als auch für die Arbeitsumgebung geeignet ist. Die Glashängeleuchte 'ITI' von Claudio Bellini birgt zwei Möglichkeiten der Lichtdiffusion: aussen aus satiniertem Kristall und innen aus gefärbtem Glas. Um verschiedene Lichteffekte zu schaffen, kann die Lichtquelle mit einem Hebel innerhalb der Leuchte bewegt werden. Auch die Hängelampe 'Saturno' von Architettura Laboratorio aus farbigem Aluminium verströmt ihr weiches Licht aus zwei unterschiedlichen Quellen. Sie ist deshalb für Wohnumgebungen und Computermonitore geeignet.

Dumoffice
Wand/Deckenleuchte Surve
Kunstglas
Leuchtstoff
l. 75cm b. 22cm
Belux AG, Schweiz

Dumoffice
Hängeleuchte Whoosh
Mattiertes Glas
2 x 40w
38cm x 20cm x 7.5cm
Dumoffice, Niederlande
Prototyp

Dumoffice wurde 1997, drei Jahre nach Wiebe Boonstras, Martin Hoggendijks und Marc van Nederpelts Abschluss an der Designakademie Eindhoven in den Niederlanden, gegründet. Ihre Arbeiten zeichnen sich durch ein witziges und frisches Design von Alltagsgegenständen aus. Sie werden nun, nachdem die Grenze der limitierten Serienproduktion mit den frühen Objekten überschritten ist und sie kommerziell sehr erfolgreich sind, durch Belux und Hidden von sdb Industries als Massenprodukt aufgelegt. 'Whoosh', eine Pendelleuchte, und 'Surve', eine Halterung für zwei röhrenförmige Leuchtmittel, sind hervorragende Beispiele dieser Dualität. Erstere ist die kreative Umsetzung eines eingefrorenen Moments der Bewegung. Sie verweist auf Fotos von Pablo Picasso, auf denen er mit einer Taschenlampe virtuelle Bilder malt. 'Surve' auf der anderen Seite ist, während sie den 'Funken einer erleuchtenden Idee' (Robert Thiemann, Frame Magazin) bewahrt, ein hochtechnisierter Gegenstand des Industriedesigns.

Mauro Marzollo
Hängeleuchte, Volo
Glas, Metall
3 x 60w
h. 47cm Ø. 38cm
Murano Due, Italien

Tobias Grau
Hängeleuchte Oh China
60w Halogen
Verstellbare Höhe Ø. 9cm
Tobias Grau, Deutschland

Tobias Grau
Hängeleuchte, Project X
Aluminium, Opalglas
150w Halogen
Verstellbare Höhe Ø. 40cm
Tobias Grau, Deutschland

'Project X' von Tobias Grau ist eine höhenverstellbare Hängeleuchte mit zwei verschiedenen Lichtwirkungen und einer schlichten äusseren Formgebung. Intensives, aber nicht blendendes Licht wird nach unten durch Opalglas geleitet und gleichzeitig wird ein weiches Licht durch farbiges Glas nach oben verstrahlt. Auch hier hat ein führender Designer/Hersteller die Notwendigkeit erkannt, eine Leuchte zu gestalten, die zum Arbeiten und Wohlfühlen gleichermaßen geeignet ist.

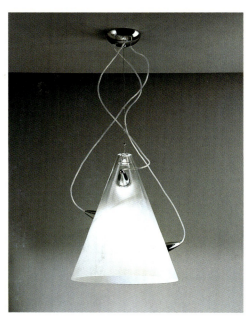

Marco Carenini
Hängeleuchte Lubia
Polypropylen
h. 23cm Ø. 6cm
Sparbirne 21w
Prototyp

 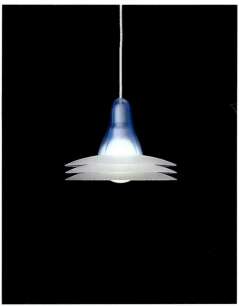 

Isao Hosoe
Leuchte Vola
Ätzglas, Polycarbonat
Verchromtes Metall
75w Halogen
h. 7–10cm l. 24cm
Luxo Italiana, Italien

Isao Hosoe und Peter Solomon
Leuchte Onda
Aluminium,, Polykarbonat
Perforiertes Metall
2 x 54w HFG5
h. 1.6cm b. 50cm l. 170cm
Luxo Italiana, Italien

Makoto Kawamoto
Leuchte Frozen
Polykarbonat, PVC
Verzinktes Aluminium
40w e-14 Leuchtmittel
h. 22.5cm b. 21cm t. 21cm
Aliantedizione, Italien
Kleinserie

Isao Hosoe und Peter Solomon
Arbeitsleuchte Arca Dome Suspension
Aluminium, ABS, Polypropylen, Stahl
2 x 55w Leuchtmittel
h. 10–60cm l. 120cm
Luxo Italiana, Italien

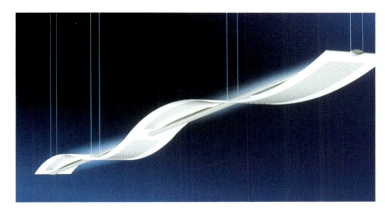

Sigi Bussinger und Iwan Seiko
Lichtinstallation Alpha
1000 Kunststoffflaschen
150w Powerstar
Ø. 180cm
Unikat

Henrik Kjellberg, Mattias Lindqvist
Hängeleuchte IKEA PS
Verchromter Stahl, Polykarbonat
Polypropylen, h. 48cm Ø. 35cm
IKEA, Schweden

Ralph Ball
Tischleuchte Very Light Box
Edelstahl, 4 x 60w Leuchtmittel
h. 25cm b. 25cm l. 32cm
Ligne Roset, Frankreich

Ralph Ball
Leuchte Golden Delicious
Schale aus Metacrylat mit Birnen
60w Leuchtmittel
h. 20cm Ø. 30cm
Ligne Roset, Frankreich

Fabrice Berreux
Leuchte Watt Colonne
Lackierter Metallsockel, Glühbirnen
9 x 25w
h. 190cm Ø. 28cm
Sockel 30 x 30cm
dix heures dix, Frankreich

Neil Austin
Leuchte Cuplight
Trinkbecher, Kupferdraht
Ø. 60cm
Mo-billy, Grossbritannien
Kleinserie

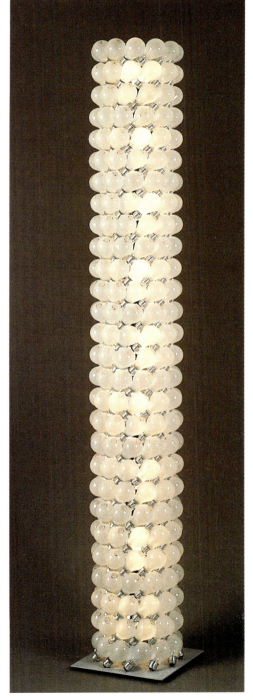

Ingo Maurer GmbH, Deutschland

Ingo Maurer
Leuchte Bellissima Bruta
Rote, grüne und blaue Leuchtdioden
40w, h. 50cm

Knuth Eckhard und Ingo Maurer
Hologramm Holzonski
Glas, Metall, Edelstahl
35w, h. 18cm b. 13cm

Ingo Maurer
Leuchtglocken Pierre ou Paul
Aluminium, Stahl, Gold/Platin
300w, Ø. 100–120cm

Ingo Maurer
Lichtskulptur Red Ribbon
Aluminium
Halogen, l. 400cm
Unikat

Ingo Maurer
Lichtskulptur Yaki Mei
Papier, Stahl, Silber, Ventilatoren
l. 700cm Ø. 80cm
Unikat

Ingo Maurers bestechend schöne 'Blumenvase', die 'Bellissima Bruta', entfaltet ihre poetische Ausstrahlung durch den Einsatz höchst moderner Technologie. Rote und grüne Leuchtdioden wurden mit blauen kombiniert, um ein weiches weisses Licht zu erzeugen.

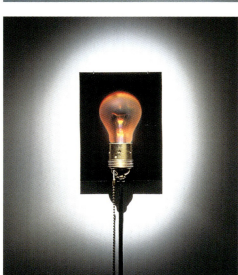
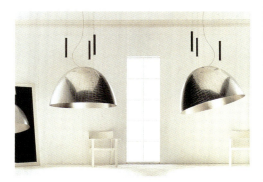
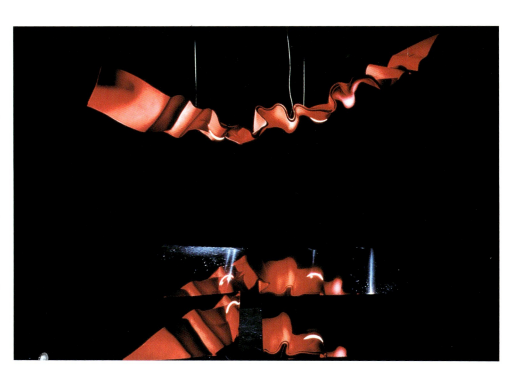
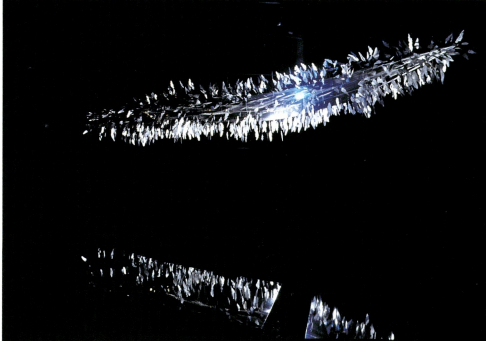

Ingo Maurer
Leuchte Max Mover
Aluminium, Fiberglas
Max 100W, Ø 150cm

Matteo Thun
Leuchte Sphera T20
Glas, Holz, Chrom
60w Leuchtmittel
Grösse 1: h. 61cm
Grösse 2: h. 42cm
Leucos, Italien

Karim Rashid
Deckenleuchte Kovac Lamp
Muranoglas, verchromter Stahl
75w Leuchtmittel
Höhe variiert, Ø 40.5cm
Karim Rashid Industrial Design, USA

Rechte Seite:
Karim Rashid
Tischleuchte Kovac Lamp
Muranoglas, verchromter Stahl
75w Leuchtmittel
h. 45.7cm Ø 40.6cm
Karim Rashid Industrial Design, USA

Arik Levy
Lichtinstallation Rewindable light
Snowcrash, Schweden

Vesa Hinkola
Markus Nevalainen
Rane Vaskivuori
Leuchte Globlow LED
Stahl, Nylon
Snowcrash, Schweden

'Globlow LED' ist eine Weiterentwicklung der früheren 'Globlow'-Leuchte für Snowcrash. Die Designer Vesa Hinkola, Markus Nevalainen und Rane Vaskivuori wollten herausfinden, ob man das Konzept des lebendigen Lichts weiterentwickeln kann. Die ursprüngliche Leuchte blies sich beim Einschalten auf. Ihr Nachfolger enthält Leuchtdioden und Mikroprozessoren, um ein interaktives Licht zu erzeugen, wobei verschiedene Lichtsequenzen über ein Computerprogramm gespeichert werden können. Mit einer Fernbedienung oder einem Handy kann man sich verschiedene Programme von der Snowcrash-Website herunterladen.
www.snowcrash.se

Marc Krusin
Kronleuchter Bulbed Wire
Glasplatte, Fassungen, Kabel
8 x 15W Osram Nitra
h. 120–180cm Ø. 70cm
Kleinserie

Philippe Starck
Cicatrices des Lux 3, 5 + 8
Kristallgläser, Glasplatten
Leitfähige Beschichtung
3/5/8 x max 35W
h. 80 - 120cm
Flos, Italien

Zur Borderlight Show in Mailand versammelte sich eine Gruppe junger Designer. Einige von ihnen stellten zum ersten Mal aus. So entstand eine Leuchtenkollektion, die vor allem durch die Reduktion dekorativer Elemente und eine dezidiert schlichte Formgebung geprägt war. Ziel war es, ein Design zu entwickeln, das sich auf Struktur und Material beschränkt und damit neue und überraschende Formen und Effekte möglich macht. Marc Kruisins 'Bulbed Wire' ist die Abwandlung des häuslichen Kronleuchters. Die Tatsache, dass er aus Kabelgehäusen und Glühbirnen besteht, die von einer runden Glasplatte gehalten werden, verwandelt eine gängige Designidee in ein völlig neues Produkt.

„Das Leben besteht aus einer unaufhörlichen Folge von Leidenschaften und Verletzungen. Die 'Cicatrices des Lux'-Kollektion ist der Versuch, ein surrealistisches, kristallines und lumineszentes Wesen einzufangen". So lautet Philippe Starcks Beschreibung seines neuen Entwurfs für Flos.

Taco Langius
Leuchtobjekt Yuck 2
Gel, PVC
Lichtschlange
h. 4cm b. 30cm l. 60cm
Codice 31, Italien
Kleinserie

Andrea Branzi
Leuchte Cactus
Bronze, rostfreier Stahl, Glas
60w
h. 50cm t. 32cm
Design Gallery Milano, Italien

Marco Carenini
Leuchte Jim
Acryl
h. 31cm ⌀. 21cm
Energiesparbirne 21w
Prototyp

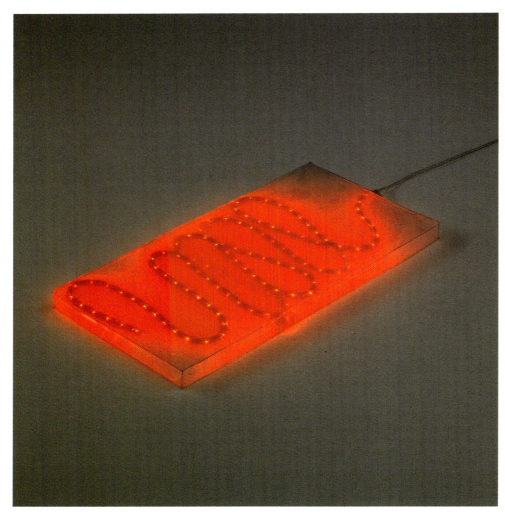

Valter Bahcivanji
Leuchtobjekt T Kiluz
Stahl, Polypropylen
60w
h. 25cm Ø. 13cm
Agora e Moda Ind. Com. Ltda, Brasilien

Valter Bahcivanji
Stehleuchten Two Points
Polypropylen, rostfreier Stahl
40w
h. 180cm t. 28cm
Agora e Moda Ind. Com. Ltda, Brasilien

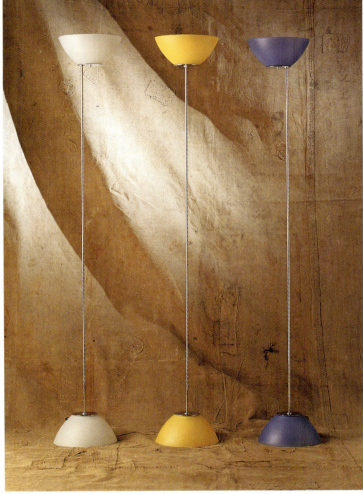

Sergio Brioschi
Leuchtobjekt Nomade
Polycarbonat, ABS
50w/60w Leuchtstoffschlange
9/10cm Länge
Antonangeli Illuminazione, Italien

Jaap van Aarkel
Tapeten-Leuchte
Tapete, Kunststoff
h. 42cm b. 13cm t. 11cm
Droog Design, Niederlande
Prototyp

Büro für form
Leuchte Flapflap
Eisen, Kunststoff
25–40w
h. 50/80cm
Next Design GmbH, Deutschland

Jaap van Aarkels 'Tapeten'-Leuchte für Droog Design spielt mit der Idee von Subtraktion und Addition. Der Teil der Tapete, der für den Lampenschirm benutzt wird fehlt auf der dahinterliegenden Wand.

Bernard Brousse
Leuchte Ellipsis
Polyurethan, Technopolymer
Max 20WE 27 Fluo E1
h. 29.5cm b. 48cm
Baleri Italia SpA, Italien

Toni Cordero
Stehleuchte Nuvola
Perforierter Metallfuß auf Marmor
Transluzenter Kunststoff
Max 300w + max 54w
h. 220cm l. 35cm t. 30cm
oLuce, Italien

Toni Cordero
Wandleuchte Nuvola
Transluzenter Kunststoff
Max 100w x 3
l. 80cm b. 50cm t. 18cm
oLuce, Italien

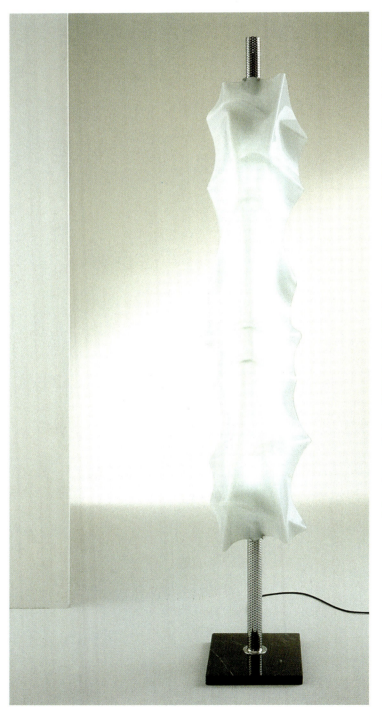

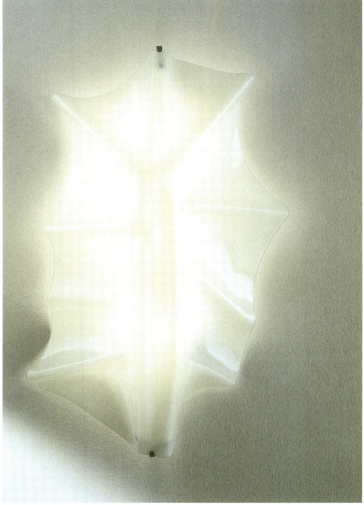

Tsutomu Kurokawa, OutDeSign
Leuchtenserie Flow
Polykarbonat
Tischleuchte: h. 43cm b. 22.5cm
Hängeleuchte: h. 21cm b. 22.5cm
Wandleuchte: h. 32.5cm b. 16.5cm t. 21cm
Daiko Electric Co. Ltd, Japan

OutDeSign wurde von Tsutomu Kurokawa gegründet, nachdem er sich von Masamichi Katayama getrennt hatte und H-Design aufgelöst wurde. Die 'Flow'-Leuchtenserie erregte aufgrund ihrer besonderen poetischen Qualität die Aufmerksamkeit De Lucchis. Kurokawa entdeckte die Schönheit, die eine Leuchte ausstrahlt, wenn sie durch Spiegel kontinuierlich vervielfältigt wird. Er versuchte, mit einem einzigen Leuchtkörper seine Idee der sich reflektierenden Lichter zu realisieren. Doppelte Lampenschirmschichten, die zur Hälfte aus Spiegelfolie bestehen, reflektieren das Licht auf Wand und Decke. So entsteht ein helles Lichtspiel mit raffinierten Effekten in einem transparent wirkenden Raum.

Paolo Ulian
Tischleuchte Palombella
Stahl, Gummi
Energiesparbirne
h. 50cm b. 35cm t. 8cm
Prototyp

Arik Levy
Leuchte Alchemy
Glas, Metall
20w Halogen
h. 18cm Ø. 13cm
Tronconi, Italien

Fabrice Berreux
Leuchte Pise
Vier Lampenschirme
Lackierter Metallfuss
4 x 60w
h. 200cm, Fuss: 48 x 32cm
dix heures dix, Frankreich

Steven Holl
Wandleuchte Kiasma
Aluminium
150w R7s Halogen
l. 134cm h. 12cm t. 12cm
FontanaArte, Italien

Steven Holl
Wandleuchte Triple
Aluminium, Glas
3 x 60w E14
h. 55cmb. 43cm t. 6cm
FontanaArte, Italien

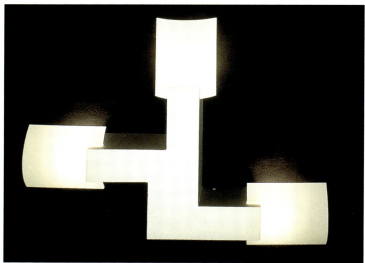

Maurizio Peregalli
Steh- und Bodenleuchte Star Cube Terra
Stahl, Polykarbonat
250w
h. 176cm b. 22cm l. 22cm
Zeus, Italien

Jorge Garcia Garay
Bibliotheksleuchte Isis
Acryl
60w
h. 16cm b. 8cm t. 14cm
Garcia Garay SL, Argentinien

Jorge Garcia Garay
Bibliotheksleuchte Libra
Acryl
60w
h. 16cm b. 8cm t. 14cm
Garcia Garay SL, Argentinien

Kazuhiro Yamanaka
Wandleuchte
What a little Moonlight can do
Aluminiumplatte
12v Halogen
h. 120cm b. 158cm t.4mm
Kleinserie

Jorge Garcia Garay
Wandleuchte Embassy
Eisen, Metacryl
2 x 36w
h. 13cm l. 132cm t.11cm
Garcia Garay SL, Argentina

Johanna Grawunder
Leuchte F6 / Fractals Collection
Aluminium
30w
h. 18cm b. 18cm l. 120cm
Memphis, Italien

Jan van Lierde
Wandleuchtensystem Secret
Stahl, Aluminiumguss
Dulux L 1 x 18w 1 x 55w
Kreon NV, Belgien

Luc Vincent
Wand/Deckenleuchte Square Moon
Aluminium, Polykarbonat
4 x 18w TC-L
h. 24.2cm b. 24.2cm t.5.5cm
Modular Lighting Instruments, Belgien

Ernesto Gismondi
Tischleuchte E-light
Polykarbonat, Nylon
Messing, Aluminium
Micro 3w
b. 32.5cm h. 57.5cm
Artemide SpA, Italien

Ernesto Gismondi
Wandleuchte Megan wall
Stahlblech
2 x 14–35w
l. 58.3–148.3cm
Artemide SpA, Italien

Ernesto Gismondi
Deckenleuchte Megan Suspension
Stahlblech
2 x 28–54w
l. 59cm
Artemide SpA, Italien

Ernesto Gismondi
Bodenleuchte Megan Floor
Aluminium, Stahlblech, Polykarbonat
4 x 55w
h. 185cm b. 59cm t. 39cm
Fuss: 48cm
Artemide SpA, Italien

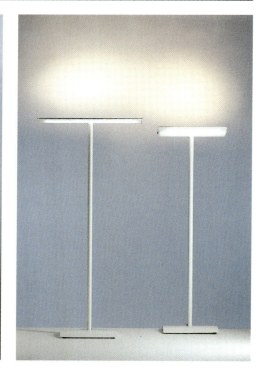

Ernesto Gismondi, der Gründer und Geschäftsführer von Artemide, hat 'E-light' entworfen. Dank der Mikrolichttechnologie gehört sie zur Kategorie der Niedrigenergieleuchten. Angesichts der wiederholten Warnung, dass wir Energie nicht verschwenden sollen, ist es sehr beruhigend, dass ein führender italienischer Leuchtenhersteller diesen problematischen Aspekt zum Teil seiner Designphilosophie gemacht hat.

Michael Horsham, Herausgeber des Internationalen Design Jahrbuchs 1999, schrieb: „Die Beleuchtung von Wohnräumen, die nicht das nationale Versorgungsnetz belastet – in welchem Land auch immer – ist eine Aufgabe, der Designer, Hersteller und Ingenieur mit dem gleichen Bestreben nachgehen sollten, ähnlich der Verwendung von Energiesparbirnen". Michele De Lucchi räumt ein, dass es „ein paar grosse schwarze Wolken am Horizont" gäbe. Seine Zukunftsvorstellung ist mit den Aspekten von Umweltverschmutzung und nachhaltiger Entwicklung verbunden. „Ich glaube, wir müssen optimistischer werden und dennoch mit einem tiefen Bewusstsein leben, dass bestimmte Dinge nicht aufgeschoben werden können."

Bruno Gecchelin
Lichtsystem Light Air
Stahlblech
28w/54w
h. 4cm b. 24cm l. 170cm
iGuzzini Illuminazione, Italien

Felice Dittli
Deckenleuchte Box
Aluminium, Glas
2 x 14w
h. 20–50cm b. 47–120cm
l. 96.9cm
Regent, Schweiz

Felice Dittli
Deckenleuchte Tool
Aluminium
36/58w
h. 3–7.6cm b. 1.5–3.8cm
l. 50.3–127.8cm
Regent, Schweiz

James Irvine
Hängeleuchte Float Rectangular
Aluminium, Polykarbonat
39w
h. 100–160cm b. 103cm
Artemide, Italien

James Irvine
Hängeleuchte Float Circular
Aluminium, Polykarbonat
39w
h. 100–160cm Ø 60cm
Artemide, Italien

Lievore, Altherr, Molina
Deckenleuchte Hopper 60–80
Aluminium, Glas
2 x 150/250w Halogen
Ø 60–80cm
Metalarte, Spanien

Christophe Pillet
Deckenleuchte Easy Mechanics Sky
Metall lackiert, verchromt
150w/20w Leuchtstoff/250w Halogen
h. 27.5cm Ø. 55cm
Tronconi, Italien

Tronconi, ein traditioneller Leuchtenhersteller, wurde 1956 gegründet. Erst in den siebziger Jahren fing das Unternehmen an, renommierte Designer zur Mitarbeit einzuladen. Heute wird es von Fabrizio Tronconi geleitet. Er begann, mit einigen jungen Designern zusammenzuarbeiten, um eine Kollektion schlichter und funktionaler Leuchten, die allen Anforderungen in Bezug auf Form und Technologie gerecht werden sollten, zu produzieren. 'Easy Mechanics Sky' ist eine Hängelampe von Christophe Pillet, die ein diffuses Licht verströmt. Sie ist durch das Gegengewicht, das am Trafo befestigt ist, höhenverstellbar.

Antonio Citterio und Oliver Loew
Leuchte Plaza
Aluminiumguss, Prismaglas
Max 300w R75 HDG
Ø. 56cm t. 11.5cm
Flos, Italien

Konstantin Grcic
Deckenleuchte Hertz
Aluminium, Polykarbonat
h. 30cm l. 35.5cm b. 35.5cm
Halogen
Flos, Italien

Jasper Morrison
Leuchten O1 und O2
Eisen, Aluminium, Polykarbonat

O1: max 100w E27 1AA
2 x 18w 2911 FSD
Ø. 38cm t. 6cm

O2: max 60w E14 IBP
13w G249 1FSQ
Ø. 30cm t. 5cm
Flos, Italien

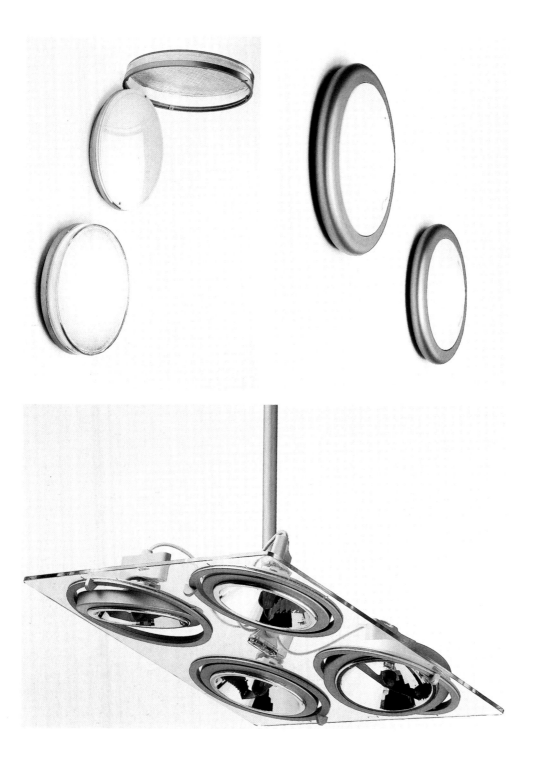

Asahara Sigeaki
Wandleuchte Karma IM
Aluminiumguss
70w/150w metal halide
h. 32cm b. 33cm
Lucitalia, Italien

Asahara Sigeaki
Wandleuchte
Aluminiumguss, Glas
Max 150w / 23w Leuchtstoff
h. 25cm b. 25cm Ø. 17cm
Lucitalia, Italien

Ross Lovegrove
Leuchte Agaricon
Polykarbonat, Seidenfinish
150w
h. 28cm Ø. 40cm, Fuss 8.5cm
Luceplan, Italien

Dominique Perrault
Gaëlle Lauriot-Prevost
Stehleuchte M.A.
Stahl, rostfreies Metallnetz
300w R7s Halogen
h. 240cm
FontanaArte, Italien

Andrea Branzi
Stehleuchte Anfora
Bronze, Marmor, Glas
100w Halogen
h. 250cm t. 42cm
Design Gallery Milano, Italien

Roberto Lazzeroni
Stehleuchte Taller Ghost
Weisses Porzellan, Metall
150w Halogen
h. 195cm b. 36cm t. 24cm
Luminara, Italien

Andrea Branzi
Bodenleuchte Bottiglia
Bronze, Marmor, Glas
100w Halogen
h. 245cm t. 42cm
Design Gallery Milano, Italien

Alfredo Häberli
Stehleuchte Carrara
Polyester Kunstharz
Leuchtstoff / Metallhalidbirne
Grösse 1: h. 210cm Ø. 20cm
Grösse 2: h. 180cm Ø. 20cm
Luceplan, Italien

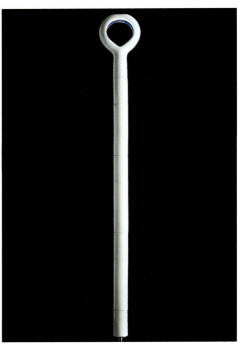

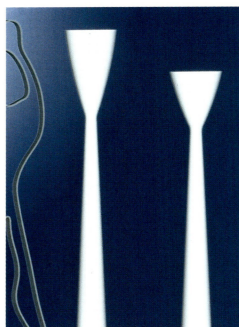

Matthias Bader
Stehleuchte Matteo
Mattiertes Aluminium
12W 220V
h. 150–200 cm t. 25cm
Pallucco Italia SpA, Italien
Prototyp

Marco Carenini
Leuchte Cap
Aluminium
h. 160cm
Energiesparbirne 21W
Prototyp

King Miranda Associati
Leseleuchte Diogenes
Aluminium
50W/150W Halogen
h. 176.6cm
Belux AG, Schweiz

'Diogenes' ist eine neue Idee von King Miranda Associati, eine Leuchte, die Leselicht und indirektes Licht ermöglicht. Eine leistungsstarke Halogenbirne sorgt für allgemeine Beleuchtung. Für direktes Leselicht ist in den Leuchtenkörper eine zusätzliche, nicht blendende und genau ausrichtbare Niedrigvolthalogenlampe integriert. Die beiden Lichtquellen können unabhängig voneinander reguliert werden.

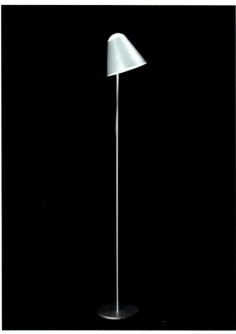

Tobias Grau Design
Tischleuchte Bill
Aluminium
50w Halogen
h. 52cm l. 69cm
Tobias Grau, Deutschland

Tobias Grau Design
Tischleuchte Soon
Polykarbonat
50w Halogen
h. 52cm l. 67cm
Tobias Grau, Deutschland

Andreas Ostwald und Klaus Nolting
Stehleuchte Minyas
Verchromtes Stahlrohr, Opalglas
100w Halogen
h. 158cm b. 97cm Ø. 24cm
ClassiCon, Deutschland

Joan Gaspar Ruiz
Arbeitsleuchte Atila
Aluminium, Polykarbonat
100w Leuchtmittel, 13w Leuchtstoff
l. 90.5cm
Marset Iluminacion, Spanien

Yaacov Kaufman
Tisch/Bodenleuchte Naomi
Aluminium, Stahl
60w Leuchtmittel/75w Halogen
l. 141cm (gross)
Lumina Italia, Italien

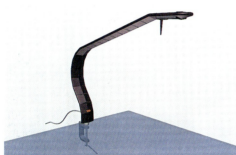

Zumtobel
Wandleuchte Ledos
Edelstahl, Mattglas
24V
l. 10cm b. 10cm t. 4cm
Zumtobel Staff AG, Österreich

Zumtobel
Strahler Phaos
Aluminiumguss
64 SMD-LEDs
h. 20cm b. 20cm t. 3cm
Zumtobel Staff AG, Österreich

Zumtobel
Deckenleuchte Active Light Field
Metall, Glas
Leuchtstoff
l. 37–46cm b. 37–64.75cm
Zumtobel Staff AG, Österreich

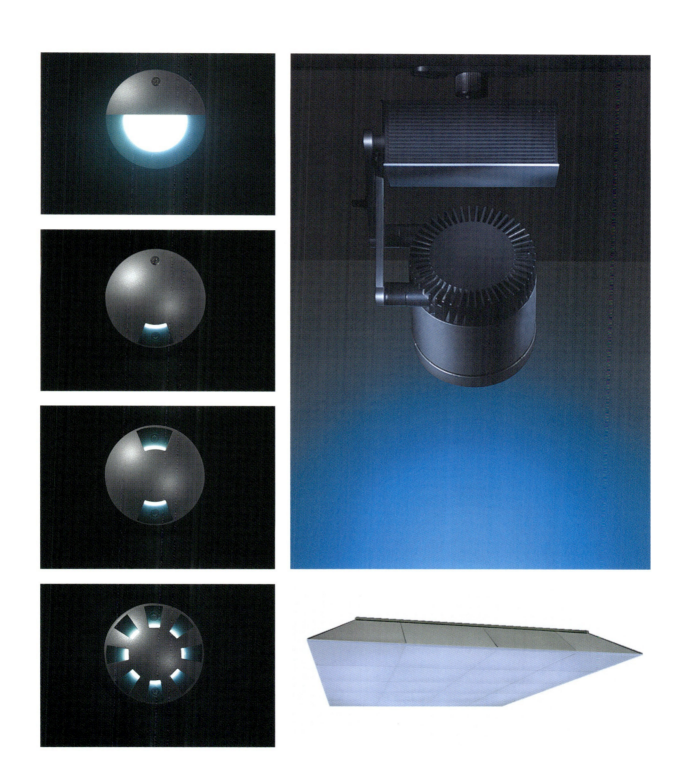

tischdekor

Es ist bemerkenswert, wie wenig sich die Auswahl im Bereich Tischdekor innerhalb des Internationalen Design Jahrbuchs im Laufe der letzten Jahre verändert hat. Der persönliche Geschmack des Herausgebers hat zur ein oder anderen Veränderung in der Schwerpunktsetzung geführt – manchmal zugunsten des Ornamentalen, manchmal als Betonung der funktionalen Strenge im skandinavischen Design. Dennoch bleibt ein Glas immer ein Glas und eine Gabel immer eine Gabel. Mario Bellini, Gastherausgeber des Internationalen Design Jahrbuchs 1990 hat in diesem Zusammenhang festgestellt, dass Gegenstände, die eng mit dem menschlichen Körper oder mit gesellschaftlichen Ritualen verbunden sind, immer eine Ähnlichkeit mit vorhergehenden Modellen haben. Auch wenn sich unser Lebensstil im Laufe der Zeit verändert hat – eine Studie des renommierten MIT Instituts besagt, dass in den 50er Jahren eine Durchschnittsfamilie eine Stunde zum Abendessen am Tisch saß, während es heute nur noch ungefähr 16 Minuten sind – scheint sich das nicht auf den Stil des Tischdekors auszuwirken.

Mehr als jede andere Kategorie ist Tischdekor seit jeher mit dem Kunsthandwerk assoziiert. Als solches ist es eher künstlerischen Einflüssen unterworfen als dem Design. Bei einem gedeckten Tisch ist die Funktion und der Inhalt fast identisch, und eigentlich gibt es nur neue Technologien, die sich in diesem Bereich abzeichnen. Die Oberflächenbeschaffenheit lässt die Objekte lebendig werden, und das ist das Unterscheidungsmerkmal.

Die Gestaltung von Geschirr oder Porzellan beruht oft auf einer jahrelangen Tradition und die Entwicklung der jeweiligen Form erklärt sich meist schlichtweg aus der Tatsache, ob sie am funktionalsten ist. Rotweingläser oder Cognacschwenker besitzen ihre Form aus gutem Grund, denn Wein oder Branntwein kann in ihnen atmen und reifen. Jean Nouvel schrieb: „Nichts ist für mich ein grösserer Alptraum, als wenn jemand versucht, die Form eines Weinglases zu verändern, nur um einem neuen oder moderneren Stil gerecht zu werden. Es aus kommerziellen, marktbedingten oder wirtschaftlichen Erwägungen anders zu formen, kommt der Verwässerung seines Inhalts, einer Banalisierung von Design gleich". (Vorwort aus dem Internationales Design Jahrbuch von 1995).

Michele De Lucchi misst dem Design einer Vase genauso viel Bedeutung bei wie der Gestaltung eines Möbelstücks oder eines elektronischen Produkts. De Lucchi erklärt: „Ich glaube, dass es sehr wichtig ist, eine Ausgewogenheit in Bezug auf die Dinge zu haben, denn auf diese Art und Weise ist es bei einer positiven Form egal, ob ich eine Vase entwerfe oder ein multifunktionales Arbeitsgerät". Diese Haltung kommt auch in der wohlüberlegten Auswahl für dieses Buch zum Tragen.

De Lucchi mochte sowohl die traditionell gefertigte Serie von Arnolfo di Cambio als auch die sehr schön gearbeiteten mundgeblasenen Glasobjekte von Aldo Cibic. Auch die Verwendung experimenteller Materialien schlägt sich in der Auswahl nieder. Der 'Lovenet'-Tischaufsatz von Oz Design besteht aus Kunstseidenfasern, die mit Harz gehärtet wurden, während Kristiina Lassus sich an Schalen aus Stroh versucht. Zu den innovativen und nützlichen Entwürfen zählen das Partyglas von Massimo Lunardon und das Picknickset 'Short break on the run' von Thomas Rosenthal. Um der Bedeutung des Kunsthandwerks im Tischdekor gerecht zu werden, entschied sich De Lucchi für die traditionelle indische Cire perdu-Technik von Satyendra Pakhalé und für die Unikate aus mundgeblasenem Murano-Glas von Emmanuel Babled. Ein herausragender Entwurf in der Kategorie Tischdekor, das auch schon in Mailand Begeisterung auslöste, ist 'Not made by Hand, Not made in China' von Ron Arad, das als einziges Produkt die technologische Weiterentwicklung in dieser Kategorie darstellt. Durch den Einsatz computergesteuerter Laserstrahlen haben Ron Arad und sein Team neue provokative Gestaltungsperspektiven entwickelt.

Die Zukunft des Tischdekors, mit Ausnahme von ein paar modischen Veränderungen und der Verwendung neuer Materialien, wird voraussichtlich seine Kontinuität in der bewährten Form bewahren. Dennoch gibt es einen neuen Stern am Horizont, und zwar das Geschirr 'smart'. Das 'Counter Intelligence Project' von MIT erforscht neue Technologien für das Wohnumfeld und hat nun einen Teller patentieren lassen, der tatsächlich Kalorien zählen kann.

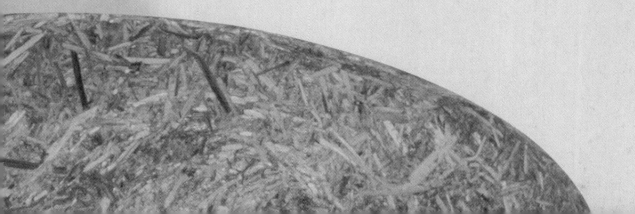

Jean-Marie Massaud
Pfeffermühle Pepe
Polypropylen, Keramik
h. 17.5cm Ø 7.5cm
Authentics, Deutschland

Marc Newson
Salz- und Pfeffermühle Gemini
Buchenholz
h. 12.5cm Ø 8.5cm
Alessi SpA, Italien

Rechte Seite:
Ka-chi Lo
Zahnstocherbehälter Polar Molar
Keramik
h. 9cm b. 8cm t. 3cm
Prototyp

Tischdekor

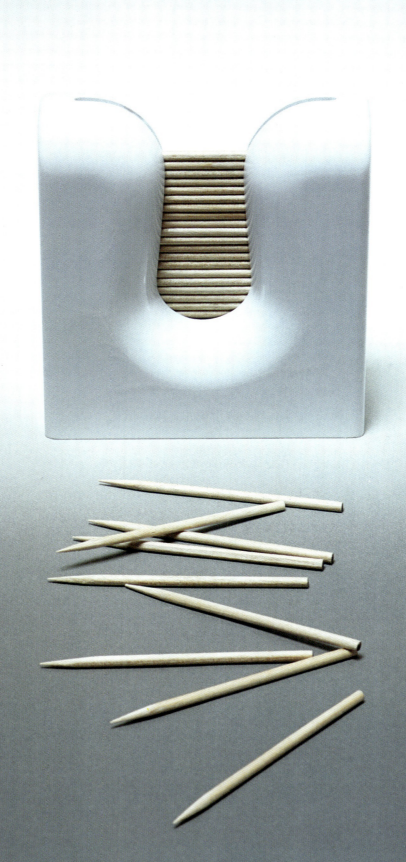

Sebastian Bergne
Besteck Slope
Edelstahl
Driade SpA, Italien

Paola Navone
Suppen- und Vorlegelöffel Paloma
Edelstahl
h. 33.6cm / h. 22.7cm
Driade SpA, Italien

Borek Sipek
Besteck Hebe
Edelstahl, Kunststoff
Arzenal, Tschechien

Claus Jensen
Servierlöffel Eva Solo
Aluminium, Kunststoff
h. 30cm Ø 9cm
Eva Denmark A/S, Dänemark

Tischdekor

Enzo Mari
Schalen Campanella
Glas, Metall, Holzl
Diverse Grössen
Arnolfi di Cambio, Italien
Kleinserie

Marta Laudani und Marco Romanelli
Geschirr Mediterraneo
Keramik
Diverse Grössen
Driade SpA, Italien

Tischdekor

Gijs Bakker
Tablett Balance
Stahl
h. 3cm Ø 41cm
Meccano, Niederlande

Bastiaan Arler
Tablett Teevee
Keramik
h. 3.5cm l. 40cm b. 30cm
Britefuture, Italien
Kleinserie

Tischdekor

Britefuture ist ein junges italienisches Unternehmen. Seine Designphilosophie: Kleine Objekte sollen in einer frischen Herangehensweise durch halbindustrielle Techniken gefertigt, gestaltet und dann vermarktet werden.

Thomas Rosenthal
Picknickset Vario+
Kunststoff
h. 35cm l. 36cm
Rosenthal AG, Deutschland

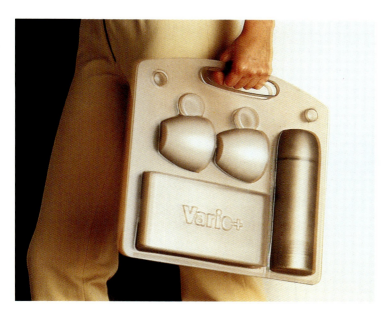

Ely Rozenberg
Tafelaufsatz Tamnun
Federstahl, Reissverschlüsse
t. 7cm Ø 58.5cm
Oz, Italien
Kleinserie

Ole Palsby
Obstkorb Concept
Edelstahlgeflecht
WMF, Deutschland

Tischdekor

Alessandro Bianchini
Dekoschale Lovenet
Umwickelter Kupferdraht, Kunstharz
h. 48cm b. 65cm l. 57cm
Oz, Italien
Kleinserie

Menr Kunstwerk als Tischdekor können die 'Container' von Alessandro Bianchini von der Decke hängen und gleichen dann riesigen Wespennestern. Jede dieser organischen Formen ist ein Unikat. Der biegsame Kupferkern der Faser wird in einer Reihe Zufallsmuster gesponnen und verwebt und dann mit Kunstharz gehärtet, bis das Objekt seine endgültige Form erhält.

Andrea Branzi
Obstkorb Solferino
Edelstahl
h. 23cm Ø 23cm
Alessi SpA, Italien

Kristiina Lassus
Schale Strawbowls
Gepresstes Stroh
Grösse 1: h. 13.5cm Ø 30cm
Grösse 2: h. 10cm Ø 22cm
Alessi SpA, Italien

Rechte Seite:
Andrea Branzi
Vasen Genetic Tales
Porzellan
h. 18cm Ø 5cm
Alessi SpA, Italien
Kleinserie

Tischdekor

Barbora Skorpilova und Jan Nedved
Vase Malá zubatá
Aluminium
h. 30cm b. 9.5cm t. 9.5cm
Giga, Tschechien
Kleinserie

Henryk Lula
Vasen
Terracotta
h. 32cm Ø 46cm
Kleinserie

Barbora Skorpilova und Jan Nedved
Vase Rastr
Aluminium
h. 30cm b. 9.5cm t. 9.5cm
Giga, Tschechei
Kleinserie

lemongras
Schale
Nylonkordel
Ø 20–50cm
lemongras design studio, Deutschland

Ron Arad
Vase Not Made by Hand, Not Made in China
Polyamid
h. 5–34cm Ø13cm
Kleinserie

'Not Made by Hand, Not Made in China' treibt das organische Design auf die Spitze. Ron Arad verleiht seiner Serie, bestehend aus Vasen und Leuchten, nicht nur eine natürliche Form, sondern zieht sie in einer künstlichen Hülle langsam heran, bis sie endgültig ausgebildet sind. Diese Objekte sind nicht gegossen, nicht geformt, nicht zusammengesetzt und auch nicht geschliffen, da Arad, gemeinsam mit Geoff Growther, Yuki Tano und Elliott Howes, eine neue Technik entwickelt hat, mit der seine Modelle in einer Art Tank mit Hilfe computergesteuerter Laserstrahlen 'wachsen' können. Mit dem Computer wird ein dreidimensionales Modell entworfen und solange animiert, bis es die gewünschte Form hat. Dann wird es auf eine Maschine übertragen, die daraus Tausende von horizontalen Querschnitten macht. Eine Plattform wird in einen Tank bis zur Tiefe der jeweils neuen Schicht heruntergelassen, gleichzeitig wird zusätzliches Material – entweder Pulver oder Harz, jedoch nie beides zusammen – zugegeben. Über die noch frischen Lagen wird ein Laserstrahl geleitet, der die verschiedenen Schichten miteinander verbindet. Über einen Zeitraum von Stunden oder Tagen wird das Objekt auf diese Art und Weise fertiggestellt, dann aus seinem Inkubator heraus genommen und zum Leben erweckt. Ron Arad Associates haben die Lücke geschlossen, die sich bislang zwischen dem, was mit dem Computer entworfen und geformt werden konnte, und dem, was am Ende realisiert wird, befand. Dennoch ist ihnen klar, dass diese Experimente angesichts der rasanten technologischen Entwicklung erst am Anfang stehen.

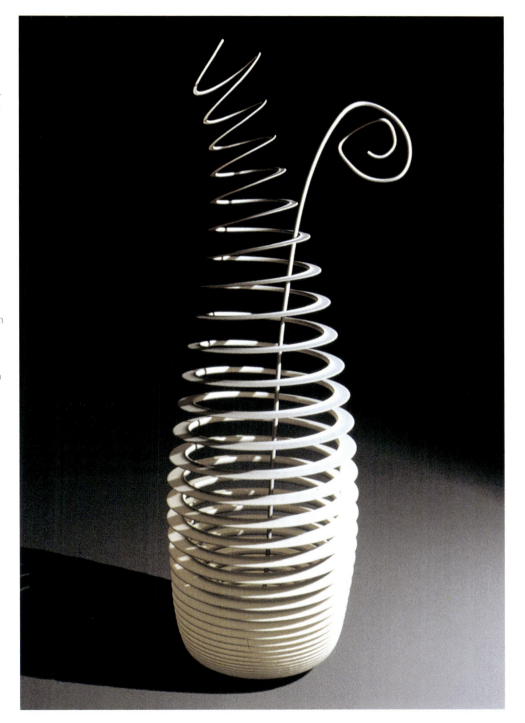

Tischdekor

Marc Boase
Schale Noodle Bowl
Porzellan
h. 10cm Ø 20cm
Maplestead Pottery Services
Grossbritannien

Marc Boase
Schale Dip Bowl
Porzellan
h. 10cm Ø 20cm
Maplestead Pottery Services
Grossbritannien

Borek Sipek
Geschirr Verna
Porzellan
Ø 26cm, 24cm, 19cm, 16cm
Arzenal, Tschechien

Marco Susani und Mario Trimarchi
Objekte Metallia
Poliertes Zinn
h. 6-18cm
Serafino Zani srl, Italien

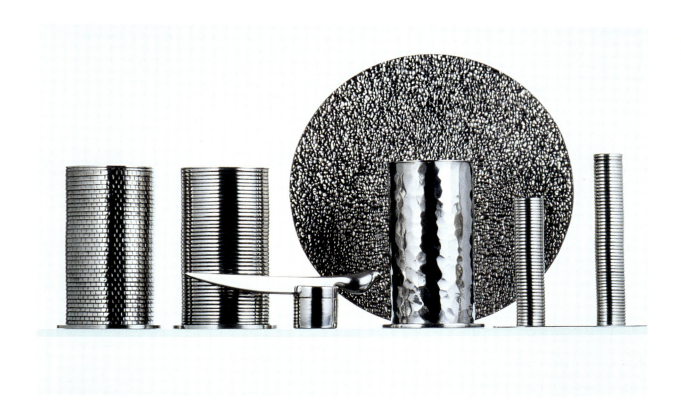

Monica Guggisberg und Philip Baldwin
Glasschalen Fili d'Arianna
Geblasenes Glas
Grösse 1: h. 39cm Ø 19cm
Grösse 2: h. 21cm Ø 28cm
Venini, Italien
Kleinserie

Nucleo
Kerze Cerapura
Paraffin
h. 41cm Ø 21cm
Nucleo Global Design Factory, Italien

Tischdekor

In den letzten paar Jahren gab es unzählige Neuinterpretationen von Kerzen, die gleichzeitig Kerze und Kerzenständer sind. Droog hat im Jahr 2000 dem Konzept von Timo Breumelhof, dessen 'Paraffin Table' sich beim Abbrennen ganz auflöst, einen neuen Impuls verliehen. Auch die Nucleo Global Design Factory hat diese Idee erfolgreich weiterentwickelt, indem man Wachs einfärbte und daraus eine Vase formte. 'Cerapura' ist ein Entwurf, der die Sinne anspricht, denn das Licht der Flamme macht das Objekt zu einem strahlenden Mittelpunkt.

Ronan Bouroullec
Kerze Candle Syst
Paraffin
h. 45cm b. 25cm l. 35cm
Backstage, Frankreich

Jacob de Baan
Kerzenleuchte Luccichio
Aluminium
h. 22.5cm Ø 20cm
D4 Industrial Design, Niederlande

Takashi Ifuji
Nachtlicht Aqmara
Keramik
h. 13cm b. 18cm t. 27.5cm
Prototyp

Mit seinem Nachtlicht 'Aqmara' hat Takashi Ifuji ein sehr poetisches Objekt geschaffen. Während die Kerze innen herunterbrennt, verwandelt sich der auf die Wand projizierte Halbmond in einen Vollmond.

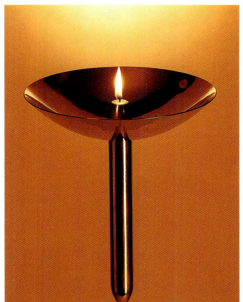

'Luccichio' ist einer der Entwürfe von Jacob de Baan aus seiner (nicht)elektrischen Kollektion. Er hat die Flamme als archaische Form der Lichtquelle als Ausgangspunkt benutzt und moderne Reflektortechnologie hinzugefügt. 'Luccichio' ist ein Kerzenhalter – eine mobile Lampe – die wie eine Taschenlampe benutzt, an der Decke aufgehängt oder an jeder beliebigen Oberfläche befestigt werden kann.

Massimo Lunardon
Vase Tulipano
Glas
h. 40cm Ø 15cm
Massimo Lunardon & Co, Italien

Rechte Seite:
Massimo Lunardon
Partyglas
Glas
h. 18cm Ø 5.5cm
Massimo Lunardon & Co, Italien

Massimo Lunardon hat zwei wirklich unangenehmen Partyprobleme gelöst: Das Glas in der einen Hand, ein Teller mit Essen in der anderen, dabei eigentlich essen wollen und, wenn es ganz schlimm kommt, das Glas auch noch verlieren. Mit einem Glas, dessen Form verändert wurde, und das man sich um den Hals hängen kann, hat er nicht nur ein Schmuckstück, sondern auch eine ganz neue Art Trinkgefäss kreiiert. Allerdings sollte man allzu enge Umarmungen vermeiden.

Tischdekor

Enzo Mari
Glas Campanella
Kristallglas
Arnolfo di Cambio Comp. Italiana
del Cristallo srl, Italien
Kleinserie

Mari Enzo
Schalen Campanella
Kristallglas
Arnolfo di Cambio Comp. Italiana
del Cristallo srl, Italien
Kleinserie

Enzo Mari
Glas Stromboli
Kristallglas
Arnolfo di Cambio Comp. Italiana
del Cristallo srl, Italien
Kleinserie

Enzo Mari
Krug Brocca
Kristallglas
h.22cm Ø 6.6cm
Arnolfo di Cambio Comp. Italiana
del Cristallo srl, Italien
Kleinserie

Tischdekor

Die Bleikristallfirma wurde 1963 von Arnolfo di Cambio gegründet. Seine Designphilosophie beruht auf der Verbindung fortschrittlicher industrieller Konzepte mit traditionellem Kunsthandwerk. Die doppelte Konzentration auf Wirtschaftlichkeit und die kulturelle Identität haben dazu geführt, dass das Unternehmen inzwischen zu den führenden in diesem industriellen Bereich zählt und darüberhinaus mit den Grössen der Designwelt zusammenarbeitet. Die zweite Auflage der 'Clearline'-Kollektion, wovon ein Teil hier vorgestellt wird, steht für die neue künstlerische Richtung, die das Unternehmen in den nächsten Jahren einschlagen möchte.

Borek Sipek
Rot- und Weissweinglas
Campanula, Magnolia
Kristallglas
Rotwein: h. 29cm Ø 8cm
Weisswein: h. 31cm Ø 7cm
Arzenal, Tschechien

Bohuslav Horak
Glas Stela
Kupfer, Kristallglas
h. 22cm Ø 10cm
Anthologie Quartett, Deutschland
Kleinserie

Bohuslav Horak
Glas Tekla
Kupfer, Kristall
h. 22cm Ø 10cm
Byra Interior Objects, Deutschland
Kleinserie

Aldo Cibic
Glas Chalice
Kristallglas
h. 27cm 22.5cm 21cm 20cm
Cibic & Partners, Italien

Aldo Cibic
Kerzenhalter
Kristallglas
Grösse 1: h. 40.5cm
Grösse 2: h. 34.5cm
Grösse 3: h. 27.5cm
Cibic & Partners, Italien

Aldo Cibic
Glaskrug
Kristallglas
h. 34.5cm
Cibic & Partners, Italien

Aldo Cibic
Glasflasche
Kristallglas
h. 42cm
Cibic & Partners, Italien

Christian Ghion
Glasvasen Insideout
h. 40cm ∅ 30cm
XO, Frankreich

Vanessa Mitrani
Vase La Mome Catch-catch
Glas, Metall
h. 27cm ∅ 25cm
Ligne Roset, Frankreich

Vanessa Mitrani
Vase, Lola Molotov
Glas, Metall
h. 24cm ∅ 14cm
Ligne Roset, Frankreich

Karim Rashid Dekanter Blob Glas h. 26cm Ø 18cm Leonardo, Deutschland	**Karim Rashid** Dekanter Spoo Glas h. 25cm Ø 14.5cm Leonardo, Deutschland	**Karim Rashid** Deanter Dive Glas h. 31cm Ø13cm Leonardo, Deutschland
Karim Rashid Glasschale Flip h. 25cm Ø 15cm (6in) Leonardo, Deutschland	**Karim Rashid** Glasschale Loop low h. 20cm Ø 29cm Leonardo, Deutschland	**Karim Rashid** Glasschale Loop high h. 25cm Ø 23.5cm Leonardo, Deutschland

Tischdekor

Seitdem die Formel der Glasherstellung – das Mischen von Salz (Natrium), Knochen (Kalzium) und Sand (Kieselerde) – vor über 4500 Jahren entdeckt wurde, ist sie eine unaufhörliche Inspirationsquelle für Kunsthandwerker und Designer. Glas zeichnet sich zugleich durch seine isolierenden und elastischen Qualitäten aus, ist transparent und ist, selbst wenn es leicht erscheint, so schwer wie Stein. Glas ist ein sehr lebendiges Material und für eine Gruppe von Designern ist es zum Material schlechthin geworden. Christian Ghion, Karim Rashid, Vanessa Mitrani und Danny Lane haben dieses Jahr wichtige Objekte produziert. Lanes unverwechselbares und imposantes Design spielt mit einem paradoxen Effekt des Glases: Es wiegt ungefähr 2570 kg pro Kubikmeter, scheint aber optisch keine Masse zu haben. Er hat eine Technik entwickelt, die das Licht auf optimale Weise bricht. Die Verwendung eines neuen Materials mit niedrigem Eisengehalt unterstützt die spektrale Qualität seiner Arbeit. Er meint dazu: „Das bedeutet, dass ich nun schwere Objekte in grossen Formaten herstellen kann und die prismatischen Spiegelungen sind mit dieser Technik noch viel stärker." Karim Rashid hält Glas für eines der schönsten natürlichen Materialien in der Gestaltung eines modernen Interieurs. Es müsse wie eine Flüssigkeit in organischen Formen gestaltet werden. Die sinnlichen Kurven und ätherischen Farbabstufungen der 'Leonardo'-Serie sollen die Bedeutung von Schönheit und Material durch ihre weiche, solide, ergonomische, sinnliche und angenehme Form unterstreichen.

Emmanuel Babled
Glasflakon Primaire N° IX
Geblasenes Glas
Ø 45cm
Covo srl, Italien
Kleinserie

Emmanuel Babled
Vasenserie Edizioni
Geblasenes Glas
h. 19–40cm Ø 50cm
Covo srl, Italien
Kleinserie

Danny Lane
Glasobjekt Crab Bowl
Geschmolzenes und gebrochenes Glas
h. 18cm l. 72cm t. 40cm
Unikat

Vielleicht empfindet Emmanuel Babled den grössten Respekt für die poetische, zugleich geheimnisvolle Ausstrahlung des Glases. Seine mundgeblasenen Vasen wurden alle in Murano von einem Meister dieses Metiers, der die Entwürfe Bableds entsprechend umzusetzen weiss, hergestellt. Dennoch ist Babled der Überzeugung, dass er und der Glasbläser nur im Dienste des Materials selbst stehen. Das Endergebnis kann vorher nur begrenzt festgelegt werden, und es ist diese Spannung zwischen der menschlichen Vorstellungskraft und dem Augenblick der Schöpfung, die er in der Arbeit mit diesem Material ganz besonders interessant findet. Veränderungen können nur im allerletzten Moment im Ofen vorgenommen werden, wenn das Glas noch formbar ist und bevor es zu kristallieren beginnt. Babled nutzt diesen Augenblick, um 'ein Fragment des Emotionalen festzuhalten'. Es geht ihm nicht nur darum, ein schönes Objekt mit einer originellen oder modernen Form zu kreieren, sondern er möchte jedem Objekt einen ganz persönlichen Ausdruck verleihen.

Tischdekor

Ettore Sottsass
Tafelaufsatz Namus
Bleikristall, schwarzer Marmor
h. 18.9cm Ø 21cm
Arnolfo di Cambio Comp. Italiana
del Cristallo srl, Italien
Kleinserie

Ettore Sottsass
Vase Manaus
Bleikristall
h. 34.8cm Ø 13cm
Arnolfo di Cambio Comp. Italiana
del Cristallo srl, Italien
Kleinserie

Oscar Tusquets Blanca
Vorspeisenset Tableta
Bleikristall
h. 3.4cm b. 29.8cm l. 29.8cm
Arnolfo di Cambio Comp. Italiana
del Cristallo srl, Italien
Kleinserie

Oscar Tusquets Blanca
Kerzenhalter mit Blumenvase Fioreluz
Bleikristall
h. 34cm b. 28cm
Arnolfo di Cambio Comp. Italiana
del Cristallo srl, Italien
Kleinserie

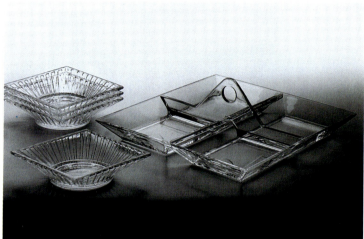

Paolo Zani
Blumenvase Sumo
Pyrex und Glas
h. 40cm Ø 13cm
FontanaArte, Italien

Abhängig von der Länge der Blumen kann der Wasserbehälter von Paolo Zanis Blumenvase 'Sumo' entfernt, der externe Zylinder auf den Kopf gestellt und der Wasserbehälter in einer anderen Position wieder eingesetzt werden.

Carsten Jøergensen
Glasschale Hot Pot
Glas
Ø 22.1cm
Bodum, Schweiz

Tischdekor

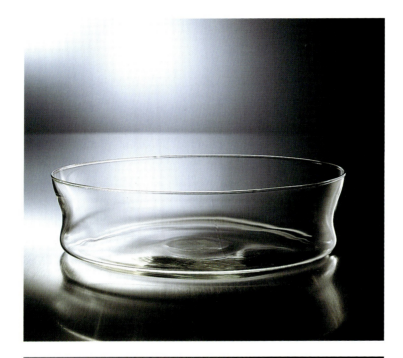

Satyendra Pakhalé
Deko-Objekt K:dai 1 and 2
Recyceltes Metall, Wachs
h. 5.5cm Ø 18cm
Kleinserie

Satyendra Pakhalé
Deko-Objekt C:da
Recyceltes Metall, Wachs
h. 15.5cm Ø 10cm
Kleinserie

Tischdekor

Michele De Lucchis Interesse am Wechselspiel von Design und Kunsthandwerk bewog ihn dazu, Satyendra Pakhalés Kollektion von Tischaufsätzen und Vasen auszuwählen. Pakhalé hat eine alte indische Metallgusstechnik verfeinert, um zeitgenössische Objekte zu produzieren. Ein Kern wird aus einer Mischung feinen sauberen Sandes und Lehm hergestellt. Traditionellerweise wird Ziegenmist in Wasser mit Erde eingeweicht, zermalmt und mit Lehm zu gleichen Teilen vermischt. Diese weiche Mixtur stellt die Grundmasse dar. Wenn sie getrocknet ist, wird sie benutzt, um ein Wachsmuster zu kreieren. Ein spezielles natürliches Wachs wird über einem offenen Feuer zum Schmelzen gebracht und durch ein feines Tuch in ein Gefäss mit kaltem Wasser gegossen, wodurch es sich wieder verfestigt. Das Wachs muss absolut frei von Verunreinigungen gehalten werden. Als nächstes wird es durch ein Sieb gedrückt, und es enstehen 'Wachsschnüre', deren Durchmesser beliebig variiert werden kann. Diese Wachsschnüre werden um den Kern herumgewickelt, eine nach der anderen, bis die ganze Oberfläche bedeckt ist. In früheren Zeiten hätte der Künstler in der warmen Sonne gesessen, um Lehmkern und Wachsüberzug in der Temperatur einander anzugleichen. Die ganze Form wird schließlich mit einer Mischung aus Lehm, Sand und Kuhdung zu jeweils gleichen Teilen bedeckt und dann gebrannt. Einfache Metalle wie Messing, Bronze, Kupfer etc. werden miteinander verschmolzen und in die gebrannte Lehmform gegossen. Das Wachs löst sich dann während des Prozesses auf.

textilien

Unter allen Kapiteln des Internationalen Design Jahrbuchs stellt das Textilkapitel den Gastherausgeber vor die grösste Herausforderung. Es ist nicht nur ein Bereich, mit dem er meistens nicht so vertraut ist, die Produkte lassen sich auch ausserordentlich schwer beurteilen, wenn man sie nicht konkret zur Hand hat. Stoffe muss man anfassen können. Hat man sie nur als Abbildung vorliegen, kann man die Haptik des Gewebes nicht beurteilen, was eigentlich die Grundvoraussetzung bei der Bewertung der Stoffe ist. Der Gastherausgeber kann also nur aufgrund ästhetischer Erwägungen und Innovationskriterien seine Entscheidungen treffen.

Dieses Jahr gab es eine grosse Auswahl: Massenproduzierte Polsterstoffe von Bute und De Padova, Computerdesign von Carol Westfall, kreative Wandbehänge von Yehudit Katz, experimentelle Materialanwendungen von Masayo Ave, Santos und Adolfsdóttir, kreative Entwürfe von Claudy Jongstra sowie eine grosse Auswahl an Teppichen von Asplund und Lignet Roset – um nur einige zu nennen. Dieses Mal drängte die Dominanz der japanischen Beiträge die anderen Nominierungen nicht in den Hintergrund. Auf den folgenden Seiten finden sich lediglich Arbeiten der Nuno Corporation, die traditionelles einheimisches Handwerk mit den neuesten Materialien und Herstellungsverfahren verbindet.

Das interessanteste Phänomen, das sich an der vorliegenden Auswahl ablesen lässt, ist die Weiterentwicklung des traditionellen Begriffes von Stoff. Die Grenzen verwischen sich, den , wie man sieht, gibt es Textilien als Möbel, z. B. Sodeaus 'Red Rug' und Gavoilles 'Kloc', als Gebrauchsgegenstände wie CPs 'City Tent' und, besonders hervorzuheben, 'intelligente' Textilien.

Wie schon im letzten Jahrbuch erwähnt, werden der technologische Fortschritt und die Materialentwicklung immer wichtiger. So halten auch die Textilien langsam Einzug in das 21.Jahrhundert. Es gibt nicht nur Fäden und Gewebe aus industriell hergestellten Materialien, die Erfindung 'intelligenter' Stoffe hat mitlerweile die Grenze zwischen Textilien und Produkten verwischt. So kann man z.B. einen 'Antistress Car Coat' kaufen, dessen Futter sich an die Körperform des jeweiligen Trägers anpasst, um Nacken und Kreuz zu unterstützen, oder ein 'Temperature-Jacket', mit einem von der NASA entwickelten Futter, das die Körpertemperatur permanent ausgleicht, indem es Wärme aufnimmt und abgibt. Levis experimentiert zur Zeit an der Entwicklung einer Jeansjacke mit eingebautem Keyboard und Synthesizer.

Auch pharmazeutische Textilien wurden entwickelt: Antistatische Stoffe für Patienten mit Herzschrittmachern oder feuchtigkeitspendenden Materialien für Brandverletzte. Die in Florenz ansässige Lineapiu Gruppe hat ein Gummigarn erfunden, das im Dunkeln leuchtet, indem es zuvor gespeichertes Licht reflektiert. Sie hat ein Kohlefasergarn namens 'Relax' entwickelt, das offensichtlich Stress reduziert, indem es den Körper vor einem Teil der elektromagnetischen Strahlung schützt, die von Haushaltsgeräten ausgeht.

Unsere Auswahl enthält auch die Tischwäsche der Zukunft. So entwickelte Philips im Rahmen seines Forschungsprogramms 'Culinary Art, Searching for Total Culinary Enjoyment' – Kulinarische Kunst auf der Suche nach dem absoluten Essvergnügen – eine Designidee, die neueste Technologie mit traditioneller Tischkultur verbindet: ein voll waschbares Leinentischtuch mit integriertem Stromkreis, der alle Gegenstände mit Strom versorgt, die man darauf abstellt.

Wohin nun führt uns die Entwicklung 'intelligenter' Textilien? Die Trendforscher der Firma Futuremode in New York wissen vielleicht die Antwort. Kürzlich berichtete man von den jüngsten Entdeckungen in Japan: Neue Konzepte, zu denen z. B. auch die Entwicklung eines Metallgewebes gehört, das sich falten und hinterleuchten lässt. Man kann darauf schreiben und sogar Information speichern.

Marc Newson
Teppich Marc
100% Neuseeland-Wolle, handgetuftet
Asplund, Schweden

Marc Newson
Teppich Marc De Luxe
100% Neuseeland-Wolle, handgetuftet
Asplund, Schweden

Alfredo Häberli
Teppich Carpet Lines
100% Neuseeland-Wolle
handgetuftet
Asplund, Schweden

Maria Kaaris
Teppich Soap Bubbles
100% Neuseeland-Wolle
handgetuftet
l. 160cm b. 210cm
Asplund, Schweden

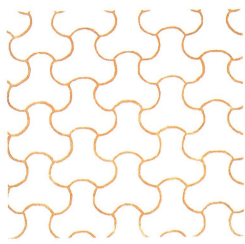

Alfredo Häberli
Teppich Lines
100% Neuseeland-Wolle
handgetuftet
Asplund, Schweden

Anki Gneib
Teppich Cheese
100% Neuseeland-Wolle
handgetuftet
Asplund, Schweden

Lars Bergström und Mats Bigert
Teppich Egg
100% Neuseeland-Wolle
handgetuftet
Asplund, Schweden

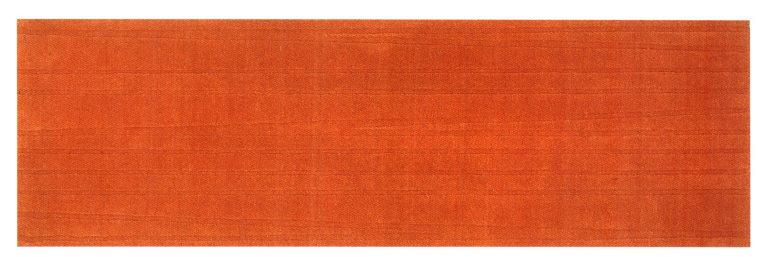

Textilien

Masayo Ave
Teppich Silent
Filz
b. 80cm l. 160–180cm
Atrox GmbH, Schweiz
Unikat

Masayo Ave
Wandteppich Quadretti
Filz
Atrox GmbH, Schweiz
Prototyp

Masayo Aves einzeln angefertigte Teppiche verbinden Traditon und Innovation. Die althergebrachte Technik des Webens erfährt eine völlige Neuerung durch einen industriell hergestellten Wollfilz. Ave macht bereits seit 1995 intensive Materialstudien und experimentiert mit Komponenten, die normalerweise in der industriellen Fertigung verwendet werden. Das verleiht den Teppichen ästhetische Qualitäten. Seit neuestem interessiert sich Masayo Ave für Polyester, das FCKW-frei produziert und wiederverwertet werden kann für nicht-gewebte Textilien wie z. B. Filz, Filtermaterial, Kunstmarmor, PET und Nylon. Durch die Entfaltung der ursprünglichen Möglichkeiten dieser Materialien entstehen Unikate mit oft unerwarteten Ergebnissen. Da Ave dem Material auf keinen Fall ein Design aufzwingen möchte, entstehen Objekte, die den Betrachter unmittelbar für sich einnehmen, indem sie nicht nur funktionieren, sondern auch an das Gefühl appellieren.

Masayo Ave
Kissen Cool
Polyesterschaum, Tüll
Grösse 1: b. 42cm l. 42cm
Grösse 2: b. 32cm l. 32cm
Atrox GmbH, Schweiz
Prototyp

Claudy Jongstra
Stoff
Merinowolle
Seidenorganza mit Metallfaden
Not tom dick & harry, Niederlande
Prototyp

Claudy Jongstra
Stoff
Merinowolle, Rohseide
Not tom dick & harry, Niederlande
Prototyp

Claudy Jongstra
Stoff
Merinowolle, Rohleinen
Seidenorganza
Not tom dick & harry, Niederlande
Prototyp

Claudy Jongstra
Stoff
Merinowolle, Tüll
Not tom dick & harry, Niederlande
Prototyp

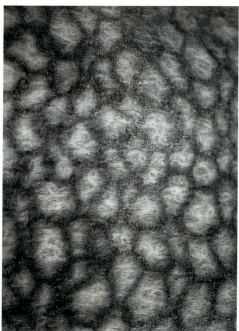

Claudy Jongstra von Not tom dick & harry arbeitet nur mit Naturmaterialien, vorzugsweise mit Filz, den sie mit Rohseide, Leinen, Kamelhaar, Kaschmir und Schurwolle verbindet. Die Stoffe wie 'Die Schöne und das Biest' sind urzeitlich primitiv auf der einen Seite, jedoch zart und kostbar wie ein Schmetterlingsflügel. Ihr Repertoire umfasst mehr als 500 Entwürfe. Zu den feineren geschmeidigeren Stoffen gehören Kombinationen aus Alpaca, Merino und metallisch glänzendes Seidenorganza. Rauher und ursprünglicher sind Mischungen aus Merinowolle und Rohleinen. Jongstra sagt: "Im Grunde genommen ist Filz die älteste Textilie der Welt und hat deswegen eigentlich kein modernes Image. Ich wollte herausfinden, ob man Filz nicht zeitgemäß verwenden kann, aber trotzdem seinen ursprünglichen Charakter respektieren, seine Festigkeit. Aus diesem Grunde arbeite ich mit rauhen unbehandelten Materialien." Jongstra hält sich eine eigene Herde seltener Schafe, um die Kontrolle über Qualität, Farbe und Mischung der Wolle nicht aus der Hand zu geben. Selbst die maschinelle Weiterverarbeitung geschieht auf Maschinen, die sie selbst hergestellt hat. Zu ihren Kunden gehören internationale Modedesigner wie Donna Karan und John Galliano, Industriedesignerin Hella Jongerius und der amerikanische Architekt Will Bruder. Kürzlich stellte sie für den letzten Star-Wars-Film die Stoffe für die Jedi-Ritter her.

Norma Starszakowna
Stoff Acts of Beauty A
Hitzebehandelt, bedruckt
h. 350cm b. 50cm
Prototyp

Norma Starszakowna
Stoff Acts of Beauty B
Seidenorganza
Hitzebehandelt, bedruckt
h. 350cm b. 50cm
Prototyp
Kleinserie

Emmanuele Ricci
Möbelbezugsstoff Wire
51% Baumwolle, 49% Acryl
b. 140cm
Lorenzo Rubelli SpA, Italien

Emmanuele Ricci
Möbelbezugsstoff Rise
51% Vi, 25% PC, 24% Seide
b. 130cm
Lorenzo Rubelli SpA, Italien

Emmanuele Ricci
Möbelbezugsstoff Bambusa
51% Baumwolle
49% Viscose
b. 140cm
Lorenzo Rubelli SpA, Italien

Emmanuele Ricci
Möbelbezugsstoff Helix
51% Viscose
25% PC, 24% SE
b. 130cm
Lorenzo Rubelli SpA, Italien

Textilien

Ane Lykke
Wandteppich Zen Se
Papiergewebe
h. 3.5cm b. 120cm l. 200cm
Prototyp

Javier Mariscal
Teppich
100% reine Neuseeland-Wolle
l. 170cm b. 240cm
Desso, Niederlande

Jeffrey Bernett
Teppich Man
100% Wolle, handgetuftet
l. 170cm b. 240cm
Ligne Roset, Frankreich

Pascal Mourgue
Teppich Smala
100% Wolle, handgetuftet
l. 200cm b. 200cm
Ligne Roset, Frankreich

Jean-Charles de Castelbajac
Teppich On Pax Joy
100% Wolle, handgetuftet
l. 170cm b. 240cm
Ligne Roset, Frankreich

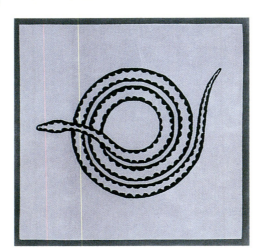

Michael Sodeau
Teppiche
Red Rug und Blue Rug
Wolle
b. 100cm l. variabel
Christopher Farr, Grossbritannien

Kristian Gavoille
Teppich Kloc
100% Wolle, handgetuftet
l. 200cm b. 200cm
Ligne Roset, Frankreich

**Stefano Marzano und
Philips Design
Tischdecke Interactive Tablecloth
Stoff, Stromkreis
Philips Electronics BV, Niederlande
Unikat**

**CP Company
City Tent/Mac
Wetterfestes Nylongewebe
SPW, Italien
Kleinserie**

Das interaktive Tischtuch ist ein Produkt aus der 'Culinary Art'-Serie von Philips. Der integrierte Stromkreis ist in das waschbare Leinentischtuch hineingewebt und kann alle Gegenstände, die man auf dem Tisch abstellt, mit Strom versorgen. Obwohl die Oberfläche des Tischtuchs selbst kalt bleibt, kann es spezielle Keramikteller warmhalten.

Die Frühling/Sommer-2000-Kollektion von CP Company gibt sich nicht damit zufrieden, einfach Mode oder nur Textilie zu präsentieren. In ihrer Serie 'Transformables: beyond clothing, an ironic aspiration to freedom' – 'Transformation: jenseits der Kleidung ein ironischer Griff nach der Freiheit' gibt es Kleidungsstücke, die sich verwandeln können: Aus einem langen Umhang wird ein Drachen, den man mit einer am Körper befestigten integrierten Leine in die Luft steigen lassen kann. Eine Jacke verwandelt sich in einen Rucksack mit vielen Taschen. Zu dem hier abgebildeten Cape gehört eine kleine Tasche mit leichten Aluminiumstangen, die man in die Säume des Capes stecken kann. So entsteht das 'City Tent', dessen Stabilität allerdings noch nicht unter extremer Wetterbeanspruchung getestet wurde.

Jasper Morrison
Stoff Melrose
Wolle
Bute Fabrics Ltd, Schottland

Jasper Morrison
Stoff Tiree
Wolle
Bute Fabrics Ltd, Schottland

De Padova
Stoff Lino 2000
54% Leinen
40% Baumwolle
6% Polyamid
De Padova, Italien

De Padova
Polsterstoff Melange 2000
80% Baumwolle
10% Viscose
6% Nylon, 4% Leinen
De Padova, Italien

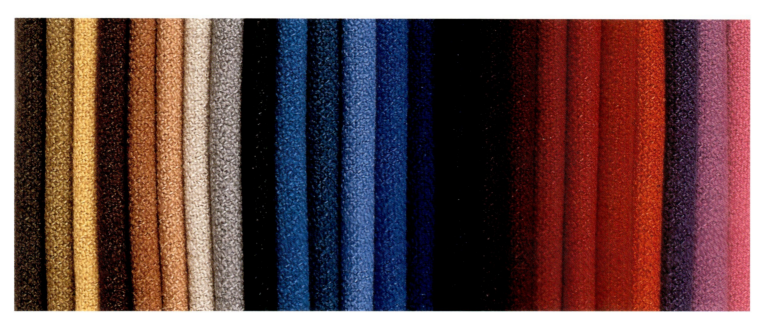

Heinz Röntgen
Dekostoff Bijoux
50% Polyester, 50% Metall
b. 170cm
Nya Nordiska Textiles GmbH
Deutschland

Yehudit Katz
Stoff Ikat
Gewachstes Leinen
Baumwolle
Bambusstäbchen
h. 226cm b. 75cm
Unikat

Yehudit Katz
Stoff Degradèe
Leinen, Kupferfäden
h. 75cm b. 68cm
Unikat

Rechte Seite:
Heinz Röntgen
Dekostoff Fukaso
33% Leinen, 33% Polyamid
34% Polyester
b. 152cm
Nya Nordiska Textiles GmbH
Deutschland

Leo Santos-Shaw und
Margaret Adolfsdóttir
Stoff SA08B2
Papier, Nylon
b. 150cm
Unikat

Leo Santos-Shaw und
Margaret Adolfsdóttir
Stoff SA0012
Polyester, Polyamid
h. 400cm b. 100cm
Unikat

Tuttu Sillanpää und
Elina Huotari
Teppich Polku I, Polku II
Filz (reine Wolle)
l. 150cm b. 220cm Ø. 160cm
Verso Design, Finnland

Thomas Sandell
Teppich Air
100% Neuseeland-Wolle
handgetuftet
Asplund, Schweden

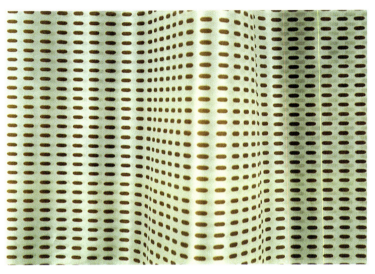
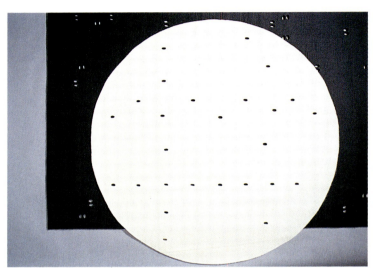

Carol Westfall
Stoff Vegetable-Cucumber Wilt
Digitaldruck auf Baumwolle
b. 148.5cm l. 103.5cm
Unikat

Carol Westfall
Stoff Animal-Protozoan
Digitaldruck auf Baumwolle
b. 148.5cm l. 274cm
Unikat

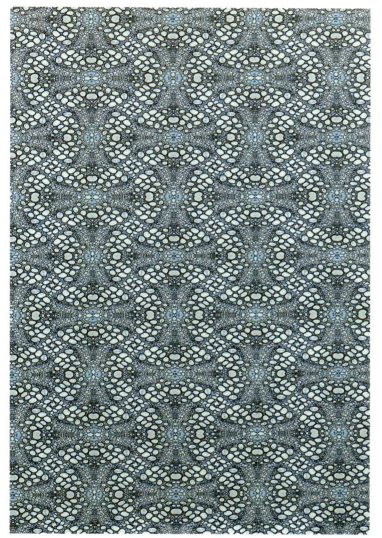

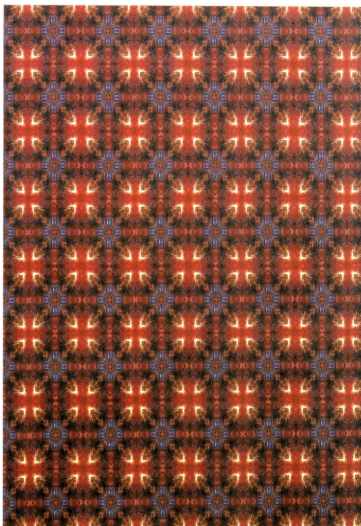

Carol Westfals Entwürfe werden am Computer entworfen und digital auf Baumwolle gedruckt.

Christine Van der Hurd
Teppich Verdi
100% Neuseeland-Wolle
b. 304.8cm l. 213.3cm
Unikat

Christine Van der Hurd
Teppich Portals
100% Neuseeland-Wolle
b. 152.4cm l. 213.3cm
Unikat

Reiko Sudo
Stoff Rubber Band Scatter
Leinen
b. 112cm
Nuno Corporation, Japan

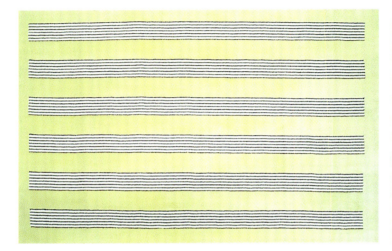

Kazuhiro Ueno
Stoff Masking Tape
Baumwolle
b. 92cm
Nuno Corporation, Japan

Reiko Sudo und Ryoko Sugiura
Stoff Southern Cross
Polyester
b. 112cm
Nuno Corporation, Japan

Yoko Ando und Reiko Sudo
Stoff Rubber Band Scatter
Polyester
b. 112cm
Nuno Corporation, Japan

In den Stoffen, die Reiko Sudo für Nuno Corporation entworfen hat, spiegelt sich die Handwerkstradition des japanischen Textildesigns. Die Beschreibung lässt eher an ein Seminar für kreative Formgebung als an massenproduzierte Stoffe von einem der bekanntesten Textilhersteller in Japan, denken.
Rubber Band Scatter: Reliefartige Formen aus Gummi werden mit einer Mischung aus Acryl und Silicon auf Leinen gedruckt.
Masking Tape: Auf den Stoff geklebte Kreppbandstreifen werden mit Farbe übersprüht und wieder abgelöst, so dass sie scharfkantige grafische Muster hinterlassen.
Southern Cross: Kleine Glasperlen werden mit Industriekleber befestigt.
Rubber Band Scatter: Reliefartige Formen aus Gummi werden mit einer Mischung aus Acryl und Silicon auf Leinen gedruckt.

produkte

„Ich habe mich immer den Veränderungen der Zeit gestellt und werde es weiterhin tun, denn dies erscheint mir als eine notwendige Bedingung zur Gestaltung von Architektur und Design", bekennt Michele De Lucchi. Seit Beginn seiner Karriere und der Gründung von 'Cavart', danach durch seine Mitarbeit bei Memphis und sein ständiges Interesse an der Entwicklung von neuen Produkten besonders auch im elektronischen Bereich, bemüht sich Michele De Lucchi, immer an der Spitze neuer Entwicklungen zu stehen. Durch seine Zusammenarbeit mit Olivetti in den späten 70er Jahren und seiner Zusammenarbeit mit Matsushita und Siemens in letzter Zeit hat De Lucchi die Bedeutung des In-house Designteams für die Entwicklung neuer Technologien entdeckt. Sein Studio hat sich einer ganzheitlichen Philosophie verschrieben, die nicht nur die Ästhetik der Gegenstände umfasst, sondern auch dem Entwicklungsprozess 'von der Analyse zum Konzept und von der Forschung zur Umsetzung' grosse Aufmerksamkeit schenkt. In Gesprächen über Leistung und Rückschritt bei der Herstellung der Produkte zu Beginn des Informations- und Telekommunikationszeitalters erklärte De Lucchi, dass diejenigen erfolgreich sein werden, deren Erfolg auf einem fundierten Forschungsprogramm basiert. „Das Ausmaß des Erfolgs hängt heute nicht mehr von Produktionskapazitäten ab, sondern von der Fähigkeit, Ideen zu haben, sie weiter zu entwickeln und umzusetzen"

Während sich sozio-kulturelle Trends verändern und der Lebensstil erfüllter, schneller und abwechslungsreicher wird, entwickeln alle führenden Hersteller intelligente Produkte mit dem Ziel, dem Konsumenten mehr Zeit für kreative Aktivitäten zu ermöglichen. Whirlpool arbeitet an einem Internetkühlschrank mit integrierter Nahrungsmittelübersichtsfunktion. Der Inhalt des Kühlschranks wird registriert und dann können alle Lieferungen direkt per E-mail vom Supermarkt angefordert werden. Mikrowellengeräte werden entworfen, die Barcodes lesen, Fertiggerichte abwiegen und zur gewünschten Zeit zubereiten können. Sunbeam hat kürzlich vernetzte Haushaltsgeräte angekündigt. 'Thalia', eine Koppelung von Kaffeemaschine, Wecker, Mixer und Badezimmerwaage, wurde entwickelt, um mit uns zu interagieren und alle Bedürfnisse nach dem Aufwachen zu erfüllen. In seinem kürzlich erschienenen Buch 'When things start to think' prophezeit Neil Goshenfeld, Professor am MIT, dass es nicht allzu lange dauern wird, bis eine vernetzte Küche Versicherungsunternehmen mit Daten über Essgewohnheiten zur entsprechenden Ermittlung von Versicherungsprämien versorgen könnte.

Angesichts der drohenden Enthumanisierung der Lebenswelt durch die Allgegenwart des Computers mussten Wege gefunden werden, um das Gleichgewicht zwischen technischem Fortschritt und menschlichem Anliegen wieder herzustellen. Seit Apple den iMAC herausgebracht hat, wurde das Design der Produkte schlichter und benutzerfreundlicher, das Innenleben jedoch zunehmend komplexer. Philips ist auch seit langer Zeit dafür bekannt, innovative Elektronik mit traditioneller Ästhetik zu verbinden Der Philips-Alessi-Serie gelang es, auf revolutionäre Weise Farbe und menschliche Wärme zurück in die sterile Hightech-Küche der 90er Jahre zu bringen. Zur Zeit beschäftigt man sich bei Philips mit einem langfristig angelegten, strategischen Design-Projekt, das eine humanere Formgebung für die explosionsartig anwachsenden Angebote im Bereich der Internetangebote und der mobilen Kommunikation zum Ziel hat. Philips Consumer Communications und Philips Design befragten Nutzer, Händler, Konsumenten und die Medien, um eine Zukunft zu definieren und zu gestalten, die sich stärker an humanen Gesichtspunkten orientiert. Die Konsumenten wollen ihre Produkte kontrollieren, nicht umgekehrt. Stefano Marzano, Geschäftsführer von Philips Design, schreibt, dass idealerweise die neue Intelligenz, die uns umgeben wird, sich in uns unterstützende oder begleitende Objekte, die uns kennen, die lernen mit unseren Vorlieben und Abneigungen umzugehen, so wie es früher ein Diener getan hätte, entwickeln wird. Auf diese Weise steht es ihrem Arbeitgeber frei, sich der Kunst, wissenschaftlicher Forschung, dem gesellschaftlichen Umgang, der Gastfreundschaft, Reisen oder auch ehrenamtlichen Aktivitäten zu widmen.'

Die Auswahl für das Internationale Design Jahrbuch hebt einige dieser Aspekte hervor. Leon@rdo von Ariston mit WRAP (Web Ready Appliance Protocol) bringt das Internet ins Haus. Matsushita hat eine Reihe von Produkten aus traditionellen und vertrauten Materialien geschaffen, die unsere Vorstellung von Frühstück in physiologischer und psychologischer Hinsicht verändert. In Zusammenarbeit mit Whirlpool und Corian hat Jam eine vollständig interaktive Küche mit weichen Kanten und warmen Oberflächen entworfen. Philips hat den 'Café Duo' herausgebracht, der nicht so sehr wie eine Maschine aussieht, sondern vielmehr wie ein freundlicher Kellner, der an der Wand lehnt und Kaffeetassen auf einem Tablett bereithält. Auch wenn das vollautomatische und mit dem Internet verbundene Zuhause der Zukunft noch keine Realität ist, steht es vielleicht schon vor der Tür.

Als das Jahrbuch in Druck ging, hat die Beisam-Stiftung (Metro) über die Zeitung nach einer technologisch versierten multilingualen Familie gesucht, die sich bereit erklärt, in einem mit neuester Technik ausgestattetem Haus zu wohnen. Unter den vielen modernen WRAP-Anwendungen, mit denen es ausgerüstet ist, befindet sich auch ein Kühlschrank, der eigenständig Lebensmittel bestellt, sowie ein Bad, das mögliche Krankheiten diagnostizieren kann. Alle täglichen Aktivitäten der Familie werden auf einer extra dafür geschaffenen Website (www.futurelife.ch) im Internet gezeigt. Wir können nur hoffen, dass dieses Experiment sich als Inspiration und nicht als Warnung entpuppt.

Marc Berthier/Design Plan Studio
Radio Pebble Objects
Aluminiumgehäuse
h. 2cm b. 6cm l. 9cm
Spirix-Lexon, Frankreich

Marc Berthier/Design Plan Studio
Diktiergerät Pebble Objects
Aluminiumgehäuse
h. 2cm b. 6cml. 9cm
Spirix-Lexon, Frankreich

Marc Berthier/Design Plan Studio
Taschenrechner Pebble Objects
Aluminiumgehäuse
h. 2cm b. 6cm l. 9cm
Spirix-Lexon, Frankreich

Marc Berthier/Design Plan Studio
Wecker Pebble Objects
Aluminiumgehäuse
h. 2cm b. 6cm l. 9cm
Spirix-Lexon, Frankreich

Marc Berthier/Design Plan Studio
Organizer Pebble Objects
Aluminiumgehäuse
h. 2cm b. 6cm l. 9cm
Spirix-Lexon, Frankreich

Marc Berthier/Design Plan Studio
Taschenlampe Pebble Objects
Aluminiumgehäuse
h. 2cm b. 6cm l. 9cm
Spirix-Lexon, Frankreich

Marc Berthier/Design Plan Studio
Schreibset Pebble Objects
Aluminiumgehäuse
h. 2cm b. 6cm l. 9cm
Spirix-Lexon, Frankreich

Geoff Hollington, Richard Arnott
David Townsend Elliot, Francis R. Skop Jr.
Fotosystemkamera Advantix T700
Kunststoff
h. 6,5cm b. 9,2cm t. 3,6cm
Eastman Kodak Company, USA

Hideki Kawai
Unterwasserkamera Ixus X-1
Polykarbonat, ABS-Kunststoff, Edelstahl
h. 7,5cm b. 10,5cm l. 4,7cm
Canon Inc., Japan

Kaoru Sumita
Digitalkamera, DSC-F505
Magnesiumguss
h. 6,2cm b. 10,7cm l. 13,5cm
Sony Corporation, Japan

Yasuhiko Miyoshi
Tragbarer MD-Player, MD-ST55 (S) (A) (R)
Aluminium, ABS-Kunststoff
l. 7.8cm b. 7.1cm
Sharp Corporation, Japan

Die Sharp Corporation beschäftigt weltweit mehr als 60.000 Menschen in 33 Ländern und 66 Fabriken. Der Konzern ist international dafür bekannt, Produkte auf einem hohen technologischen Standard anzubieten, die sich gleichzeitig durch Eleganz und Modernität auszeichnen. Das Unternehmen wurde 1912 von Tokuji Hayakawa gegründet, um Metallobjekte entsprechend einem Patent für Metallschnallen zu produzieren. Die Sharp Trademark ist auf Hayakawas Erfindung des 'Ever-Sharp'-Stiftes zurückzuführen. Trotz dieser bescheidenen Anfänge ist das Unternehmen mittlerweile der weltgrösste Hersteller für LCD-Anzeigen und erschließt durch die Entwicklung einzigartiger Produkte aus den Bereichen industrieller Elektronik und Haushaltselektronik bis hin zu Bürotechnologie jedes Jahr neue Märkte. Sharp stellt den Menschen weiterhin in den Mittelpunkt. Die Bedürfnisse des Kunden werden erforscht und das Produktdesign reflektiert diese Kriterien. In einer zunehmend technologisierten Welt, an deren Ausgestaltung wir verstärkt teilhaben, hat Sharp erkannt, dass der Anwender paradoxerweise eine einfache Schnittstelle zwischen sich selbst und der Komplexität dieser Welt benötigt. Die Sharp-Designphilosophie lautet, Objekte zu produzieren, die sich durch 'Klarheit und Verlässlichkeit' einerseits sowie durch 'Freundlichkeit und Spaß im Gebrauch' andererseits auszeichnen.

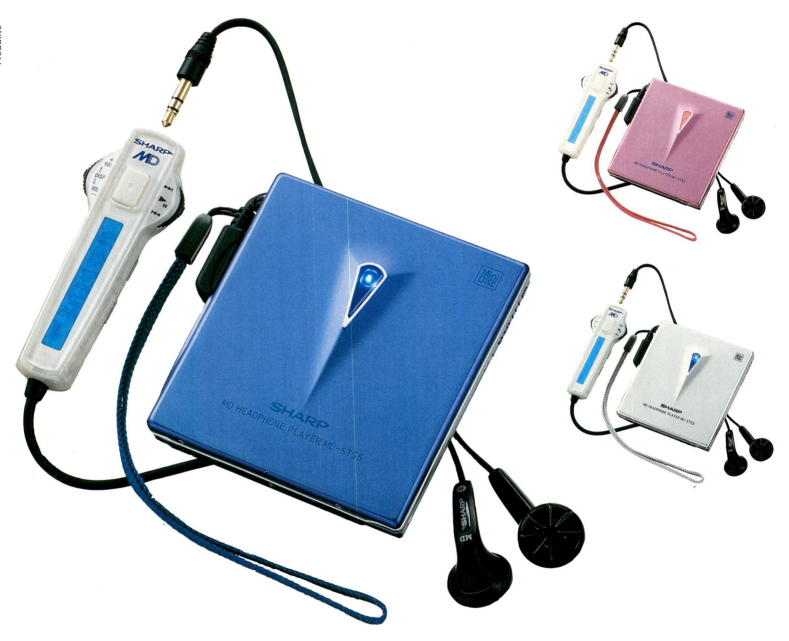

Kunihiro Okhi
Personal Digital Assistant MI-C1-A
Kunststoff
h. 1.55cm b. 3.6cm t. 8cm
Sharp Corporation, Japan

Yumiko Takeshita
Faxgerät UX-E800
ABS-Kunststoff
h. 12.7cm b. 33.8cm t. 26.5cm
Sharp Corporation, Japan

Sachio Yamamoto, Katsunori Kume, Junichi Saitou
MPEG 4 Digitale Videokamera VN-EZ5
Aluminium, Kunststoff
h. 8.5cm t. 4.82cm
Sharp Corporation, Japan

Philips
Kopfhörer HS 700
Outdoor Sport Earphones
Kunststoff
h. 10cm b. 5cm t. 1.5cm
Philips Electronics BV, Niederlande

Produkte

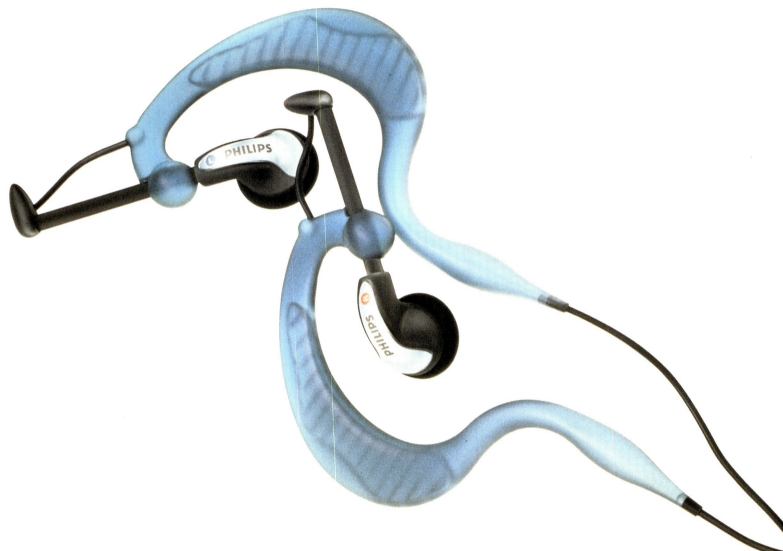

International als Anbieter innovativer Elektronik anerkannt, glaubt Philips an 'humanware' und 'hardware'. Als die Firma 1920 mit der Massenproduktion von Konsumgütern begann, führte der damalige Geschäftsführer Louis Kalff eine Marktforschungsstudie durch, um die Unterschiede des Konsumentengeschmacks weltweit aufzuzeigen und diese in den bereits revolutionären Entwürfen zu berücksichtigen. Doch erst 1980 mit der Ernennung von Robert Blaich zum Direktor des Philips Büros für Industriedesign, wurde eine Unternehmenspolitik eingeleitet, wonach das Design eines jede Produkts nicht nur nützlich und pragmatisch sein sollte, sondern auch verstärkt die privaten und persönlichen Ansprüche des modernen Konsumenten zu erfüllen hatte.

Stefano Marzano, Geschäftsführer von Philips Design seit 1991, ist dennoch der Schöpfer des 'High Designs', das eine Ausweitung dieses Konzepts bedeutet. 'High Design' ist eine Philosophie, die innerhalb des gesamten Unternehmens propagiert wird. Marzano glaubt, dass uns viele menschlichen Werte abhanden gekommen sind. Industriedesign sei in der Hauptsache mit der Produktion pompöser Gimmicks beschäftigt, weniger mit den Bedürfnissen der Konsumenten. Er zitiert Ezio Manzani von der Domus Akademie: „Wir haben vergessen, dass wir es sind, die die Gegenstände kraft unserer geistigen Fähigkeiten und unserer praktischen Fertigkeiten geschaffen haben". Er gibt zu Bedenken, dass die Menschen die Technologie generell fürchten.

Als Geschäftsführer von Philips Design sei er dafür verantwortlich, diese Berührungsängste zu mildern. Indem traditionellere Formen verwendet werden und mit einem Team aus Soziologen, Anthropologen und Psychologen daran gearbeitet wird, bei der Gestaltung der Objekte den menschlichen Benutzer vor Augen zu haben, gelang es Philips, die Kluft zwischen Technologie und Alltagskonsument zu überbrücken. Damit wurde eine Corporate Identity geschaffen, um 'sinnvolle Objekte zu entwickeln, die die Menschen in ihren alltäglichen Tätigkeiten unterstützen, die gleichzeitig die Werte, an die sie glauben, ausdrücken und die ihre Emotionen und Kreativität stimulieren'.

Philips
Thermometer HF 370 Sensor Touch Temple
Kunststoff, Metall
h. 17.5cm b. 4.3cm t. 3.3cm
Philips Electronics BV, Niederlande

Philips
Telefon+Basisstation Kala™ Digital
Kunststoff
h. 16.3cm b. 5.3cm t. 3.5cm
Philips Electronics BV, Niederlande

Philips
Hautpflegegerät
Cellesse SenseActive HP 5231
Neopren
h. 16cm b. 11.6cm t. 8.8cm
Philips Electronics BV, Niederlande

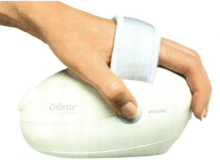

Frederick Lintz
Walkie-Talkie Olympe
ABS-Kunststoff
h. 16.7cm b. 3.7cm l. 6.7cm
Spirix Lexon, Frankreich

TKO Design
Handy One Touch Easy DB™
ABS-Kunststoff, Gummi, Polymer
l. 11.4cm b. 5.2cm t. 2.8cm
Alcatel Telecom, Frankreich

Siemens
Handy S35I
ABS-Kunststoff
h. 2.1cm l. 11.8cm b. 4.5cm
Siemens AG, Deutschland

WAP-Verbindungseinheit
Unifier IC35
ABS-Kunststoff
h. 2.05cm l. 10.8cm b. 8.6cm
Siemens AG, Deutschland

'S35' gehört zur neuen Generation der Siemens-Mobiltelefone. Es ist handtellergross, wasserdicht und widerstandsfähig. Die 'IC35'-Verbindungseinheit bietet alle Funktionen eines Laptops und ist mit dem Internet über das Handy verbunden. Musik kann gespeichert und über Kopfhörer wiedergegeben werden.

Claus-Christian Eckhardt
Handy Bosch 310
ABS-PC Silikon, Chrom, Edelstahl
h. 12.4cm b. 4.4cm t. 2.4cm
Bosch Telecom GmbH, Deutschland

Claus-Christian Eckhardt
Handy Bosch 1886
ABS-PC Silikon, Chrom, Edelstahl
h. 11.2cm b. 4.4cmt. 2.2cm
Bosch Telecom GmbH, Deutschland

Design 3 Produktdesign
Drahloses DECT-Telefon T-Easy C410
ABS-Kunststoff
Telefon: h. 14.8cm b. 5.2cm t. 3.2cm
Basis: h. 12cm b. 9.5cm t. 7.3cm
Deutsche Telekom AG, Deutschland

Hannes Wettstein
Armbanduhr Futura
Titan-Nitrogen
b. 4.5cm l. 2.5cm t. 0.9cm
Ventura Design, Schweiz

Massimo Canalli
Monats-Dauerkalender Endless
l. 42cm b. 42cm
Nava Design SpA, Italien

Hannes Wettstein
Armbanduhr Ego Calculator
Titan-Nitrogen
t. 0.9cm Ø 4.3cm
Ventura Design, Schweiz

Hannes Wettstein
Armbanduhr Ego Chronometer
Titan-Nitrogen
t. 0.9cm Ø 4.3cm
Ventura Design, Schweiz

Linde Design
Chronograph Mexx City
Edelstahl
Ø 4.2cm
Mexx Time, Dänemark

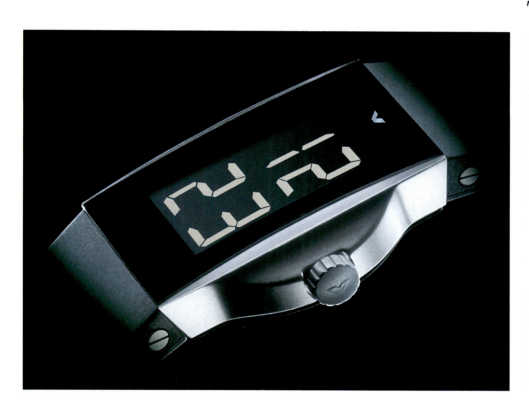

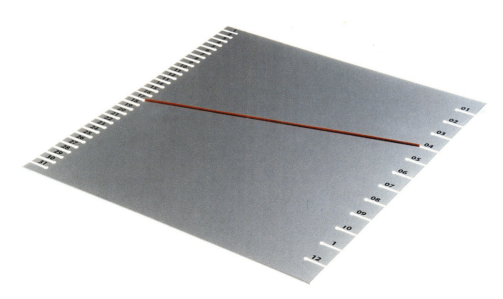

Apple Computer Inc.
Apple Cinema Display
Kunststoff
h. 47.9cm b. 58.8cm t. 21cm
Apple Computer Inc., USA

Apple Computer Inc.
Computer PowerMac G4 Cube
Kunststoff
h. 24.8cm b. 19.5cm t. 19.5cm
Apple Computer Inc., USA

Apple Computer Inc.
Apple Power G4
Kunststoff
h. 43cm b. 22.6cm t. 46.7cm
Apple Computer Inc., USA

Lunar Design
Sony Home Monitor
ABS-Kunststoff
h. 37cm b. 37.3cm t. 42.4cm
Sony Corporation, USA

Philips
Monitor Philips 1999/2000 CRT
Kunststoff
h. 44.7cm b. 44cm t. 39.6cm
Philips Electronics BV, Niederlande

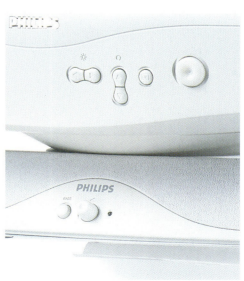

Philips
LCD-Monitor Philips Brilliance 151AX
Acryl
h. 41.8cm b. 40.2cm t. 17.6cm
Philips Electronics BV, Niederlande

Lunar Design
HP Multimedia PC
ABS-Kunststoff
Tower: h. 37cm b. 24.05cm t. 35.5cm
Flachbildschirm: h. 44cm b. 39cm t. 21cm
Hewlett Packard Company, USA

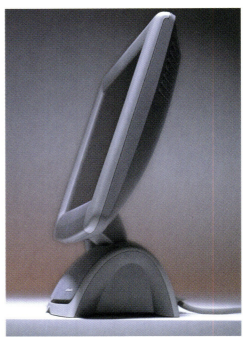

Siemens
Computermaus ID Mouse
Kunststoff
Siemens AG, Deutschland

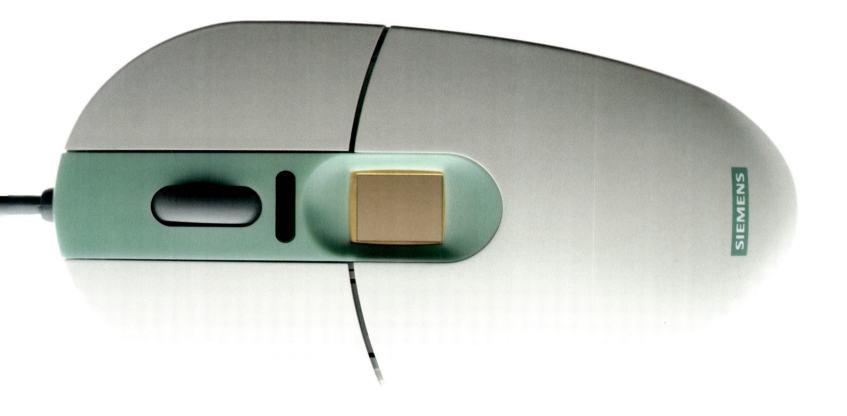

Die ID Mouse erkennt den Fingerabdruck ihres Besitzers. Sie lässt sich unter Windows schnell installieren, doch muss der Benutzer zuerst seinen Fingerabdruck als Referenz abspeichern. Sensoren schaffen dann eine Simulation des Abdrucks und schafft damit ein visuelles Passwort.
Die Designabteilung von Siemens – heute ein unabhängiges Designstudio mit dem Namen Designafairs – hat sich schon frühzeitig auf die Gestaltung von User Interfaces spezialisiert. Dies ermöglicht dem Studio in so komplexen Bereichen wie Medizintechnik, Kommunikationstechnology und digitalen Medien sehr erfolgreich zu arbeiten.

Mitsuhiro Nakamura
CD-Walkman D-EJ01
Magnesiumlegierung
h. 2.15cm l. 13.85cm b. 13.62cm
Sony Corporation, Japan

Noriaki Itai
DVD-Player + 7"-LCD-Monitor DV-L70S
Kunststoff
h. 2.54cm b. 18.8cm t. 14.1cm
Sharp Corporation, Japan

Shinichi Obata
VAIO Musik-Clip MC-P10
Kunststoffgehäuse
h. 2cm b. 12cm t. 2cm
Sony Corporation, Japan

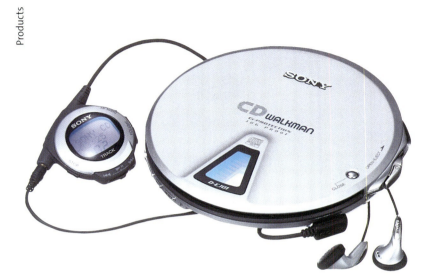

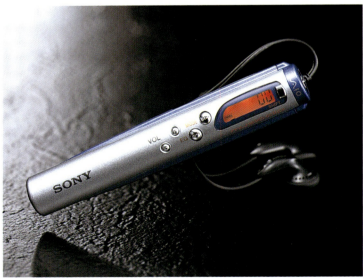

Das 'MC-P10 Music Clip' kann digitale Musik, die entweder aus dem Internet heruntergeladen oder von einer Audio CD überspielt wird, speichern und abspielen. Eine Stunde Musik in ungefähr drei Minuten übertragen werden.

Yoshinori Inukai
Farb-Flachbettscanner CanoScan FB636U
Aluminium, ABS-Kunststoff, Glas
h. 3.9cm b. 25.6cm l. 37.25cm
Canon, Japan

Yoshinori Inukai
Farb-Flachbettscanner CanoScan FB330P/FB630P
ABS-Kunststoff, Glas
h. 3.9cm b. 25.6cm l. 37.25cm
Canon, Japan

Airi Itakura
Farb-Flachbettscanner CanoScan FB1210U
ABS-Kunststoff, Aluminium
h. 9.25cm b. 28.6cm l. 46.1cm
Canon, Japan

Oba Haru
VAIO-PC PCV-L720
ABS-Kunststoff
LCD-Display: h. 33cm b. 43cm t. 17.5cm
VAIO Smart-Tastatur: h. 3.5cm b. 38cm t. 17.5cm
Sony Corporation, Japan

Im Vergleich zu anderen LCD-Bildschirmen, gewährt der Neigungswinkel vom LCD-Bildschirm des 'PCV-720' eine grössere Beweglichkeit, da nicht nur der Bildschirm, sondern auch der Sockel mittels eines Scharniers mit der Tastatur verbunden ist. Oba Haru wollte einen Computer entwerfen, mit dem entspannter gearbeitet werden kann, als würde man ein Buch lesen.

Toshiyuki Kita
28" TFT LCD-Fernseher LC-28HD 1
Aluminium
h. 44.8cm b. 69.08cm t. 6cm
Sharp Corporation, Japan

Philips
Fernseher New Vision 1
Kunststoff
h. 37cm b. 41cm t. 38cm
Philips Electronics BV, Niederlande

Philips
Fernseher FL-7 Design Line Silver Gloss 32" widescreen TV
Kunststoff
h. 104cm b. 92cm t. 60cm
Philips Electronics BV, Niederlande

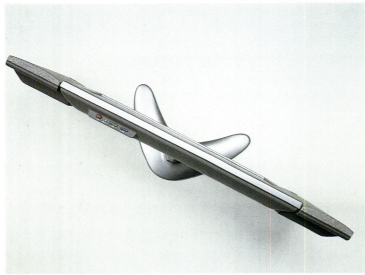

Der 'New Vision 1' mit 12"-Fernsehbildschirm erfüllt einen Konsumentenwunsch, der durch Marktforschung ermittelt wurde: Bedürfnisse und Wünsche einer bestimmten sozialen Zielgruppe wurden definiert. Daraufhin hat man einen Fernseher für den Schlafraum entworfen, in den eine analoge Uhr und eine Raumbeleuchtung integriert sind.

Yamaha Product Design Laboratory
Flügel Yamaha Disklavier pro 2000
Fichte, Kirschbaum, Ahorn, Aluminium, Eisen
h. 102cm b. 155cm t. 227cm
Yamaha Corporation, Japan
Kleinserie

NAC Sound
Lautsprecher Atun
Keramik
h. 74cm b. 20cm
NAC Sound srl, Italien

NAC Sound
Lautsprecher Seth
Keramik
h. 32cm b. 14cm
NAC Sound srl, Italien

NAC Sound
Lautsprecher Isis
Keramik
h. 74cm b. 20cm
NAC Sound srl, Italien

NAC Sound
Lautsprecher Zemi
Keramik
Ø 24cm
NAC Sound srl, Italien

NAC Sound verbindet innovatives Design mit den neuesten Lautsprecherentwicklungen. Die Produkte verbreiten eher einen sphärischen als einen konischen Klang, und die patentierte akustische 'Omnidirectional Technology' ermöglicht es dem Benutzer, diese Lautsprecher überall im Raum aufzustellen. Die ursprünglichen Entwürfe waren hauptsächlich aus Keramik. Heute experimentiert das Unternehmen mit vielen anderen Materialien wie Aluminium, Kohlenstofffasern und Holz. Ein NAC-Produkt kann sofort anhand seiner Form identifiziert werden. Sie ist entweder lang und zugespitzt oder kugelförmig, denn NAC Sound nutzt Formgebungen, die nicht nur durch ihre Ästhetik definiert sind, sondern auch noch den Vorteil haben, den Irritationen durch mechanische Vibrationen oder ungewünschte Resonanz nicht zu unterliegen.

AVC Design Centre
**Tragbarer DVD-Player
mit LCD, DVD-LA75
Kunststoff**
h. 24.8cm b. 18,5cm l. 14cm
Matsushita Electrical Industrial Co. Ltd, Japan

Nobuhiro Fujii
Staubsauger
Kunststoff, Gummi
h. 102cm
Sharp Corporation, Japan

Luigi Molinis
Ventilator und Temperaturregler Frend
ABS-Kunststoff
h. 45cm b. 76.5cm t. 17.5cm
Rhoss SpA, Italien

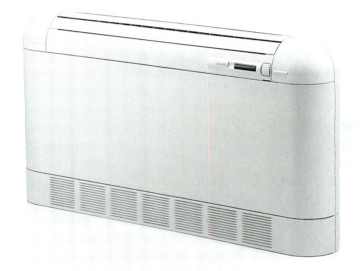
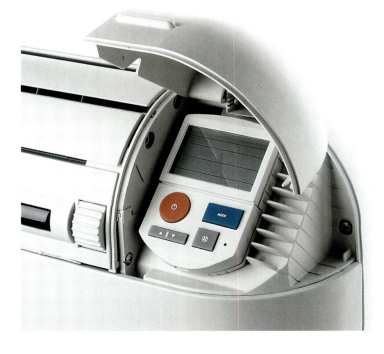

Tomoki Taira
Microwelle Half Pint R-120D
ABS-Kunststoff, Stahl
h. 36cm b. 36.5cm t. 36.2cm
Sharp Corporation, Japan

Die Mikrowelle 'Half Pint R-120D' ist ein Lifestyle-Gerät, das es in vielen Farbvarianten gibt. Mit seiner kompakten Grösse eignet es sich ideal für den Einsatz im Home-Office und anderen räumlich begrenzten Orten. Die Aufnahmekapazität ist jedoch nicht reduziert worden, so dass das Gerät ohne weiteres auch in der Familienküche eingesetzt werden kann.

Carsten Jørgensen
Elektrische Kaffeemaschine Santos
Polykarbonat
h. 32cm Ø 18cm
Bodum AG, Schweiz

Massimo Iosa-Ghini
Espressomaschine 'T'
h. 41cm b. 28cm t. 24cm
Tuttoespresso, Italien

Kazuhiko Tomita
Teekanne Ciacapo
Gusseisen
h. 13cm b. 18cm Ø 14cm
Covo srl, Italien

Philips
Kaffeemaschine
Café Duo HD 7140/42
Kunststoff, Metall
h. 25cm b. 17cm t. 17cm
Philips Electronics BV, Niederlande

Stefano Giovannoni
Kanne Alibaba
Pmma-Glas
h. 25cm Ø 17.5cm
Alessi SpA, Italien

Ann Morsing, Beban Nord
Zeitungsständer/Papierkorb
Faserplatte
h. 30cm b. 43cm t. 31cm
Box Design AB, Schweden

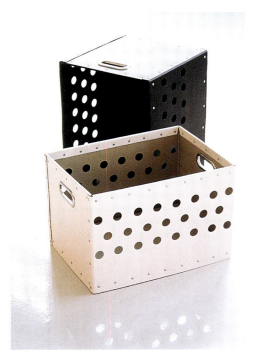

Henrik Holbaek, Claus Jensen
Eiswürfelbehälter Eva Solo
Edelstahl, Kunststoff
h. 7cm Ø 17cm
Eva Denmark A/S, Dänemark

Henrik Holbaek, Claus Jensen
Zitronenpresse Eva Solo
Glas, Edelstahl, Kunststoff
h. 18cm Ø 11cm
Eva Denmark A/S, Dänemark

Henrik Holbaek, Claus Jensen
Thermoskanne Eva Solo
Edelstahl, Kunststoff
h. 27cm Ø 13cm
Eva Denmark A/S, Dänemark

Henrik Holbaek, Claus Jensen
Messerblock Eva Solo
Aluminium, Kunststoff
h. 26cm b. 7.5cm
Eva Denmark A/S, Dänemark

Sam Hecht, Naoto Fukasawa, IDEO
Matsushita Küchenutensilien-Kollektion
ABS, Porzellan, Edelstahl verzinnt, Glas

Wasserkessel
h. 24cm Ø 20cm

Entsafter
h. 10cm Ø 8cm

Toaster
h. 15cm b. 18cm t. 16.5cm

Eierkocher
h. 16cm Ø 5,7cm

Reiskocher
h. 20.5cm Ø 20cm

Kaffeemaschine
h. 25cm Ø 9.5cm

Als Antwort auf den sich verändernden Lebensstil der durchschnittlichen japanischen Familie wurde von Matsushita die Küchenutensilien-Kollektion von IDEO entwickelt. Das Frühstück ist nunmehr eine Mischung aus westlichen und östlichen Traditionen und setzt sich aus einer reichen Auswahl von verschiedenen Lebensmitteln zusammen, die meistens sozusagen 'auf dem Sprung' gegessen werden. Nur waren die Geräte, um schnelle Gerichte vorzubereiten, bisher kaum verfügbar. Das Briefing des Unternehmens für die Entwicklung dieser Serie sah vor, dass die Utensilien schmal und kompakt gestaltet werden sollten, damit sie an unterschiedlichen Orten entweder in der Küche oder direkt auf dem Esstisch benutzt werden können. Auch sollte die Anzahl der Komponenten begrenzt sein, um die Geräte besonders praktisch zu machen.

Der 'Rice maker' ist der erste Reiskocher, der auch zum Mahlen benutzt werden kann. Die beiden Teile können auseinandergenommen und unabhängig voneinander benutzt werden. Der 'Juicer'-Entsafter wurde auf ein Minimum reduziert. Der Saft wird in demselben Glas zubereitet, aus dem er später getrunken wird. Im 'Egg Steamer' können Eier durch Dampf weich oder hart gekocht werden, was allein von der Wassermenge abhängig ist. Der Deckel dient später als Eierbecher.

Paolo Ulian
Küchenmesser Pane e Salame
Stahl, Aluminium, Holz
h. 4cm b. 1.5cm l. 33cm
Zani & Zani, Italien

Paolo Ulian, Guiseppe Ulian
Pizzamesser Rotella Tagliapizza
Stahl
h. 8cm b. 2cm l. 26cm
Zani & Zani, Italien

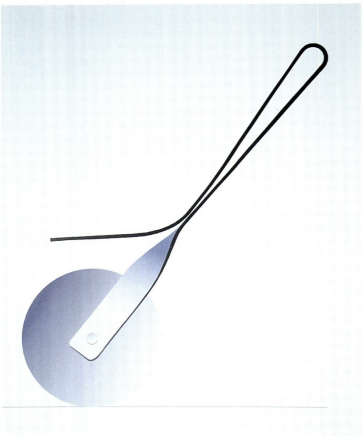

Asher Stern
Schachspiel mit Trinkgläsern
Red vs. White
Holz, Aluminium, Glas
l. 44cm b. 44cm
Kleinserie

Jürgen Schmidt
Schnurloser Schraubenzieher
b. 6cm l. 20cm t. 6cm
Metabowerke, Deutschland
Prototyp

Tobias Koeppe
Papierscheren Cassini
Zink, Stahl, ABS-Kunststoff, PMMA
h. 0.85cm b. 6.2cm l. 21cm
Lerche, Deutschland

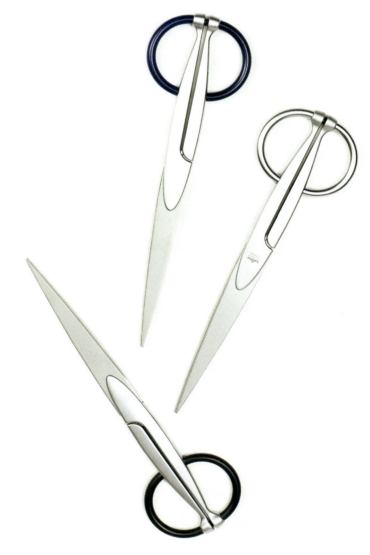

Philips
Rasierapparat
Philishave Quadra Action 6000 Series
Stahlgehäuse
h. 14.5cm b. 5cm t. 7cm
Philips Electronics BV, Niederlande

Shinichi Sumikawa
Zahnbürste Swan
Kunststoff
h. 20cm b. 1cm t. 15cm
Iridium, Korea

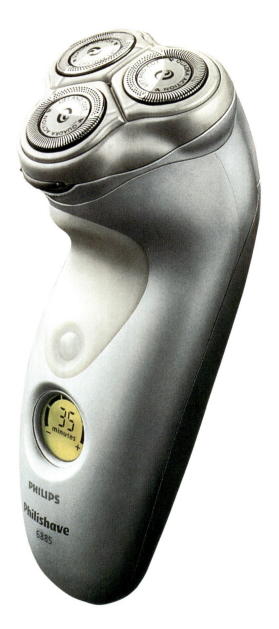

Ippei Matsumoto
Schwammwaage
Schwamm, LED-Anzeige, Kunststoff
h. 5cm b. 29cm t. 25cm
IDEO, Japan

Makoto Hashikura, IDEO Japan
Mousepad Keyboard
Neopren, ABS-Kunststoff
h. 1.2cm b. 38cm t. 16cm
Matsushita Electric Corporation, Japan

Makoto Hashikura, IDEO Japan
Computermaus
h. 2.5cm b. 8cm t. 2.5cm
Matsushita Electric Corporation, Japan

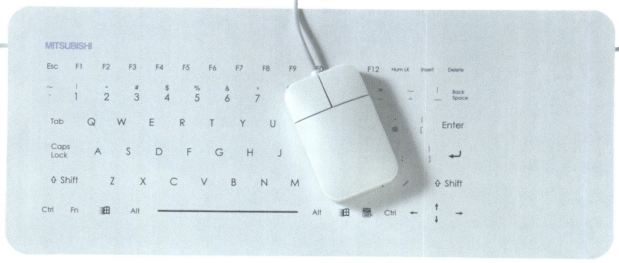

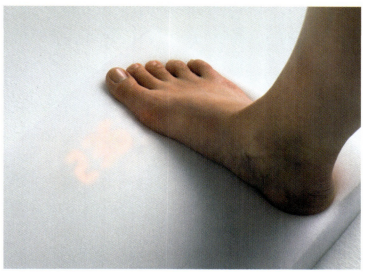

Im Herbst 1999 organisierte IDEO und das Diamond Design Management Network Workshops für Designer verschiedener Unternehmen aus unterschiedlichen Branchen, um die emotionalen Reaktionsweisen der Menschen auf die Produkte, die sie umgeben, und ihre intuitive Interaktionsweise zu erforschen. Die Entwürfe, die in diesen Workshops entstanden, wurden in einer Ausstellung mit dem Titel 'With-out Thought – design for the unconsciousness' gezeigt. Jedes Objekt spielt nicht nur mit den Erinnerungen und Gefühlen, sondern spricht auch die Sinne an. Die Schwammwaage ist weich und reagiert per LED-Anzeige sanft auf das Gewicht. Das Mousepad 'Keyboard' ist gleichzeitig eine Tastatur, so dass auf derselben Arbeitsoberfläche entweder getippt oder geklickt werden kann.

Luigi Trenti
Schreibutensilien Collezione Egosphere
Kunstharz, Stahl, Gold/Platin
Francesco Pineider SpA, Italien

dai design
Kugelschreiber IHAG
Aluminium, Edelstahl
l. 14cm Ø 1cm
Hergestellt für:
IHAG Zürich AG, Schweiz

Shibuyo Ito und Setsu Ito
Ständer für Schreibutensilien How
Kunststoff
h. 10cm b. 8.5cm l. 8.5cm
Nava Design SpA, Italien

Shibuyo Ito und Setsu Ito
Behälter für Schreibutensilien How
Kunststoff
h. 7cm b. 10cm . 10cm
Nava Design SpA, Italien

Shibuyo Ito und Setsu Ito
Schreibunterlage How
Kunststoff
b. 70cm l. 50cm
Nava Design SpA, Italien

Shibuyo Ito und Setsu Ito
Schreibunterlage How
Kunststoff
b. 70cm l. 50cm
Nava Design SpA, Italien

Shibuyo Ito und Setsu Ito
Scotchtape-Abroller How
Kunststoff
h. 7cm b. 10cm l. 10cm
Nava Design SpA, Italien

David Farrage und Goeran Jerstroem
Digital-Thermometer Vicks Comfort Flex
ABS-Kunststoff, Kryton-Gummi, Acryl
b. 0.3cm l. 13cm
OXO International, USA

Smart Design
Scall Thumbscript Concept
Silikon, Polyurethan, Metall
h. 7.6cm b. 5.3cm l. 1.9cm
OXO International, USA
Prototyp

David Farrage, Vanessa Sica, Kevin Lozeau
Luftbefeuchter Kaz Health Mist
Polypropylen
h. 15.24cm b. 33cm
OXO International, USA

David Farrage
Bürsten OXO Good Grips Scrub Line
Polypropylen, Santopren, Nylon
OXO International, USA

David Farrage, Dean Chapman, Davin Stowell
Computergesteuertes Pillenset Medimonitor
Kunststoff, LCD screen
h. 3.6cm b. 22.8cm l. 12.2cm
OXO International, USA

Kazuyo Komoda
Spielzeug La Tavola Imbandita ('Lair')
Baumwolle, Polyurethanschaum, Aluminium, Holz
h. 50cm b. 135cm t. 80cm
Edition Galleria Luisa Delle Piane, Italien

Lamberto Angelini
Schalenkoffer Frog
Polypropylen
Gross: h. 62cm b. 27cm l. 80cm
Klein: h. 54cm b. 24cm l. 69cm
Roncato SpA, Italien

Design Team Mandarina Duck
Gepäcktrolley Frog Jr.
Polypropylen, Stoff
h. 55cm b. 40cm t. 20cm
Mandarina Duck Plastimoda, Italien

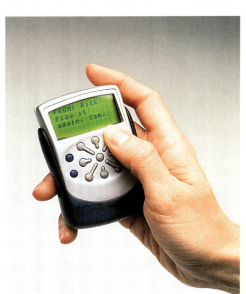

TKO Design
Waschmaschine Titan
Stahl, Polymer
h. 85cm b. 60cm t. 60cm
Monotub Industries, Grossbritannien
Prototyp

Jam Design
Küchenkonzept Corian
Jam Design and Communications Ltd
Grossbritannien

Christophe Pillet
Küchensystem Aerosystem
Edelstahl, Glas, Nussbaum, Aluminium
Ciatta a Tavola, Italien

Das junge britische Designerteam Jam arbeitete mit den grossen Produktherstellern Corian, Whirlpool und Linbeck Rausch Lighting zusammen, um eine Konzeptküche zu entwickeln, die 1999 bei 100% Design in London ausgestellt wurde. Diese Installation demonstriert, dass die Küche der Zukunft intelligent, vollautomatisch, multifunktional und flexibel sein wird. Diese Küche kann alle profanen Aufgaben übernehmen und damit dem Benutzer mehr Zeit für andere Aktivitäten verschaffen.

Der Entwurf bestand aus einem hochtechnischen Kernelement zur Kühlung, Lagerung und Zubereitung der Gerichte, an dem man auch essen kann, während mit den Whirlpool-Produkten gezeigt wurde, auf welche Weise Temperaturregulierung, Beleuchtung und elektronische Kontrollsysteme weiterentwickelt werden können.

Merloni Elettrodomestici
Computer Leon@rdo
Novakval ABS-Kunststoff 5V
h. 20cm b. 25cm l. 35cm
Ariston, Italien

Sacha Winkel
Waschbecken Soap
Kunststoff
h. 33cm l. 80cm t. 45cm
Boffi, Italien

Die Zukunft der häuslichen Technologie liegt in der Hand von WRAF (Web Ready Appliances Protocol). Ein vernetzter Haushalt kann mit elektronischen Anwendungen und der Umwelt auf der Basis jedes Telekommunikationsnetzwerkes verbunden werden. Auch der Internetzugang ist dank Leon@rdo möglich. Das Ariston Digital Service Centre überwacht den Energieverbrauch des Haushalts und dient als Frühwarnsystem. Die Haushaltsgeräte können auch Selbstdiagnosen ausführen und die Ergebnisse an das Center weitermelden. Da der Leon@rdo ein Homecomputer ist, kann man mit ihm ausserdem E-mails versenden, Lebensmittel bestellen, neue Rezepte aus dem Internet herunterladen oder den Ofen programmieren (E-cooking).

Claudio Silvestrin
Küche Xila
Laminat, Setasil, HPG, Polyester
Boffi, Italien

Val Cucine
Küche Ricicla Laminato
Aluminium, Laminat, Holz
Val Cucine SpA, Italien

Claudio Silvestrin
Waschbecken Adda
Keramik
h. 17.5cm Ø 50cm
Boffi, Italien

Es gehört zur Philosophie des Unternehmens Val Cucine, die Umwelt zu respektieren. Die Küchen sind aus natürlichen Materialien hergestellt und alle Produktionstechnologien basieren auf Werkstoffen, die maximale Recyclingfähigkeit bieten. Darüber hinaus steht das Unternehmen in engem Kontakt mit 'Bioforest', einem Verband, der zur Förderung von nachwachsenden Rohstoffen gegründet wurde. Kürzlich wurden zwei Wiederaufforstungsprogramme in Brasilien und Ecuador finanziert. Diese sind jedoch nur Beispiele für das allgemeine Engagement, Wälder zu erhalten und aufzuforsten, damit Kohlendioxyd abgebaut wird, das bei der Möbelproduktion entsteht.

Norbert Wangen
Küchen Cube 2000
Edelstahl, Holz
h. 93cm b. 70cm l. 234cm
Norbert Wangen, Deutschland

Nobert Wangens kompakter 'Cube 2000' enthält alles, was in einer Küche benötigt wird: Kühlschrank, Geschirrspüler, Ofen/Mikrowelle, Spüle und Stauraum. Die bewegliche Arbeitsplattee kann zur Seite geschoben und als Tisch benutzt werden, während Spüle und Herdplatten zum Vorschein kommen.

Bulthaup
Küche System 25
Edelstahl, Linoleum
Diverse Grössen und Kombinationen
Bulthaup, Deutschland

Giampaolo Bendini
Badewanne Spoon
Exmar (Marmor, Kunstharz)
h. 48cm b. 101cm
Agape srl, Italien

Giampaolo Bendini
Armatur Fez 40
Messing verchromt
Agape srl, Italien

Giampaolo Bendini
Armatur Fez 260
Messing verchromt
Agape srl, Italien

Maximillian Burton
Tiolettenbürste OXO good grips
Polypropylen, Santopren
Nylon, ABS-Kunststoff
h. 45.7cm b. 14cm
OXO International, USA

Rechte Seite:
Stefano Giovannoni
Saugglocke Johnny the Diver
Thermokunststoff, Kunstharz
h. 26cm Ø 13.3cm
Alessi SpA, Italien

Roderick Vos
Küchenbehälter
Bricks for the House
Glasierte Keramik
h. 11.4cm b. 11.4cm l. 11.4cm
Driade SpA, Italien
Kleinserie

Martin Szekely
Blumentopf
Brique à Fleurs à Vallauris
Ton
h. 52.5cm Ø 46.5cm
Galerie Kreo, Frankreich

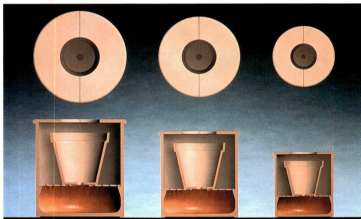

Emma Quickenden
Heizkörper Hot Water Bottle
Gummi
h. 76cm l. 51cm
Prototyp

Emma Quickenden
Heizkörper Fire Place
Pressstahl
h. 76cm b. 51cm
Prototyp

Dick Van Hoff
Betonofen
Beton, Metall
h. 100cm b. 52cm l. 80cm
Van Hoff Omptwerper, Niederlande
Prototyp

Emma Quickenden hat unsere Heizungen emotional 'erwärmt,' indem sie die Typologie dieser Geräte neu erfunden hat. Die hässlichen Metallgehäuse wurden durch Entwürfe ersetzt die nostalgisch und behaglich anmuten und die, wie Emma Quickenden hofft, zum Zentrum eines jeden Raumes werden. Die Wärmflasche ist aus Gummi. Das Wasser fließt durch Metallröhren innerhalb der flexiblen Form, die zum Halten, Drücken, Anlehnen und sogar Riechen einlädt.

BMW-Design
Leichtkraftrad C1
BMW AG, Deutschland

Produkte

Was kann das wohl sein? Ist es ein Motorroller mit Dach oder ein Auto ohne Seitenteile? Was auch immer es ist, dieser Hybrid ist für den modernen Pendler gedacht, der sich die Freiheit wünscht, die ihm ein Zweirad bietet: Der Benutzer kommt auch bei dichtem Verkehr gut voran und mit der Sicherheit, die ein Dach über dem Kopf verspricht. Sicherheit war eine der wichtigsten Überlegungen für BMW, als das 'C1'-Leichtkraftrad entwickelt wurde. Im Dach ist ein Überrollbügel eingebaut, der sich in Crashtests bewährt hat.

Der Motor springt nicht an, bevor der Sicherheitsgurt angelegt wurde. Über dem Vorderrad ist ein Vorsprung, der die Auswirkungen im Falle eines Frontalzusammenstoßes abfangen kann. In Schulterhöhe sind seitliche Schutzstangen angebracht, so dass jeder Stoß vom Rahmen aufgefangen wird und so den Fahrer schützt. Es ist ein interessantes Design, das Aufmerksamkeit auf sich zieht. Doch gibt es auch Nachteile. Aldan Walker, Herausgeber von Blueprint und passionierter Fahrradfahrer, schreibt, dass das 'C1' ein oder zwei beunruhigende Eigenschaften habe. Durch den turmartigen Rahmen fühlt sich der Fahrer in Kurven aus der Balance gebracht. Ausserdem ist die Front sehr breit, was die Sicht nach vorne einschränkt. Man kann nicht sehen, was das Vorderrad macht. Auf lange Sicht sind dies jedoch Probleme, die mit den entsprechenden Erfahrungswerten aus der Praxis beseitigt werden können.

Marc Newson
Fahrrad Biomega
Aluminium
h. 100cm b. 56cm l. 183cm
Magis srl, Italien

Stile Bertone S.P.A
Mountain Bike MTB fully suspended
Karbon- und Magnesiumrahmen
h. 100cm b. 56cm l. 175cm
Stile Bertone SpA, Italien

Honda
Autostudie Neukom

Honda
Autostudie Fuya-jo oder Sleepless City

Wir sind Zeugen einer beeindruckenden Transformation der äußeren Formen und inneren Komponenten von Autos. An dieser Entwicklung des Designs kann die fortgeschrittenste Vision einer neu entstehenden Welt abgelesen werden. Die Innovationen im Bereich der Form, des Stils und der Mobilität schaffen neue Konzepte für die städtische und ländliche Lebenswelt. Der Passagierraum wird bei den Studien von Honda entweder ausschließlich zum Abteil, in dem man sich fortbewegt oder zu einem speziellen Wohnraum.
Honda bezeichnet 'Neukom' als Kommunikationskapsel. Nur Glas scheint den Passagier zu umgeben, was eine Panoramasicht ermöglicht, während die drehbaren Sitze einen Treffpunkt auf Rädern schaffen.
Der 'Fuya-jo' oder 'Sleepless City' wurde für das junge Publikum, das gerne Spaß hat, konzipiert. Beifahrer, die in halb stehender Position mitfahren, nehmen am aufregenden Fahrvergnügen teil, als würden sie auf einem Skateboard oder auf Inlinern stehen. Das Steuer ähnelt einer Drehscheibe, das Armaturenbrett dem Mischpult eines Diskjockeys. Zusammen mit den kraftvollen Lautsprecherboxen in den Türen scheint das Auto ein Mini-Diskothek auf Rädern zu sein.

Christopher C. Deam
Wilsonart International
Inside Design
Wohnwagen
Aluminium (aussen), Laminat (innen)

Fiat
Autostudie Eco-Basic

Dieser Wohnwagen ist das Ergebnis der Zusammenarbeit zwischen Wilsonart International (einem Hersteller von dekorativen Oberflächenprodukten), Inside Design (einem Unternehmen, das sich der Förderung des zeitgenössischen Designs durch Produktentwicklung, spezielle Veranstaltungen und Bildungsmedien verschrieben hat) und Christopher Deam (einem allmählich international anerkannten Mitglied der neuen Gruppe amerikanischer Designer).

Der Aluminiumanhänger ist schon seit langer Zeit ein nicht mehr wegzudenkendes Symbol amerikanischer Mobilität geworden. Diesem Modell aus dem Jahr 1948, das als Herzstück der International Contemporary Furniture Fair 2000 in New York entwickelt wurde, steht eine neue Zukunft bevor. Jim Huff von Inside Design ist der Auffassung, dass die Inneneinrichtung nie so attraktiv wie die Aussenwände war und beschloss, sie anzupassen. Um den Innenraum auszukleiden, benutzte Deam laminiertes Holz, weil dieses Material leicht, widerstandsfähig, kostengünstig und warm in der Berührung ist, insbesondere auch als Kontrast zum 'kalten' Aluminium. Obwohl man Laminat lange Zeit nur mit Fertighäusern in Verbindung brachte, hält Deam für das einzig richtige Material, das 'auf nostalgische Weise bekannt, aber doch modern, sogar futuristisch' ist. Das Resultat ist ein Designklassiker, der neu erfunden wurde, um der jüngeren Ästhetik zu entsprechen.

Dank seines Motors, der sparsam und umweltfreundlich konzipiert ist, verbraucht der 'Eco-Basic' nur 3 Liter Diesel auf 100 Kilometer. Seine aerodynamische Form und ein 'Start and Go'-System, wodurch der Motor sich nach 4 Sekunden Stillstand ausschaltet und automatisch wieder startet, wenn das Gaspedal betätigt wird, machen den 'Eco-Basic' zum idealen Kompaktauto für die Stadt der Zukunft.

Designer Biografien und Register

Lodovico Acerbis was born in Italy in 1939 and studied Economics and Business Studies at Milan University. In 1963 he joined the family firm of which he is now president. Acerbis International SpA was founded in 1870 as a carpenter's shop but it quickly expanded to industrial proportions and became one of the first companies to use architects for furniture design. Acerbis has earned a reputation for blending modern design with avant-garde technology, working with the finest materials and best designers. A number of Acerbis products have been awarded the Milan Compasso d'Oro Award, and are on permanent display in the Victoria and Albert Museum, London; Die neue Sammlung Staatliches Museum fur Angewandte Kunst, Munich; the Museum of Contemporary Art, Chicago; and in the City Hall, Shanghai. **49**

Werner Aisslinger was born in 1964 in Berlin. He founded his own design company in 1993 and since then has carried out various furniture projects for Italian companies such as Magis, Cappellini and Porro. His 'endless shelf' won the Bundespreis Produkt design and in 1997 his 'Juli' chair for Cappellini was acquired as part of the permanent design collection at MoMA, New York. Aisslinger has also carried out corporate architecture concepts and projects for Lufthansa and Mercedes Benz. **43, 48, 64**

Gunilla Allard was born in 1957. She worked as a stage designer and property manager for the film industry during the early 1980s before attending the University College of Arts, Crafts and Design in Stockholm to study interior architecture. Today she continues to work as a stage designer and is also well-known in Sweden for furniture design. She has been awarded the Excellent Swedish Form prize in 1991, 1992, 1996 and 1999. **33**

Harry Allen received a Masters in Industrial Design from the Pratt Institute, New York. He worked for Prescriptive Cosmetics before opening his own studio. He immediately received success with his 'Living Systems' furniture line which he showed at the ICFF in New York and which led to commissions including the Sony Plaza and the North Face Store in Chicago. He has also earned international recognition for his interior design projects most notably the Murray Moss shop in New York – which he is currently expanding – and the 'Dragonfly Selects' jewellery store in Taiwan. He has recently completed new offices for Metropolis magazine and for the Guggenheim Museum, New York. Product designs include a medicine chest for Magis, various articles for Wireworks and lighting designs for George Kovacs and IKEA. His use of innovative material can be seen in his series of ceramic foam lamps which are on display in MoMA, New York and which he showed in the Mutant Material in Contemporary Design exhibition in 1994. **61**

Emilio Ambasz was born in 1943 in Argentina but studied at Princeton University after which he took up a post as curator of design at MoMA, New York. From 1981 to 1985 he was President of the Architectural League and taught at Princeton's School of Architecture. He has also been visiting professor at Ulm Design School in Germany. In 1992 he was awarded first prize at the Universal Exhibition, Seville and his works are represented in museums worldwide, including MoMA and the Metropolitan Museum, New York. In 1989 there was a major retrospective of his architectural work at MoMA. **29, 33**

Yoko Ando was born in Shibuya, Tokyo. He trained as a graphic artist at the Musashino Art University and is currently working for NUNO Corporation. He has exhibited work within Japan and at the 'L'Asie en Rose' Fashion show in Manila, the Philippines. **177**

Lamberto Angelini founded Angelini Design in Bologna in 1980. A graduate in mechanical engineering, he worked for two years at the Volkswagen Style Centre, Wolfsburg, Germany, and from there moved into product design. The first Angelini products were all vehicles but the company now works across many areas for a diverse range of clients such as Acquaviva, Ducati, Motobechane, BMW, Castelli, Fogacci, Marcato, Mandarina Duck and Goldoni. **210**

Ron Arad was born in Tel Aviv in 1951. He studied at the Jerusalem Academy of Art, and from 1974 to 1979 at the Architectural Association, London. In 1981 he founded One Off with Caroline Thorman and in 1983 designed their first showroom in Neal Street, Covent Garden, London. Early pieces include the Rover Chair, the vacuum-packed Transformer Chair and the remote-controlled Aerial Light. Later work explored the use of tempered steel, in the Well-Tempered Chair and the Bookworm. In 1988 Arad won the Tel Aviv Opera Foyer Interior Competition with C. Norton and S. McAdam, and formed Ron Arad Associates with Caroline Thorman and Alison Brooks in order to realize the project. As well as the design and construction of the new One Off design studio, furniture gallery and workshop in 1991, projects have included furniture design for Poltronova, Vitra, Moroso and Driade; the design of various interior installations; the interiors of the restaurants Belgo and Belgo Centraal in London, domestic architectural projects and the winning competition entry for the Adidas Stadium, Paris (unbuilt). In 1994 Arad established the Ron Arad Studio in Como, Italy, to expand on the production of limited edition handmade pieces. Arad was a guest professor at the Hochschule in Vienna from 1994 to 1997 and is currently Professor of Furniture and Product Design at the Royal College of Art in London. In 2000 his work was the subject of a major retrospective at the V & A Museum, London. **31, 35, 141**

Architettura Laboratorio is an industrial design group founded by Andrea Cacai, Maurizio Giordano and Roberto Grossi. These three architects have worked together and exhibited at Milan since 1992. They have collaborated with Colombo Design, Gruppo IPE and Gruppo Scaroni. **88**

Neil Austin was born in 1958 and studied furniture design at Buckinghamshire College, England, where he is now a course leader in Furniture and Related Product Design. After graduation he worked as a professional draughtsman, and was then Design Director for a London furniture company. He regularly exhibits in conjunction with Mo-billy and has shown his work in New York, Milan and Hamburg, as well as throughout the UK. **95**

Masayo Ave was born in Tokyo in 1962 but now lives in Milan. She studied architecture at Hosei University in Japan but after practising for some time, moved to Milan and graduated with an MA in Industrial Design from the Domus Academy in 1990. In 1992 she established Ave Design Corporation, based in Tokyo and Milan, and has won various awards in architecture and design. Clients have included international companies such as Authentics while her own design collection was launched by Atrox GmbH in 2000. **162, 163**

François Azambourg was born in France in 1963 and studied Industrial Design in Paris. He has designed furniture and interiors for various Parisian shops, has produced work for VIA and numbers Cappellini, Plank, O Luce and Chainey among his most recent clients. He has also been involved in the development of new materials for Mandarina Duck, Hermès and Vuitton. In 1999 he was named Young Creator of the Year. **29**

Shin and Tomoko Azumi studied industrial design at Kyoto City University of Art and the Royal College of Art, London. In 1996 they were finalists in the Blueprint/100% Design Awards. They founded Azumi's in 1995, undertaking projects for British, Italian and Japanese clients. They have exhibited at Sotheby's and at the Crafts Council, London. They are also frequent exhibitors at both the Cologne and Milan Furniture Fairs. **28**

Jacob de Baan graduated from the Gerrit Rietveld Academy of Art in 1987 and worked in Amsterdam until 1991, when he moved to Germany to work for Team Buchin Design. In 1995 he moved back to Amsterdam and started the D4 Agency whose clients include the Dutch Ministry of Finance, Jumbo, NOVEM, Osram and Philips. **145**

Emmanuel Babled was born in France in 1967, and today lives and works in both Milan and Venice. He studied at the Istituto Europeo di Disegno in Milan, then worked for several years with Prospero Rasulo and Gianni Veneziano at Studio Oxido in Milan. He has been working as a freelance designer since the early 1990s for clients such as Fine Factory, Steel, Casprini, Wedgwood, Waterford Crystal Ltd, Kundalini and Rosenthal. Since 1995 he has also been an independent producer of Murano glass vases and ceramic items. Using different kilns and collaborating with the master glass-blower, Livio Serena he has produced unique pieces for IDEE Co. Ltd, Tokyo. **153**

Matthias Bader was born in 1970, trained as a toolmaker and then studied interior design at the Fachhochschule in Kaiserlautern, graduating in 1997. He worked for Hartz and Hermes and planned showrooms for Villeroy and Bosch worldwide. In 1999 he set up his own office and in 2000 joined forces with Andrea Winkler in Karshule, specializing in shop planning and design. Current clients include Pallucco and Phos Design. They have recently exhibited in Cologne and Milan. **123**

Valter Bahcivanji was born in Brazil in 1958 and studied Industrial Design. He has designed furniture, household and technological goods and has been involved in product development for the domestic and office markets. His work is represented in the Museu da Casa Brasileira, São Paulo, Brazil. **103**

Gijs Bakker was born in 1942 in The Netherlands. He studied Industrial Design in his home country and in Sweden. In 1966 he set up a studio in Utrecht with his wife, thereafter working as a freelance designer for clients such as Polaroid and Rosenthal. He has been Professor at the Design Academy, Eindhoven from 1987 and in 1993 he founded Droog Design with Renny Ramakers. Since then they have exhibited yearly in Milan and recent clients have included Mandarina Duck, Flos, Salviati and Levi's. **133**

Philip Baldwin see Monica Guggisberg

Ralph Ball studied furniture design at Leeds College of Art and received a MDes from the Royal College of Art, London, where he now has been appointed Senior Tutor. He taught at various design schools through the UK and between 1981 and 1984 was a designer with Foster Associates. He is now a partner in his own firm Naylor-Ball Design Partnership. Ball's works can be found at the Contemporary Applied Arts and Crafts Council, the Victoria and Albert Museum, London and MoMA, New York. He was one of only seven European designers to be selected by Nobou Nakamura to develop furniture concepts for Japan. **94**

Barber Osgerby Associates was founded in 1996 by Edward Barber and Jay Osgerby who met when they were studying together at the Royal College of Art, London. The practice has designed interiors for residential and commercial premises and has had furniture manufactured by Cappellini and the Conran shops. Its latest project is the Soho Brewing Company – a microbrewery and restaurant in London. The two were awarded Best New Designers in 1998 at the International Contemporary Furniture Fair in New York. Recent Projects include a pharmacy and herbal apothecary interior and a flagship hair salon for Trevor Sorbie. **38**

Martine Bedin was born in Bordeaux, France, in 1957 and studied first at the Ecole d'Architecture de Paris, then in Florence. In 1978 she joined the Radical Design group and briefly collaborated with Ettore Sottsass before participating in the founding of the Memphis Group in 1981. Since 1982 she has divided her time between her design/architecture studio in Milan and Paris, where she teaches. In design her focus is furniture and lighting but since 1988 she has also worked on many architectural projects in France. She has taught and exhibited internationally and is the recipient of many awards. **80**

Giampaolo Bendini was born in 1945 and studied architecture at Milan Polytechnic, after which he worked in architecture and industrial design. He was involved with public housing and restoration but also commercial and industrial sites. In product design he is particularly interested in the office and bathroom sectors and has been responsible for style at Bugatti and Lotus. Since 1973 he has been Agape's art director. Under his directorship, five Agape items have won the Design Plus Award. **218**

Claudio Bellini was born in Milan in 1963. He graduated in Architecture and Industrial Design from Milan Polytechnic in 1990 and worked at Mario Bellini Associates until 1996, working on a diverse range of projects. In 1997 he founded Atelier Bellini, a new consultancy devoted to industrial design. His recent clients include Vitra, Heller, Artemide, Fiat, Venini, Driade, Rosenthal and Iguzzini and Fritz Hansen. **46, 88**

Mario Bellini was born in 1935 and graduated in architecture from Milan Polytechnic in 1959. He began to design products and furniture in 1963 and has collaborated with numerous Italian and international manufacturers. Completed architectural projects include the Milan Trade Fair Extension; the Tokyo Design Centre; the Schmidtbank Headquarters in Germany; and the Natuzzi Americas Inc. Headquarters in North Carolina. As well as for architectural work, Bellini is well known for his exhibition design. He has lectured at leading design schools worldwide and since 1995 has taught in the School of Architecture at the University of Genoa. He was the editor of Domus from 1986 to 1991. Examples of his products can be seen in most major design collections including MoMA, New York. Bellini has received many awards including seven Compasso d'Oro prizes. **32**

Sebastian Bergne studied industrial design at London's Central School of Art and Design and Royal College of Art, and worked in Hong Kong and Milan before forming his own practice, 'Bergne: Design for Manufacture' in 1990. His clients include Cassina, Vitra, Oluce, Authentics and Driade. He is a visiting tutor at Central Saint Martin's College of Art and Design and the London Institute as well as lecturer at the Royal College of Art. He was a jury member for the Design Week Awards in 1991 and has been a frequent guest on jury panels worldwide. He has taken part in numerous group shows in London, New York, Hamburg, Tokyo and Brussels, most recently 'Mutant Materials in Contemporary Design' at MoMA, New York in 1995 and in 1997 a one-man show at the International Contemporary Furniture Fair in New York. **130**

Lars Bergström was born in 1962 in Stockholm and studied at the Royal Academy of Fine Arts. Since 1986 he has worked in collaboration with Mats Bigert (b.1965) and they have exhibited widely throughout the world. **161**

Jeffrey Bernett founded Studio B in New York in 1995. In 1996 he presented an award-winning range of furniture accessories and objects at the New York Furniture Fair. He works in many areas, including interior architecture, furniture, lighting, graphic design and corporate image. His client list includes Authentics, B&B Italia, Cappellini, Dune, Hidden/sdb, Ligne Roset and Troy. He also lectures at schools in the US. **61, 168**

Thomas Bernstrand was born in Stockholm in 1965. He studied at the University College of Arts, Crafts and Design, the Danish Designskole and the Inchbald School of Design, London, graduating in 1989. His work is frequently exhibited throughout Scandinavia and in London. In 1998 he won the Young Swedish Design Award. **85**

Fabrice Berreux was born in France in 1964. After graduation from the Ecole Nationale des Beaux Artes in 1986 he worked in interior architecture, founding the group 18 Aout in 1987. In 1991, 18 Aout was reformed and enlarged into dix heures dix who have exhibited with VIA and whose designs are held in the collection of the Musée des Arts Décoratifs, Paris. Fabrice Berreux has taught throughout France and has recently been collaborating with other designers on various lighting projects. **95, 110**

Marc Berthier is an internationally known industrial designer. He has received the Premio Compasso d'Oro in 1991 and 1994; the Form design award in Germany in 1995, 1997 and 1998; the Design Plus in 1999 and has also been awarded the Grand Prix National de la Creation Industrielle by the French Ministry of Culture. **180**

Dinie Besems was born in 1966 and studied at the Gerrit Rietveld Academy, Amsterdam, graduating in 1992. Besems has exhibited often in The Netherlands and has won several awards for applied arts. **85**

Jurgen Bey was born in The Netherlands in 1965 and studied at the Design Academy, Eindhoven where latterly he has taught. As an independent designer he has worked for Levi's and the New York Times Magazine and has participated in exhibitions in New York, Germany, Paris, and The Netherlands. **84, 85**

Francesco Binfaré was born in 1939 in Milan where he still lives and works. From 1969 to 1976 he was a director at Centre Cassina. In 1980 he set up the Centre for Design and Communication for the realization of works such as Wink by Toshiyuki Kita, Feltri by Gaetano Pesce, the Collezione Il Cileo for Venini and designs for De Padova by Vico Magistretti. He has taught at the Domus Academy, Milan and the Royal College of Art, London, and held seminars and conferences in major institutions worldwide. His own client list includes Adele C, Cassina and Edramezzei. **45**

Riccardo Blumer was born in Italy in 1959 and graduated in architecture from Milan Polytechnic. He is a practising architect and also designs furniture. His Lalegerra chair, designed in collaboration with Alias, was awarded the Compasso d'Oro in 1998. **26**

Marc Boase was born in 1973 and graduated in 3D Design for Production from the University of Brighton, England, in 1997. He specializes in product, furniture and interior design and in 2000 was a finalist in the Peugot Design Awards. **142**

Cini Boeri graduated from Milan Polytechnic in 1951 and for some years collaborated with Marco Zanuso. In 1963 she set up her own studio concentrating on civil and interior architecture and industrial design. Her architectural projects in Italy and abroad include apartments, houses, shops, showrooms and office buildings. Her projects are represented in museums worldwide, and she has won many awards, including the Compasso d'Oro twice. **48**

Jörg Boner is a product designer and member of the Design Group N2 based in Lucerne, Switzerland. He has exhibited in Hamburg, Cologne and Lucerne, and collaborated with Christian Deuber on a project for Dorbracht Interiors. He has also designed products for Hidden/sdb and is currently engaged in work for Hidden. **34, 64**

Pierre Bouguennec was born in Brittany and moved to New York in 1987 where he trained as a cabinetmaker before starting practice as an architect. From 1989 to the present he has worked in his own studio, Boum Design, where he has carried out interior design, furniture and lighting projects. In 1998 his lamp, 'Plug In' was manufactured by Ligne Roset in France and won two awards at the Furniture Fair in Paris. Bouguennec is also a member of Samba Inc. He is currently working on a series of modular modern spaces. **58–9**

Erwan Bouroullec was born in Quimper, France, in 1976 and studied industrial design at the Ecole Nationale Supérieure des Arts Appliques and the Ecole Nationale des Arts Decoratifs. Since 1998 he has been collaborating with his brother Ronan. **38, 41, 45, 145**

Ronan Bouroullec was born in Quimper, France, in 1971. He graduated in applied and decorative art and has worked on a freelance basis since 1995, designing objects and furniture for Cappellini, Liagre, Domeau et peres, Ex Novo, Ligne Roset and Galerie Neotu. He was awarded Best Designer at the International Contemporary Fair, New York in 1999. **145**

Box Design AB was founded in Stockholm in 1986 by Ann Morsing and and Beban Nord. Ann Morsing studied in San Francisco and the National School of Art & Craft, Stockholm, after which she worked for IKEA and Matell Arkitekter AB. Beban Nord studied art history and woodmanship in Stockholm. Before co-founding Box Design he worked in the Joinery at the Royal Palace, Stockholm and Svenska Rum Arkitekter. They have exhibited many times in Italy and Scandinavia. **200**

Todd Bracher studied industrial design at St John's University, New York and furniture design at the Danish Design School, Copenhagen, graduating in 2000. He has acted as a consultant for various American and Italian companies and was Senior Designer for Eernstein Design Associates New York from 1996 to 1998. Since 1998 he has been consultant designer for Posman Collegiate Bookstores Inc., New York. **24**

Andrea Branzi was born in 1938 in Florence. He studied architecture, then founded the avant-garde group Archizoom Associates together with Gilberto Corretti, Paolo Deganello and Massimo Morozzi in 1966. From 1974 to 1976 he was involved with Global Tools, and in the late 1970s set up CDM, a Milan-based group of design consultants. He worked with Studio Alchimia and Memphis, designing furniture and objects and preparing shows and publications. He founded the Domus Academy in 1983 and has been its cultural director and vice-president. He teaches and holds conferences at universities in Italy and abroad, and has held many one-man shows at the Milan Triennale and at galleries worldwide. In 1987 Branzi won the Compasso d'Oro prize. **102, 122, 138, 139**

Sergio Brioschi was born in Italy in 1960 and studied design at Milan Polytechnic. From 1981 to 1984 he worked for the architect and industrial designer Mario Bellini. In 1985 he began working with the designer Antonio Citterio and has designed for many prestigious clients including B&B Italia, Arc Linea, Olivetti, Vitra and Antonangeli. **104**

Britefuture, led by Bastiann Arler, is an Italian design team which creates sculptural objects, concerned with mechanics, assembly, purity of material and form. Dutch-born Bastiann Arler has also lived and worked in Japan, Italy and Sweden. Before establishing Britefuture, he worked as a freelance designer for such clients as IKEA, Iittala Glass, Whirlpool, and on behalf of Studio de Lucchi for Olivetti and Fiat. **134**

Bernard Brousse was born in Bordeaux, France, in 1948. From 1970 to 1980 he worked as a deep sea diver for French, Brazilian, British and Norwegian companies. In the early 1980s he started working in wood and design. Since 1989 has run a workshop where he designs and makes prototypes of lamps and furniture for different French and Italian companies. **105**

Büro für form was founded in 1998 by the German designers Constantin Wortman and Benjamin Hopf. They work in the fields of interior and product design, particularly lighting and furniture. Objects play with the perception of the viewer and aim to blend organic shape with geometric elements. In 2000 they exhibited for the first time in Milan and Cologne. **104**

Maximillian Burton was born in London in 1966. He studied Industrial Design at Manchester Metropolitan University and the Royal College of Art, London, graduating in 1992. After working for Pankhurst Design in London, the work from his Master's show was included in an exhibition at MoMA, New York and at the 'One Hundred Years at the RCA' show. He worked briefly for Hollington Associates, London, before joining Smart Design in 1995, where he is a senior designer. Since then he has worked on various independent projects which span both product and furniture design. **218**

Sigi Bussinger was born in 1965 in Munich. He studied wood carving and since 1989 has been working as a sculptor and performing artist. **94**

Bute Fabrics was founded nearly fifty years ago on the Isle of Bute, Scotland, and it is among the company leaders in the industry. Fabrics fall into three groups: project driven, off the peg and bespoke, such as the ten miles of fabric ordered for Chek Lap Kok Airport, Hong Kong. Specializing in wool rich blends, Bute upholstery fabrics are used in auditoria, corporate interiors, hotels and restaurants, airports and lounges, banks and governmental buildings. **171**

Louise Campbell graduated from the London College of Furniture in 1992 and completed further study at the Danish Design School's Institute of Industrial design in 1995. The following year she set up her own studio in Copenhagen and has since been involved in various projects including setting up the 'Walk the Plank' project with Sebastian Holmback and Cecilia Enevoldsen. **22, 74, 75**

Massimo Canalli studied design in Milan and then moved to New York to work with Wajskol Inc. He currently works as a graphic designer in Michele De Lucchi's studio but also has his own Milan based studio where he works on corporate image, packaging, editorial design and web design. **187**

Chiara Cantono studied architecture and industrial design at Milan Polytechnic. She formed her own design studio in 1993, her work being based on experimentation with and study of new materials and technologies. In 1997 she created a new collection using material which up until then had been used solely in Formula 1 car racing and in the aeronautical industry. The following year Cantono presented 'Alicia' a collection of lamps which react to light like fibre optics. She has also collaborated with companies such as Brunati Italia and the Busnelli Industrial Group. **50**

Marco Carenini was born in Zurich in 1968 and studied architecture and design. In 1996 he set up the studio B&C Design where he is working independently in furniture, product, graphic and corporate design. **91, 102, 123**

Caroline Casey studied fashion and textile design at Sydney College of the Arts, graduating in 1986. Since then she has worked for may companies in New York, London and Sydney as a fashion, interior and furniture designer. In 1999 she had a solo exhibition at the Powerhouse Museum, Sydney. **18**

Jean-Charles de Castelbajac is a Parisian couturier. Born in 1949, he has been creating garments since the age of 19, searching for a pure, elemental, visual language. In 1979 he began diversifying into other areas of design and has recently worked with Ligne Roset. He has taught at Central Saint Martin's School of Design, London and the Academy of Applied Arts, Vienna. **168**

David Chipperfield was born in London in 1953 and graduated from the Architectural Association in 1977. He became a member of the Royal Institute of British Architects in 1982 and after collaboration with Douglas Stephen, Richard Rogers and Norman Foster, founded David Chipperfield Architects in 1984. The studio's activities are varied, ranging from furniture design to interior architecture and urban planning. In 1987 he opened an office in Tokyo, followed by ones in Berlin and New York. He has since been able to undertake projects for Issey Miyake, the Neues Museum, Berlin and the Hotel Shore Club, Miami. Recent projects include plans for the enlargement of the San Michele cemetery in Venice and the Museum of Art, Davenport USA. He has won many awards and also been Professor of Architecture at the Staatliche Akademie, Stuttgart and visiting professor at various institutions. **54**

Aldo Cibic was born in Schio, Italy, in 1955 and moved to Milan in 1979 to work with Ettore Sottsass, participating in the foundation of the Memphis group. In 1989 he set up his own independent design practice, Cibic & Partners, a studio whose interior design and architecture projects range from department stores to cinemas, public works to private residences. **150**

Antonio Citterio was born in Meda, Italy, in 1950 and has been involved in industrial and furniture design since 1967. He studied at Milan Polytechnic and in 1973 set up a studio with Paolo Nava. They have worked for B&B Italia and Flexform, among others. In 1979 they were awarded the Compasso d'Oro. In 1987 Terry Dwan became a partner in Studio Citterio Dwan, and interior design projects have included schemes for Esprit and offices and showrooms for Vitra. Among work in Japan, in partnership with Toshiyuki Kita, are the headquarters in Kobe for World Company, the Corente Building in Tokyo, and the Diago headquarters in Tokyo. Citterio has taught at the Domus Academy in Milan and participated in many exhibitions including independent shows. In 1993 he designed the exhibition 'Antonio Citterio and Terry Dwan' promoted by Arc en Rêve in Bordeaux, which travelled to Osaka and Tokyo in 1994. In 1996 Antonio Citterio participated in numerous design competitions including the corporate design for the Commerzbank pilot branches in Germany, the new retail environment for Habitat in Paris and the restructuring of the existing Line 1 metro system of Milan. Recent projects include interior architecture for Cerruti, Emanuel Ungaro SA, the UEFA headquarters, B&B Italia and Zegna Sports clothing store. In 1999 Antonio Citterio & Partners was established as a multidisciplinary architecture and design studio with offices in Milan and Hamburg. **47, 62, 72, 120**

Toni Cordero was born in Italy in 1937. After studying architecture in Turin he opened a design office in 1962. Architectural clients have included Olivetti, Fiat, Blumarine, Kenzo, the Banco Mediceo del Filarete, and the Turin Automobile Museum. His furniture and design work includes collaborations with Acerbis, Driade, Artemide and Sawaya & Moroni. **106**

Carlo Cumini was born in Udine in 1953 where he lives and works. He studied at the Marinoni Technical School and started working for the family firm. When Horm was established he became the main furniture designer, concentrating on design in solid wood. Since 1991 he has also worked for Luc-e and Nuova Auras. He has collaborated with Alberto Freschi and Carlo Biancolini; he continues to work in the design field, investigating new materials. **81**

dai design and identification was founded in Zurich in 1987 as a design agency, specializing in architecture, interior design and corporate identity. **208**

Lorenzo Damiani was born in 1972. He studied architecture at Milan Polytechnic and since then has taken part in many exhibitions and competitions. In 1999 he represented Milan in the Design section at the Biennale of Young Artists and the Meditteranean. **73**

Christopher C. Deam, principal of San Francisco-based CCD Architecture and Furniture Design, is a Milan-trained architect whose furniture designs have generated many awards and international recognition. He received the Editor's Award for Furniture Design in 1997 and his work is in the permanent collection of the San Francisco Museum of Modern Art; it has also been exhibited widely. **226**

Design 3 Produktdesign was founded in Hanover in 1987 as the German office of Moggridge Associates (London) and ID Two (San Francisco). In 1990 it became an independent company when the others joined IDEO. In 1999 the studio moved to Hamburg. **186**

Christian Deuber is one of the founder members of the N2 group in Lucerne, Switzerland. While training as an electrical engineer, he gained experience in lighting design and set up his own studio, Pharus Lighting Design. He has designed lighting for Driade, Palluccoitalia and bathrooms for Dornbracht Interiors with Jorg Boner. Most recently he has designed for Hidden/sdb. **64**

Jane Dillon was born in the UK in 1943 and studied interior design at Manchester College of Art and Design followed by an MA at the Royal College of Art, London. Since graduation in 1968 she has developed an international client list which includes Olivetti, Casas Barcelona, Habitat, Heals, Thonet, Cassina, Herman Miller and Ercol. In 1972 she formed a design partnership with Charles Dillon – Studio Dillon has had a range of own brand products since 1997. Recent projects have included seating design for the Science Museum, London, consultancy work for the Globe Theatre, London and a collection for W. Lusty and Sons. She teaches at the Royal College of Art and is currently involved in projects with Guy Mallinson Furniture Ltd and Keen Group Ltd. **19**

Felice Dittli studied design in Basel, Switzerland specializing in interior decoration, products and construction design. In 1988 she set up her own studio and now works in interior decoration and product design. She has had various exhibitions and won several awards. **117**

Designer Biografien und Register

Dante Donegani and Giovanni Lauda established their design company in 1993. Donegani graduated from the Faculty of Architecture in Florence after which he worked for Corporate Identity Olivetti. Since 1993 he was been the Director of the Design Master Course held at the Domus Academy. He has collaborated with firms such as Memphis, Stildomus and Luceplan and has won several major awards for his architectural schemes such as the Manhattan Waterfront, New York (1988) and the Berlin Wall Prize (1987). Lauda has a degree in architecture and works in the fields of interior, exhibition and industrial design for companies such as Artas, Play Line and Sedie and Company. He was a member of Morozzi and Partners until 1994 when he became responsible for the Design Culture course in the Industrial Design Master Course at the Domus Academy. He has curated numerous exhibitions including 'Il Design Italiano dal 1964–1990' which was held at the Triennale of Milan in 1996. **68, 69**

Rodolfo Dordoni was born in Milan in 1954, where he studied architecture. He is involved in art direction, corporate identity, interior design, and furniture and lighting design. His client list includes Acerbis, Arteluce, Artemide, Cappellini, Dolce & Gabbana, Driade, Ferlea, Flos, Molteni, Moroso and Venini. **56**

Dumoffice is based in Amsterdam and consists of the designers Weibe Boonstra, Martijn Hoogendijk, and Marc van Nederpelt. All three graduated in 1994 from the Design Academy Eindhoven and have produced work for Belux of Switzerland and sdb Industries, The Netherlands. They have exhibited in Milan and are also represented in the Stedelijk Museum, Amsterdam and the San Francisco Museum of Modern Art. Their aim is to produce work which is unorthodox with an element of wit. **89**

Knuth Eckhard was born in Hamburg in 1945 and studied art history and theatre. While working as a dramatic advisor, he found that he preferred working as a light designer. He first employed laser technology in 1979 to 1980 and attended the School of Holography in San Francisco. In Munich he built a machine for 360° holography and his hologram of the crown of the Holy Roman Emperors was the focal point for the Millennium Exhibition in Austria. In 1997 he began a collaboration with Ingo Maurer and developed the Holonzki 'holographic lamp. **96**

Claus Christian Eckhardt was born in 1965 and studied industrial design at the Academy of Fine Arts, Brunswick, going on to work as an interior designer for Silvestrin Design in Munich. From 1992 to 1999 he was in charge of designing consumer electronics and communication products for the Blaupunkt design department in Hildesheim, where he was also responsible for the design of Bosch mobile phones. He is now Chief Designer and Head of Global Product Design for Bosch Telecom in Frankfurt. He has received several international awards. **186**

Cecilia Enevoldsen was born in 1970 and graduated in Industrial Design from Denmark's Design School in 1995. In the same year she established her own design company which mainly designs furniture. She exhibits often and has won several design prizes. Along with Sebastian Holmback and Louise Campbell she initiated the 'Walk the Plank' project. She lectures at the Danish Design School and has worked as an adviser at the Architecture School, Copenhagen. **22**

David Farrage was born in England and studied Industrial Design at the Royal College of Art, London. He worked for Ross Lovegrove Studio X, moved to Japan to work for the architectural and urban product manufacturer Sekisui Jushi, and moved back to London to work for FM Design. In 1996 he became Senior Industrial Designer at the New York-based Smart Design. More recently he has joined Sony at its US East Coast Design Centre. **210**

Khodi Feiz was born in Iran in 1963. He graduated from Syracuse University, USA in 1986, and worked for Texas Instruments Design Centre, joining Philips Design in 1990. He became Manager and Senior Designer for the Advanced Design Group but left to establish Feiz Design Studio in 1998. Based in Amsterdam, Feiz Design Studio has been featured in exhibitions worldwide and its current client list includes Alessi, LEGO, Loewe, LG Electronics and Polydor. **44**

Norman Foster was born in Manchester, England in 1935 and studied at the University of Manchester and Yale University. He established Team 4 in 1963 – with his late wife, Wendy, and Su and Richard Rogers – and founded Foster Associates in 1967. He is renowned for his high-tech designs, such as the Hongkong and Shanghai Bank (1979–85) and Stansted Airport (1981–89). More recent projects include the Sackler Galleries at the Royal Academy of Arts, London; the Centre d'Art Cultural, Nimes; the new headquarters for Commerzbank in Frankfurt, the remodelling of the Reichstag in Berlin and the vast new airport at Chek Lap Kok for Hong Kong. He is currently working on the new Wembley Stadium in London. His work has won over 60 awards and citations. Although primarily concerned with large-scale architectural projects, Foster is also active in furniture and product design. **53**

Nobuhiro Fujii was born in 1968 in Japan. He attended Tsukuba University and joined Sharp Corporation in 1992 as a product designer, working on home appliances. **198**

Naoto Fukasawa was born in Kofu, Japan, in 1956 and graduated from Tama Art University. He was Chief Designer at the Seiko Corporation before joining IDEO San Francisco. He returned to Japan in 1996 to become Director of IDEO, Japan. He has won many awards and his Metro stacking chair is included in the collection of the San Francisco Museum of Modern Art. His work was recently exhibited in Berlin as part of the exhibition 'Where We Stand'. He has lectured at the Royal College of Art, London, at Tama Art University and is currently retained as teacher to Matsushita Design. **202–3**

Jorge Garcia Garay was born in Buenos Aires, Argentina, and has worked in Barcelona since 1979 as the director of Garcia Garay Design. He is involved almost exclusively in lighting with an architectural design emphasis and his work can be seen in permanent collections in Europe and the United States. His work has been published in many journals, including Blueprint, Abitare and Interni. His products are distributed worldwide. **111, 112**

Kristian Gavoille was born in Brazzaville in 1956 and has lived in Paris since 1986. From 1986 to 1991, after practising as an architect with DPLG Toulouse, he collaborated with Philippe Starck on several hotel and restaurant projects and in 1992 was voted designer of the year. He has designed shops for Kookai and furniture clients include Ligne Roset and Mobilier National. **169**

Bruno Gecchelin was born in 1939 and studied architecture at Milan Polytechnic. Since 1962 he has been involved in many areas of industrial design numbering such companies as Indesit, Olivetti, Arteluce-Flos, Fiat, Antonangeli, Venini, Matsushita, Salviati and Tronconi as clients. He has won the Compasso d'Oro prize in 1989 and 1991. **117**

Massimo Iosa Ghini was born in Bologna in 1958 and studied architecture at Milan Polytechnic and in Florence. In 1985 he began working for RAI. His work with Memphis dates from 1986, the year he founded the Bolidismo movement. In industrial design he has collaborated with Cassina, Flou, Mandarina Duck, Alessi, Akfi, Ritzenhoff, WMF, Yamigawa and Hasashi Glas. **200**

Christian Ghion was born in Montmorency, France in 1958. He graduated from Etude et Creation de Mobilier, Paris in 1987 and since then has worked with Patrick Nadeau. In 1998 he started his own project concentrating on industrial and interior design for European and Japanese companies including Cinna/Roset, Neotu, 3 Suisses, Idee, Tendo and Thierry Mugler. His work has been awarded several prizes and is on show in the design collection of the major museums of New York, Los Angeles and Paris. **43, 151**

Stefano Giovannoni was born in La Spezia, Italy, in 1954 and graduated from the architecture department at the University of Florence in 1978. From 1978 to 1990 he lectured and carried out research at Florence University and also taught at the Domus Academy in Milan and at the Institute of Design in Reggio Emilia. He is the founding member of King-Kong Production, which is concerned with avant-garde research in design, interiors, fashion and architecture. Clients include Alessi, Cappellini, Arredaesse and Tisca France. In 1991 he designed the Italian Pavilion at 'Les Capitales Européennes de Nouveau Design' exhibition, which was held at the Centre Georges Pompidou in Paris. **200, 219**

Ernesto Gismondi was born in 1931 in San Remo, Italy. He studied at Milan Polytechnic and the Higher School of Engineering, Rome. In 1959, with Sergio Mazza, he founded Artemide SpA, of which he is the president and managing director. Since 1970 he has designed various lights for Artemide and in 1981 he was involved in the development of the influential Memphis group. He has sat on the boards of several national design boards and taught widely in the same field. **116**

Marco Giunta was born in 1966 and studied design and architecture at the Polytechnic of Milan. From 1992 to 1996 he acted as a consultant for Zerodisegno and Quattrocchio. Since 1994 he has taught at Milan Polytechnic and also in Antwerp and Genova. In 1995 he set up Disegni which specializes in furniture, displays for shops and packaging. **83**

Natanel Gluska was born in Israel in 1957 but currently works n Zurich and in Lefkada, Greece. He studied in Israel, the Hague and the Rietveld Academy, Amsterdam. His most recent projects include the interior of a club in Zurich, chairs for the Union Bank of Switzerland (both 1999), chairs for the Sanderson Hotel, London, and Donna Karan's shop, Madison Avenue, New York (both 2000). **14, 21**

Anki Gneib is an architect and designer based in Stockholm. Born in London in 1965, she studied at the University College of Arts, Crafts and Design in Stockholm and at Middlesex Polytechnic, UK. Since 1993 she has worked independently but has also undertaken public and private interior design jobs through Wallenstreen and Ostgren. Clients include Asplund, Fogia, Arvesund and Interstop. She has exhibited throughout Europe and Japan and won several awards. **161**

Tobias Grau was born in Hamburg. He studied economics in Munich and then design in New York, thereafter working in the product development department of Knoll International. In 1984 he began work as a freelance interior designer, and since 1985 has developed an internationally recognized and exclusive lighting range. In 1999 the first two Tobias Grau shops were opened in Hamburg and Berlin, the third in Dusseldorf in 2000.
90, 124

Johanna Grawunder is an architect based in Milan, where she has worked with Sottsass Associati since 1985, becoming a partner in 1989. Born in San Diego in 1961, she studied architecture in California, San Luis and Florence. She has collaborated with many companies including Egizia, WMF and Giotto as well as designing one-off pieces for the Venetian company Salviati and Christophile of France. **112**

Konstantin Grcic was born in 1965 in Germany. He trained as a cabinetmaker and continued his education at the John Makepeace School for Craftsmen, then studied design at the Royal College of Art, London, on a scholarship from Cassina. He worked in the studio of Jasper Morrison in 1990 and founded his own studio in Munich. Clients have included the Munich Tourist Office (in collaboration with David Chipperfield Architects UK), Agape, Cappellini, ClassiCon, Flos, Iittala, Montina and Zeritalia while recent commissions have comprised work for Authentics GmbH and Whirlpool Europe srl. **26, 120**

Group Kombinat is Sven Anwar Bibi, Mark Gutjahr and Jorg Zimmerman. They all studied design at the University of Applied Sciences, Cologne and frequently exhibited their work in both Cologne and Milan. In 2000 Group Kombinat split up but Mark Gutjahr and Sven Anwar Bibi are continuing to work together under the name Bibi*Gutjahr. **34**

Gitta Gschwendtner was born in 1972 in Würzberg, Germany. She holds at BA (Hons) in Furniture and Product Design from Kingston University, London, and an MA in Furniture Design from the Royal College of Art, London. Since 1998 she has worked as a freelance furniture, product and interior designer. **19**

Dögg Gudmundsdóttir was born in Reykjavik, Iceland and holds a Diploma in Industrial Design from the Istituto Europeo di Design in Milan. Gudmundsdóttir has held many exhibitions within Scandinavia and currently works for IKEA as a freelance designer. **24**

Monica Guggisberg and Philip Baldwin are an American/Swiss couple who have been working together for 15 years. They trained in Sweden at the Orrefors Glass School and later in the studio of Ann Wolff and Wilke Adolfsson. In 1982 they established their own design and hot glass studio near Lausanne in Switzerland. Their creations have been exhibited widely in Europe, America Japan and are to be found in many museums worldwide. **144**

Marti Guixé was born in 1964 and studied Interior Design in Barcelona, and Industrial Design in Milan. From 1994 to 1996 he was a consultant for KIDP, Seoul. Recent projects include shops for Camper in Barcelona, London and Via Montenapoleoni, and an apron and bag collection for Authentics. He has exhibited with the Droog Design collective, individually in Barcelona, Milan and Berlin and currently works between Barcelona and Berlin as a Techno-gastrosof, Tapaist and Designer. In 1999 he won the Ciutat de Barcelona Design Prize. **84, 85**

Alfredo Häberli was born in Buenos Aires, Argentina, in 1964 but moved to Switzerland in 1977. He studied industrial design in Zurich and worked as an installation designer at the Museum fur Gestaltung until 1993. Since then he has worked alone or in collaboration with Christophe Marchand for companies such as Alias, Edra, Zanotta, Thonet and Driade. He is currently developing products for Asplund, Bally, Cappellini, Iittala and Zeritalia. **38, 40, 49, 81, 122, 160, 161**

Zaha Hadid was born in Baghdad in 1950 and studied at the American University in Beirut and the Architectural Association in London. She joined the Office for Metropolitan Architecture and worked on the Dutch Houses of Parliament Extension in The Hague. She established her own practice in 1979 and in 1983 won the Hong Kong Peak International Design Competition. Recent projects include the Contemporary Arts Centre in Cincinatti and an exhibition pavilion in Weil am Rhein, Germany. She has taught at the Harvard Graduate School, Illinois University and the Architectural Association, London. She currently teaches at the Hochschule in Hamburg and at Columbia University, New York. **52**

Makoto Hashikura was born in Japan in 1972. He joined Mitsubishi in 1998 after graduating from Keio University. Since then he has designed computers and visual information projects such as LCD displays and CRT Monitors. **207**

Sam Hecht was born in London in 1969. After studying at the Royal College of Art he worked as an interior and industrial designer. He moved to Tel Aviv and joined the Studia group, then moved to San Francisco where he began collaboration with IDEO. He also completed projects for AT&T and NEC. He then worked for IDEO in Japan with clients such as NEC, Seiko and Matsushita. He won the D&AD Exhibition Category Award in 1998 for his White Box design, and moved to London to become Head of Industrial Design at IDEO. Recent projects include the Thames Water Pavilion at the Millennium Dome, Greenwich. He lectures in Japan and his work forms part of the permanent collection of MoMA, New York. **202–3**

Steven Holl is the principal of Steven Holl Architects, New York. Born in 1947 in Bremerton, Washington, he attended the University of Washington, then studied architecture in Rome and at the Architectural Association, London. He established his firm in 1989 and his work was presented in a two man show at MoMA, New York. Recent awards include the 1996 Architecture Awards for Excellence in Design. Holl's Chapel of St Ignatius in Seattle won a National AIA Award for Excellence in Design in 1997. **110**

Geoff Hollington was born in the UK in 1949. He studied industrial design at the Central School, London and environmental design at the Royal College of Art, London. In 1980 he established the Hollington studio which has such international clients as Kodak, Gillette, Ericsson and Herman Miller. His studio's products are in museum collections and have won many international awards. The studio is now a leader in the field of digital interaction design and is currently collaborating with the Science Museum, London. He is a fellow of the Royal Society of Arts, the Chartered Society of Designers and a member of the Industrial Design Society of America. **67, 181**

Bohuslav (Boda) Horak was born in Pardubice in the Czech Republic in 1954 and attended both the Zizkov Art School of Prague and the Academy of Applied Arts. In 1987 he became a member of the design group Atika, also in Prague, and in 1990 opened his own studio. His designs are produced frequently by Anthology Quartett. **149**

Isao Hosoe was born in Tokyo in 1942 and studied aerospace engineering at the Nihon University of Tokyo. Since 1967 he has lived in Milan and collaborated with Alberto Rosselli until 1974. He is Professor of Industrial Design at Milan Polytechnic. Among his many awards are the Compasso d'Oro and the Biennial of Industrial Design at Lubiana. He has exhibited many times and his works are in the permanent collections of the Victoria and Albert Museum, London; the Centre Georges Pompidou, Paris; the Chicago Athenaeum; and the Museum of Science and Technology, Milan. **92, 93**

Elina Huotari graduated with an MA from the University of Art and Design, Helsinki in 1999. Since 1996 she has worked as a designer for Ratti SpA, Italy, Studio Lasse Keltto and Verso Design Oy, Finland. Her work has been exhibited in the UK, Italy and Finland. **174**

Richard Hutten graduated in industrial design from the Design Academy in Eindhoven in 1991 and then set up his own studio. He has achieved international recognition for his innovative designs which can be seen in the permanent collections of many design museums in The Netherlands as well as in the Vitra Museum, Weil am Rhein. He has held exhibitions worldwide and Philippe Starck selected two of his products for the interiors of the Delano Hotel in Miami and the Mondrian Hotel in Los Angeles. Hutten taught product design at the Art School of Maastricht from 1996 to 1998. **34, 35**

Takashi Ifuji was born in 1969 in Gifu, Japan. After studying industrial design at the University of Tsukuba he joined the Design Laboratory at Fujitsu Ltd. In 1999 he moved to Milan and established Ifuji Design. He took part in the Salone de Mobile in Milan and was awarded the Red Dot for the Highest Design Quality in 1999, Design Zentrum Nordhein Westfalen, Germany. **145**

Yoshinori Inukai was born in Nagoya, Japan in 1964. He graduated from Kanaza College of Art in 1996 and joined Canon Inc. shortly afterwards. He has received numerous awards and in 1999 was given the IF Award in Germany as well as the IDEA 99 bronze prize, USA. **193**

James Irvine was born in London in 1958. He studied design at Kingston Polytechnic and then at the Royal College of Art, London, graduating in 1984. He moved to Milan where he was a design consultant for Olivetti design studio Milan, designing industrial products under the direction of Michele De Lucchi and Ettore Sottsass. In 1988 he worked for the Toshiba Design Centre in Tokyo but returned to Milan to open his own studio whose clients included Cappellini, BRF and SCP. From 1993 to 1998 he was also a partner in Sottsass Associati. His first personal exhibition was at the Royal College of Art, Stockholm in 1993. In 1999 he completed the design of the new city bus for the Hannover transport system, USTRA. Current clients include Artemide, B&B Italia, Magis, Whirlpool and Canon Inc., Japan. **118**

Noriaki Itai was born in Japan in 1965 and joined Sharp Corporation in 1983. He has designed electronic component-based application projects and is now in charge of product design development for television, video and DVD. **192**

Airi Itakura was born in Kanagawa, Japan in 1974. She graduated from the Women's College of Arts in 1996 and joined Canon Inc. shortly afterwards. She designs scanners and fax machines and has won the Japanese Good Design Award (1999). **192**

Setsu Ito was born in Yamaguchi, Japan in 1964. He obtained a Masters Degree in product design from the University of Tsukuba and has since published studies on product semantics and design valuations for the Japanese Society for the Science of Design. He has undertaken design research projects for the TDK Corporation, NEC Electric Co and Nissan Motor Co, and in 1989 worked for Studio Alchimia in Milan. Since 1989 he has collaborated with Angelo Mangiarotti. He is currently a consultant designer for the TDK Corporation Hitachi and Casio and since 1996 he has taught at the Instituto Europeo di Design in Milan. Some of his works are in the permanent collection of the Die Neue Sammlung Museum in Munich. **209**

Dakota Jackson has been a considerable presence in American Furniture for three decades, with furniture in the permanent collections of the Cooper Hewitt National Design Museum, the Brooklyn Museum, the American Craft Museum, the Chicago Atheneum, the London Design Museum and te Deutsche Architekturmusuem, Frankfurt. Recently Jackson has completed designing the Steinway Tricentennial Grand Piano. **81**

Hans Sandgren Jakobsen was born in 1963. He trained as a cabinetmaker before studying furniture design at the Danish Design School in Copenhagen. In 1991 he began working at Nanna Ditzel's drawing office but started his own practice in 1997. He is also a member of the design group 'Spring' and the Danish Designers MDD. Freelance clients include Via America, Fritz Hansen and Fredericia Stolefabrik. He has exhibited his work widely. **22, 23, 57**

Jam Design was formed in 1994 by A. Zala and M. Paillard. Collaborations have included work for Philips, Sony and Zotefoams Plc. 1999 saw the launch of the Flatscreen coffee table and 2000 of Panel Light, a wall mounted lamp. One off projects have included the Millennium Crib. **212**

Claus Jensen is an Industrial Designer Born in 1966 he graduated from the Danish Design School in 1992 and established Tools Design with Hans Holbaek. Holbaek was born in 1960 and graduated from the Royal Academy of Arts Architectural School in 1990. Since then they have exhibited widely throughout the world and won many awards. **131, 201**

Carsten Joergensen was born in 1948 in Denmark. He was educated at the Art and Craft School in Copenhagen where he studied painting and graphic illustration. In 1974 he started his collaboration with Bodum working as a freelance designer and later founding a department within the company which he later moved to Lausanne. **156, 200**

Claudy Jongstra was born in The Netherlands in 1962 and studied Fashion Design in Utrecht. She has designed fabrics for a diverse range of clients including John Galliano, Donna Karan, Volvo and 'Star Wars, the Phantom Menace'. She has exhibited worldwide and is represented in museums in London, New York, Belgium and The Netherlands. **164**

Yehudit Katz was born in Israel and graduated from the Bezalel Academy of Art and Design, Jerusalem. She received a postgraduate degree from the Ateneum School of art in Helsinki and has since worked on dobbies and jacquards for various mills in Israel and abroad. She has taught weaving at the Art Centre of Jerusalem and is Senior Lecturer at the Shenkar College in Ramat Gan. She received the Alix De Rothschild Foundation Prize for Fibre Arts in 1998 and has now retired from industrial design in order to research the interaction between weaving and light. **172**

Yaacov Kaufman was born in Russia in 1945, lived in Poland until 1957, and moved to Israel where he now lives and works. He studied at the Bat Yam Institute of Art and is now Professor of Industrial Design at the Bezalel Academy of Art and Design, Jerusalem. He is particularly active in the fields of furniture and lighting design and has won several international design prizes. He is currently collaborating with several Italian furniture designers and has designed for Lumina for many years. **125**

Hideki Kawai was born in Nagoya, Japan in 1967. He graduated from the Aichi College of Art in 1989 and joined Canon Inc. as an industrial designer. In 1999 he won the Good Design Award in Japan. **181**

Makoto Kawamoto was born in Japan in 1965 and graduated form Osaka's University of Arts. In 1994 he moved to Perugia, then Milan and in 1995 began a collaboration with Sawaya and Moroni. He is also active in graphic and interior design, having designed the offices for Il Cittadino in Milan in 1996. Kawamoto exhibits regularly, most recently with the Borderlight Group in Milan 2000. **93**

King Miranda Associati was founded in 1976 by Perry King and Santiago Miranda. They work in product, service, interior and exhibition design and are active in a variety of industries from consumer products to furniture, lighting to telecommunications. With clients worldwide, they founded the European Designer's Network in 1990. **27, 123**

Toshiyuki Kita was born in Osaka in 1942 and graduated in industrial design from the Naniwa College in 1964. He established his own design studio in Osaka and began working both in Milan and Japan focusing on domestic environments and interior design. In 1989 he was presented with the Delta de Oro Award in Spain. He designed the chairs and interior for the rotating theatre at the Japanese Pavilion at Expo '92, Seville. He is a visiting lecturer at the Hochschule für Angewandte Kunst in Vienna and founded a private school in the Fukui Prefecture of Japan. **194**

Henrik Kjellberg and Mattias Lindqvist are the names behind the award-winning design company Sweedish, which was founded in 1998. Henrik was born in 1971 and studied in Oslo, New York and Stockholm while Mattias was born in 1967 and studied in Stockholm and Copenhagen. Both graduated in furniture and interior architecture and their notable clients have included IKEA of Sweden. **94**

Kazuyo Komodo was born in Tokyo in 1961 and studied at the Musashino University of Art. She began her career in industrial and interior design in 1982 and since 1989 has worked in Milan. After collaboration with Denis Santachiara she established her own studio in Milan. She works, among others, for Acerbis International, Bernini, Driade, Rosenthal and Yamaha. **210**

Tobias Koeppe was born in Wolfsburg, Germany, in 1958 and trained as a metalworker. He studied industrial design in Hanover and after working in the industry for some years founded his own studio in 1996. He focuses on the creation of new product ideas and the design of high quality goods in metal, plastics, glass and porcelain. **205**

Komplot Design was founded in 1987 by Poul Christiansen and Boris Berlin and is active in the fields of industrial, furniture and graphic design. Poul Christiansen was born in Copenhagen in 1947, where he studied architecture at the Royal Academy of Fine Arts. Boris Berlin was born in Leningrad in 1953, where he studied at the Institute of Applied Arts and Design and moved to Denmark in 1983. They have exhibited widely in Europe and Asia and have won many awards in Scandinavia. Their work is in the permanent collections of the Danish National Art Foundation and the Danish Museum of Decorative Art. **22**

Geert Koster was born in The Netherlands in 1961. He studied in Groningen and Milan, graduating in 1985. Since then he has been based in Italy, collaborating with Michele De Lucchi, participating in the Solid group and co-founding the ecological design group 'o2'. For Studio De Lucchi he worked with clients such as Vitra, ENEL produzione, Telecom Italia and Mandarina Duck. In 1989 he opened his own studio in Milan, working on interiors, exhibitions, furniture and industrial design for clients such as Abet Laminati, Olivetti, Cappellini and Hidden. In 1999 he co-founded Park Studio (architecture and design). **34, 35**

Defne Koz was born in Ankara, Turkey and moved to Milan in 1989 to study for an MA in Industrial Design at the Domus Academy. She spent 1991 to 1992 at Sottsass Associati but since 1992 has undertaken independent work in interior planning and industrial design, working for Cappellini and Ala Rosa among others. Recently she has planned interiors for private and commercial customers and designed office furniture for a Turkish company. Her projects have been shown in Milan, Cologne and Istanbul. **64**

Marc Krusin was born in London in 1973 and graduated in Furniture Design from Leeds Metropolitan University. Following placements in the UK and Italy, he moved to Milan and collaborated with various prestigious international clients including Piero Lissoni's office. In 1998 he co-founded the Milan-based design group Codice 31, which has continued to expand. His clients include Bosa, Fontana Arte and Saporiti. **101**

Katsunori Kume, born in Japan in 1967, has graduated in Industrial Design from Kuwazuma Design School in 1989 and joined Sharp Corporation. He is responsible for product design development in the field of television, LCD projector, video camera and advance design development. **183**

Tsutomu Kurokawa was born in Aichi, Japan, in 1962. He studied design at Tokyo Designer School in Nagoya and trained in the offices of Ics Inc. and Super Potato Co Ltd. He established H. Design Associates with Masamichi Katayama in 1992. They are involved in interior and furniture design and have worked on a series of boutiques in Japan. They have exhibited their work internationally. In 2000 Kurokawa established Out DeSign. **107**

Vardit Laor was born in 1972 in Rehevot, Israel. She graduated from the Bezalel Academy of Art and Design, Jerusalem, in 1998 and exhibited in Milan in 2000. Her focus is on industrial, furniture and exhibition design. **29**

Danny Lane was born in Urbana, Illinois in 1955. Largely self-taught, he moved to England in 1975 to work with the stained-glass artist Patrick Reyntiens, then studied painting at Central Saint Martin's College of Art and Design in London. In 1983 he co-founded Glassworks with John Creighton and began a three-year association with Ron Arad. He has worked with metal and wood and participated in numerous museum and gallery exhibitions and international furniture shows. In 1988 he held three one-man shows in Milan, London and Paris and started producing work for Fiam Italia. In 1994 he was commis-sioned by the Victoria and Albert Museum in London to install a balustrade of stacked glass in the Glass Gallery. In 1998 he created a water sculpture for the Conrad Inter-national Hotel in Cairo and also developed the technique of blowing borosilicate glass into tubular shapes, creating a glass fountain in Shanghai. In 1999, Lane held an exhibition in London, 'Breaking Tradition', and in the past year has designed glass-based pieces for hotels in Singapore, Hong Kong and the ITN Building, London. **30, 153**

Taco Langius was born in The Netherlands in 1964 and studied in Eindhoven, then Milan. Since 1990 he has collaborated with Philips Whirlpool, Matteo Thun, Aldo Rossi Architecture and Luca Trazzi Industrial Design and Architecture. Currently he works with Lissoni Associates and is also a member of Codice 31, Milan. **102**

Designer Biografien und Register

Kristiina Lassus was born in 1966 in Helsinki, Finland. She studied interior and furniture design at the University of Industrial Arts, Helsinki and then at the National College of Arts, Crafts and Design in Stockholm. She has worked in Helsinki and Brisbane, specializing in interior and graphic design. In 1993 she set up the D'Imagio design practice and has been working with Zanotta since 1995. **138**

Marta Laudani and Marco Romanelli work together as interior and product designers. Laudani graduated in Rome in 1979. Her competition project for the piazza in the Parco dei Caduti in Rome won first prize and executive status in 1990. Romanelli took a Masters degree in design after graduating in architecture in 1983. He worked for Mario Bellini until 1985 when he became freelance. He was editor at Domus magazine from 1986 to 1994 and has been a design editor at Abitare since 1995. He works as a consultant with Driade and is art director at Montina and Oluce. Laudani and Romanelli currently work for Atlantide, Cleto Munari, Montina and Oluce. Their exhibition designs include the retrospective of Gio Ponti which was held at the 1997 Milan Furniture Fair. They have practices in Rome and Milan respectively and also work together on interior design projects. **132**

Gaëlle Lauriot-Prévost is an architect and designer. He works in various fields from urban design to product design. Since graduation in 1991 he has worked extensively with the architect Dominique Perrault and in 1996 set up his own practice. Important works have included various projects for the French National Library. Recent work has comprised the competition for the City Hall of Marseille, the book With and lighting design for Fontana Arte – all in collaboration with Dominique Perrault. **122**

Roberto Lazzeroni was born in 1950 in Pisa, Italy, where he still lives and works. After studying art and architecture in Florence, he began working in industrial and interior design. Since 1988 he has been art director of the Ceccotti Collections and he has collaborated with many companies, including Acerbis, Ciatta, Confaloneri, Driade, Moroso and Gervasoni. **122**

Lemongras design studio was set up in Munich by Carmen Cheong and Moritz Engelbrecht. Both studied at the Royal College of Art, London, although they originate from Singapore and Germany respectively. They regularly exhibit in Milan and Cologne and have handled projects for Authentics and Deutsche Telecom. **140**

Arik Levy was born in Tel Aviv and graduated from the Art Centre College of Design in Lausanne. He worked for a period in Japan before moving to Paris where he set up his own studio, 'L Design'. He took part in the 'Light Light' exhibition in Paris in 1998. **100, 109**

Morten Linde was born in 1965 and studied at the School of Arts and Crafts, Copenhagen. For two years he was involved in the design of Bang & Olufsen products before opening his own architectural practice in 1992. He has worked for Tag Heuer, Kirk Telecom, Mexx Time, Grundig TV and Hewlett Packard, France. Most recently he designed a collection of 140 watches for Mexx Time which were presented at the Basel Fair 2000. **187**

Frederick Lintz was born in France in 1971, graduating from ENSCI Les Ateliers in 1994. His preferred areas are product design, graphic design, illustration and architecture. After working for several design studios, he joined Design Plan Studio in 1997. **186**

Piero Lissoni was born in 1956. He studied architecture at Milan Polytechnic and worked for G14 Studio, Molteni and Lema. He formed his own company with Nicoletta Canesi in 1984, involved in product, graphic, interior and industrial design and architectural projects. Since 1986 he has worked with Boffi Cucine as art director, creating corporate images and sales outlets, and in 1987 began to collaborate with Porro, Living Design, Matteograssi and Iren Uffici. He worked in Japan in the early 1990s for Takashimaya Company. Since 1994 he has worked as art director for Lema and in 1995 became art director for Cappellini, starting collaboration with Cassina and Nemo. In 1996 Lissoni was appointed art director for Units, the new Boffi and Cappellini kitchen company, and opened showrooms in Paris for Matteograssi and Boffi. He was awarded the Compasso d'Oro in 1991 for the Esprit kitchen designed for Boffi. In 1998 Lissoni moved to new premises and started collaborating with Benetton. Since then he has worked on various interior design projects including the headquarters of Welonda; two hairdressing salons; two new showrooms for Cappellini; the Allegri showroom; and the Boffi Bagni showroom in Milan. **40, 47, 60, 82**

Mary Little graduated from the Royal College of Art, London. Her first collection of experimental upholstery 'Coat of Arms' was shown in London in 1994 and a piece from the collection was purchased by the Victoria and Albert Museum, London. Her work is in many private and public collections, including the Vitra Chair Museum and the Musée des Arts Décoratifs, Paris. In 1997 Mary Little and Peter Wheeler formed Bius. They design one-off limited editions and production furniture. **27**

Ka-chi Lo was born in Hong Kong in 1962 and studied Electronics and Electrical Engineering at Middlesex Polytechnic, UK, followed by Industrial Design at Central Saint Martin's College of Art, London. After graduating in 1990 he mainly worked freelance for TKO Product Design and Graham Allen Associates. From 1998 he has worked as a freelance contractor for Papa Design and David Ames Design Studio and has won various awards. **129**

Ross Lovegrove was born in 1958 in Wales. He graduated from Manchester Polytechnic in 1980 with a BA in industrial design, later receiving a Masters from the Royal College of Art, London. He has worked for various design consultancies including Allied International Designers, London and frogdesign in Germany. In 1984 he moved to Paris to work for Knoll International and became a member of the Atelier de Nimes, a group of five designers which included Gérard Barrau, Jean Nouvel, Martine Bedin and Philippe Starck. In 1986 he co-founded Lovegrove and Brown Design Studio which was later replaced by Lovegrove Studio X. Clients include Louis Vuitton, Luceplan, Tag Heuer, Philips, Sony and Apple Computers. His work can be seen in major design collections, including MoMA, New York; the Guggenheim Museum, New York; the Axis Centre, Japan; the Centre Georges Pompidou in Paris and the Design Museum in London where, in 1993, he curated the first permanent collection. Lovegrove is a visiting lecturer at the Royal College of Art, London. Current projects include the Airbus A3XX, the first class advanced interior for Japan Airlines and a diversification programme for Tag Heuer in Switzerland. He is also designing a private villa for his family in Poland. **18, 30, 121**

Henryk Lula is a sculptor, ceramicist and art restorer. Born in Poland in 1930, he studied at the Academy of Fine Arts, Gdansk, where he has held a chair since 1977. His works are held in the Polish national museums, the JFK Cultural Centre, Washington and ceramics museums in Faenza and Vallauris. He has won many awards and recent work has involved the restoration of the old city of Gdansk and Renaissance sculpture and ceramics in the Palazzo di Artus. **140**

Massimo Lunardon, born in Marostica in 1964, is an artist and designer working primarily in glass. He received a Masters in industrial design from the Domus Academy and has collaborated with designers such as Andrea Anastasio, Ron Arad, Marc Newson and Javier Mariscal. He has exhibited throughout Europe, most recently at the Glass Biennale in Venice (1998/99) as well as at the New Glass Review at the Corning Museum of Glass in New York, 1997. He has also worked with Artemide, Flos, Driade and Memphis. **146, 147**

Ane Lykke was born in Denmark in 1967 and graduated in industrial design from the Academy of Danish Design in 1996. She has worked for Design Studio Faro Designi in Rome, Bang & Olufsen and Jurgen Lehl Textile Studio, Tokyo. In 2000 she established a design studio in Copenhagen. **168**

Kendo Makihara was born in Japan in 1955. He joined Sharp Corporation in 1974 as a product designer after graduating from the design school in Nagoya. He designs home appliances and in May 2000 was made head of GUI design. **198**

Peter Maly is the head of Peter Maly Studio in Hamburg which works on product and interior design. The practice designs international furniture collections and also produces concepts and designs for trade fairs and exhibitions. Maly has received many awards and been the subject of various publications including a monograph by Form Verlag in 1995. Clients number COR, Behr, Interlubke, Thonet and Ligne Roset. He was born in 1936 and studied interior decoration at the Technical College, Detmold, after which he worked as a journalist and interior decorator for a German home service magazine. In 1970 he opened his design studio in Hamburg. **63, 72**

Christophe Marchand was born in Friburgo in 1965 and studied industrial design in Zurich where he met Alfredo Haberli. From 1988 they have been curators at the Museum fur Gestaltung, Zurich and have worked with Alias since 1993. **81**

Enzo Mari was born in Novara, Italy in 1932 and studied at the Academy of Fine Art in Milan. In 1963 he co-ordinated the Italian group Nuove Tendenze and in 1965 was responsible for the exhibition of optical, kinetic and programmed art at the Biennale in Zagreb. In 1972 he participated in 'Italy: the New Domestic Landscape' at MoMA, New York. Mari is occupied with town planning and teaching and has organized courses for the history of art department at the University of Parma and the architecture department at Milan Polytechnic. He has also lectured at various institutions including the Centre for Visual Communication in Parma and the Academy of Fine Arts in Carrara. He has been awarded the Compasso d'Oro on three occasions: for design research by an individual (1967); for the Delfina chair (1979) and for the Tonietta chair for Zanotta (1987). His work can be found in the collections of various contemporary art museums, including the Stedelijk Museum, Amsterdam; the Musée des Arts Décoratifs, Paris and the Kunstmuseum, Düsseldorf. Since 1993 he has collaborated with the KPM (Royal Porcelain Works) in Berlin, and in 1996 staged the 'Arbeiten in Berlin' exhibition at Charlottenburg Castle. **132, 148**

Javier Mariscal was born in Valencia in 1950 and studied graphic design in Barcelona. In 1988 he created the mascot for the Barcelona Olympic Games and the following year founded Estudio Mariscal. Projects have included a new image for the Swedish Socialist Party (1993), covers for the New Yorker (1993/94/96) and the mascot for the Hanover 2000 exposition. He has designed furniture collections for Moroso and a bathroom collection for Cosmic as well as the corporate image for Barcelona Zoo. He also works in animation while his wide range of projects include furniture, textiles, porcelain and sculpture for such firms as Akaba, Adex, Memphis, Alessi, Swatch and Rosenthal. Mariscal also teaches throughout the world. **168**

Mauro Marzollo was born in Venice in 1942. He studied industrial design at university and went on to work in Murano where he learned art techniques from famous master glass blowers. For some time he was head of the Design Department at Lumenform but has moved into private practice. He currently runs his own lighting design business, whose clients include Murano Due and Aureliano Toso 1938. **90**

Jean Marie Massaud was born in Toulouse, France, in 1966 and graduated from the Ateliers-Ecole Nationale Superieure de Creation Industrielle in 1990. He has worked for a range of European and Asian design consultancies. In 1994 he started his own studio concentrating on industrial and interior design for companies including Authentics, Baccarat, Lanvin, Magis and Yamaha. He has received several awards and his work is on show in the major museums of Amsterdam, Chicago, London, Paris and Zurich. **128**

Leona Matejkova see Gabriela Nahlikova

Ippei Matsumoto was born in Japan in 1973 and studied industrial design at Tama Art University. In 1997 he started to work for IDEO Japan and has received awards from IF Hannover, IDSA and ID. **207**

Ingo Maurer is widely acclaimed for his innovative and beautiful lighting designs. Born in 1932 on the island of Reichnau, Lake Constance, Germany, he trained in typography and graphic design. In 1960 he emigrated to the United States and worked as a freelance designer in San Francisco and New York before returning to Europe in 1963. He founded Design M in Munich in 1966 and since then has achieved worldwide recognition. He has exhibited widely and his works are in the permanent collections of major museums including MoMA, New York. He edited the 2000 edition of The International Design Yearbook. **96–7**

Alberto Meda was born in Italy in 1945 and studied mechanical engineering at Milan Polytechnic. In 1973 he took up the position of technical director at Kartell. From 1979 he was consultant engineer and designer for Alias, Brevetti, CSI Colomo Design and Swatch Italia. He was a project director at Alfa Romeo from 1981 to 1985 and Professor of Production Technology at the Domus Academy, Milan form 1983 to 1987. Since he began working for Alias in 1987, three of his chair designs have selected for the collection of MoMA, New York and he has been awarded the Campasso d'Oro in 1989 and 1994. **33, 36, 68**

Metalarte was founded in 1991 by Alberto Lievore, Jeanette Altherr and Manel Molina. Alberto Lievore was born in Buenos Aires, Argentina, in 1948 and studied architecture. After moving to Barcelona, he was involved in the set up of several influential design groups, including SIDI. Jeanette Altherr was born in Heidelberg in 1965 and in 1989, after graduating in Industrial Design, she began work with Alberto Lievore. Born in 1963, Manel Molina is from Barcelona and after graduating in Interior and Industrial Design he worked as a freelance designer. Metalarte is currently working for companies throughout Europe including Thonet, Disform, Perobell and Arper. They work in interior design, packaging design, product design, consultancy and art projects. **118**

Vanessa Mitrani was born in 1973 and studied at the Ecole Superieure Internationale D'Administration des Enterprises and the Ecole Nationale Superieure des Arts Decoratifs, specializing in furniture design. In 1999/2000 she spent a semester at the National Institute of Design, Ahmedabad, India, as part of an exchange programme. Professionally, she has been active in graphic design and in 1998/1999 worked with Pedro Veloso, the master glass-maker. Recently she has been working with Ligne Roset. **151**

Luigi Molinis was born in Udine in 1940 and studied architecture in Venice. He started working for Zanussi in 1969 and was head of industrial design in he electronics department for ten years. Since 1980 he has worked freelance and is based in Pordenone with a client list which includes Zanussi, Radio Marelli, Ceramica Dolomite and Rhoss. **198**

José Rafael Moneo was born in Navarra, Spain, in 1937 and graduated from Madrid's Technical School of Architecture in 1961. In 1970 he was made Professor of Architectural Theory at the Technical School of Architecture in Barcelona, where he taught until his return to Madrid in 1980. In 1984 he was appointed chairman of the Architecture Department at Harvard University and in 1990 named Josep Luis Sert Professor in Architecture. Among his best-known works are the Pilar and Joan Miro Foundation in Majorca, the Davis Art Museum, Massachusetts, the Museum of Modern Art and Architecture in Stockholm, the Auditorium in Barcelona and the Kursaal Auditorium and Congress Centre in San Sebastian (1999). **54**

Mauro Mori was born in Cromona, Italy, in 1965, and lives in Parma. He trained in architecture but works mostly in carving, especially in wood. Inspiration is gained from frequent travelling and recent clients include Cappellini. **20, 38**

Jasper Morrison was born in London in 1959. He studied design at Kingston Polytechnic, the Royal College of Art, London and the Hochschule der Kunste, Berlin. In 1986 he set up his Office for Design in London. He has designed furniture and products for companies including Alessi, Alias, Cappellini, Flos, FSB, Magis, SCP, Rosenthal and Vitra. In 1995 his office was awarded the contract to design the new Hannover tram for Expo 2000. The first vehicle was presented to the public in 1997 at the Hannover Industrial Fair and was awarded the IF Transportation Design Prize and the Ecology Award. Recent projects include furniture design for Tate Modern, London. Morrison's designs are in the collections of museums worldwide, including MoMA, New York. **38, 120, 171**

Benny Mosimann was born in Baden in 1966 and studied interior and product design at the Zurich Design School. From 1990 to 1993 he was senior designer at Greutmann Bolzern. He then spent a year travelling around the world before studying graphic design at Basel Design School. In 1998 he founded his own studio whose focus is product design, graphic design and fair and exhibition design. **76**

Pascal Mourgue was born in 1943 in Neuilly-sur-Seine, Paris and is a graduate of the Ecole Nationale Supérieure des Arts Décoratifs. He started his career at Prisunic. During the 1980s, when he was working independently, he started long-standing collaborations with several companies including Fermob, artelano, Roset, Toulemonde-Bochart, Scarabat and Cassina. He has since designed for Cartier and Baccarat; private homes for clients; shops for Roset in Chicago, Miami and Munich; and graphics for the Musée de la Poste in Paris. He has exhibited widely within Europe and in 1984 was elected 'Designer of the Year' by the Salon du Meuble de Paris. He received the Grand Prix de la Creation de la Ville de Paris in 1992 the Grand Prix de la Critique du Meuble Contemporain (1996) and the Grand Prix National de la Creation Industrielle (1996). Mourgue's work is in the permanent collection of the Musée des Arts Décoratifs in Paris. He produces sculptures, many of which have been exhibited worldwide. **26, 60, 168**

Gabriela Nahlikova has worked with Leona Matejkova since 1996. Both attended the Academy of Art, Architecture and Design in Prague, studying in the design studio of Borek Sipek. Nahlikova spent a further year at the Academie Bellende Kunsten in Maastricht. They have exhibited widely. **27, 28, 74**

Paola Navone was born in Turin in 1950. She graduated in architecture from Turin Polytechnic, her dissertation being published by Bruno Orlandini as Architettura Radicale. She worked for Alessandro Mendini, Ettore Sottsass and Andrea Branzi and as part of the the experimental groups 'Global Tools' and 'Alchimia' for whom she arranged major cultural events at the Venice Biennale of 1980. She was consultant art director to Centrokappa form 1975 to 1979 and has worked as a researcher at Centro Domus. She has acted as a consultant to Abet Laminati where she was responsible for market studies, product development and communication strategies. Other clients include Alessi, Knoll International and Fiat Auto. In 1985 she founded the manufacturing company Mondo with Giulio Cappellini. **20, 130**

Marc Newson was born in Sydney, Australia, where he studied jewellery and sculpture. He started experimenting in furniture design at college where he staged his first exhibition. In 1987 he moved to Japan and in 1991 set up a studio in Paris in 1991, working for clients such as Cappellini and Moroso. He formed a joint venture Ikepod Watch Company which manufactured a range of watches as well as aluminium furniture such as the 'Event Horizon' table and 'Orgone' chair. Since the mid-1990s he has become increasingly involved in interior design and was responsible for restaurants such as Coast in London, Mash & Air in Manchester and Osman in Cologne. In 1997 he moved to London and set up Marc Newson Ltd; he has since become involved in wider range of mass-manufactured items for Alessi, littala and Magis. He has also designed the livery and interior of the $40 million Falcon 9008 long range private jet. His designs have won many prizes and can be seen in major design collections around the world. A monograph published by Booth-Clibborn Editions was published in 1999. **128, 160, 223**

Nucleo is a team of young designers based in Torino, Italy. Now four years old, they concentrate on product and industrial design, with the aim of designing items which allow clients to use their own sense of creativity. **144**

On Industriedesign is a German design team which consists of Klaus Nolting and Andreas Ostwald. Both were born in 1964 and studied at the Fachhochschule Kiel. They have worked for various design bodies. On Industriedesign's clients include Rolf Benz, Classicon, FSM Frank Sitzmobel, Hoffmeister Leuchten and Pieper Concept. **124**

One Foot Taller are Katarina Barac and Will White. Both studied product design at Glasgow School of Art and are based in Scotland. They exhibited in New York in 2000. **30**

Oz Design was founded in 1997 by Ely Rozenberg, Michael Garelick and Alessandro Bianchini who were born in Russia, Israel and Italy respectively. The group is dedicated to design which uses only the latest materials and technologies. They exhibited for the first time in Milan in 1998. Rozenberg studied industrial design at the Bezalel Academy of Art and Design, Jerusalem. He is the design correspondent on the Biniyan ve Diur (interior design magazine) and in 1996 was awarded first prize by 'Ra'dad – the Israeli Cutlery Industry. Garelick also graduated in industrial design from Bezalel and then worked as head designer in the Bible Lands Museum, Jerusalem. He has been awarded the American Israel Foundation 'Sharet Grant' on three occasions and has also received the Brandeburg Prize for his innovative furniture designs. Bianchini studied architecture and industrial design in Venice and Rome and works on interior design projects. Since 1994 he has collaborated with various companies in Italy including Soft Line for whom he designed the 'Igloo' bed. **137**

Satyendra Pakhalé was born in India in 1967 but has been based in Europe since 1992. He studied industrial design in Bombay and then at the Art Centre College of Design in Switzerland. From 1995 to 1998 he was senior product designer at New Business Creation, Philips Design. He worked on a concept car which was a collaboration between Philips and Renault. In 1998 he established Atelier Satyendra Pakhalé in Amsterdam. He is active in fields ranging from industrial design to furniture, crafts to interior architecture, and his client list includes Curvet, Habitat, Magis, Mexx International, and Zeritalia. **157**

Ole Palsby was born in Copenhgen in 1935 and worked in finance until 1960 when he became a producer of home furnishings; in 1964 he opened an art gallery. Until 1968 he worked with a graphic designer, developing new marketing concepts and advertising programmes for design projects. In 1975 he began working as an independent designer and in 1986 opened a studio in London. He won both the Stuttgart Centre of Design Prize and the Japanese Design Prize. He has worked for many prestigious companies and won the If Product Ecology Design Award 2000. His work is held in museums and design centres worldwide. **136**

Verner Panton was born in Denmark in 1926 and studied architecture at the Royal Art Academy in Copenhagen between 1947 and 1951. From 1950 to 1952 he worked in Arne Jacobsen's architectural studio, opening his own studio in 1955. The winner of several important awards for design, he created the Panton Chair for Vitra in 1969, the Swatch Art Clock Tower in Lausanne (1996) and an interior for Erco Lighting, London (1997). A fellow of the Royal Society of Arts, Panton died in 1998. Major retrospectives were held at the Design Museum in London in 1999 and at the Vitra Design Museum, Weil am Rhein in 2000. **37**

Jiri Pelcl was born in 1950 in Czechoslovakia. He studied architecture at the Academy of Applied Art in Prague and furniture design at the Royal College of Art, London. He is the founder of the design Group ATIKA and in 1990 set up his own studio, Atelier Pelcl. Major commissions include Vaclav Havel's study in Prague Castle, St Laurence Church, Prague and the Czech Embassies in Rome and Pretoria. He has exhibited in galleries throughout the world and has been head of the School of Architecture and Design at the Academy of Applied Art in Prague since 1997. **80**

Maurizio Peregalli was born in Varese in 1951. He studied in Milan and began to work on fashion shops and showrooms including the Giorgio Armani boutiques in Milan and London as well as on the image of the chain Emporio Armani. In 1984 he founded the furniture collection Zeus where he works today as Partner and Art Director. He is also a Director of Noto which produces Zeus. **111**

Dominique Perrault is an architect, known for his refined and austere high-tech style. Born in Clermont-Ferrand, France, in 1953, he studied at the Ecole Supérieure des Beaux Artes, the Ecole Supérieure des Ponts et Education and the Ecole des Hautes Etudes en Sciences Sociales, graduating in 1980. Notable works include the Bibliothèque Nationale, Paris; the Ecole Supérieure, Marne-La-Valée; and the Olympic Velodrome, Berlin. **122**

Christophe Pillet was born in 1959 and studied in Nice and the Domus Academy, Milan. After graduating, he collaborated with Martine Bedin and Philippe Starck but has been working alone since 1993. He was named Designer of the Year in 1994 and is active in furniture design, product design, interior design, architecture and set design. His clients include, Cappellini, Moet et Chandon, Lancôme, Bally and Moroso. **119, 212**

Giancarlo Piretti was born in Bologna in 1940. He studied and later taught interior design at the Institute of Art in Bologna after which he spent 12 years as a furniture designer for Castelli SpA. In 1998 he launched the Piretti Collection, which is a highly successful office seating programme. He has twice won the Compasso D'Oro, and in 1997 launched the Torsion Collection. **36**

Paolo Piva was born in Italy in 1950 and studied architecture in Venice. He also studied in Vienna, where he now teaches at the Academy Of Applied Arts. He has designed for renowned furniture companies and for buildings. Since 1974 he has had a close association with Wittmann GmbH, Germany. **44**

Tim Power is an American architect/designer who has been living and working in Milan since 1990. Born in California in 1962, he studied architecture at the California Polytechnic State University. Having spent periods in the studios of Sottsass Associati, Superstudio and I.O.O.A., he opened his own studio in 1995. Clients include Zeritalia, Cassina/Interdecor, BRF, Poltronova, WMF, Rosenthal, and Fontana Arte. Recently his practice has begun expanding into interior and architecture work for clients in the art, media and advertising worlds. **66**

Christopher Procter and Fernando Rihl both studied at the Architectural Association in London. They are well-known for their experimental work in the use of live-edge acrylic in furniture design. Before collaboration, Procter worked with Rick Mather and Paolo Solari and the engineer Tim McFarlane; and Rihl collaborated with the landscape architect Burle Marx. They worked with Zaha Hadid on panels for the Interbuild Blueprint Pavilion and in 1996 were commissioned to design acrylic partitions for five shops in central London. Procter and Rihl's work can be seen in the design collection of MoMA, New York. They are currently designing for industry with projects underway with North American, Swedish, Italian and Brazilian companies. They are also working on several residential and commercial projects in London and a beach house in Brazil. **79**

Emaf Progetti was set up in 1982. Its chief activites are design, installations and communication for furniture makers. Its products have won awards and are owned by various museums. **48**

Emma Quickenden graduated from Kingston University's Product and Furniture course in 1999. Since then she has exhibited in London, New York and Milan and is now working freelance. Her designs reinterpret aspects from traditional domestic living. **221**

Karim Rashid was born in Cairo in 1960 and graduated in industrial design from Carleton University in Ottawa, Canada in 1982. After graduate studies in Italy he moved to Milan for a one-year scholarship in the studio of Rodolfo Bonetto. On his return to Canada he worked for seven years with KAN Industrial Designers in Toronto. Rashid was a full-time associate professor of industrial design at the University of Arts in Philadelphia for six years and has also taught at the Pratt Institute, the Rhode Island School of Design and Ontario College of Art. Since 1992 he has been principal designer for Karim Rashid Industrial Design in New York, designing products, lighting, tableware and furniture. He has won many awards including the 1999 George Nelson Award as well as the Silver IDEA Award for the Oh Chair. His work has been exhibited in museums internationally, including MoMA, New York; the Chicago Athenaeum; and the Design Museum, London. He recently held a show at the Sandra Gering Gallery called '5 Senses', exhibiting 120 limited edition ceramic sculptures and 3 Blobject sculptures. **18, 32, 98, 99, 152**

Emmanuele Ricci was born in Treviso, Italy, in 1963. He studied at Milan Polytechnic and spent a period with the architect Gianfranco Frattini, after which he set up as an independent designer. He divides his time between a studio in Milan and the Treviso hills where he carries out artistic research. Among past and present clients are Alfa Romeo SpA, Artemide SpA, Fiat SpA, Chrysler, Lorenzo Rubelli SpA, Cassina, Dolomite, Lumina and Studio Thun. **166–7**

Paolo Rizzatto was born in Milan in 1941 and graduated in architecture from Milan Polytechnic. He founded Luceplan in 1978 with Riccardo Sargatti, and from 1985 to 1987 he designed for Busnelli and Molteni and was also involved with interior architecture, planning and exhibitions, and interior design for private residences. Today he works as a freelance designer. He has collaborated with many leading manufacturers and has exhibited his work worldwide. Examples can be seen in the permanent collection of MoMA, New York. In 1990 he was invited to Japan to represent Italian design in the exhibition 'Creativitalia' in Tokyo. He has been awarded the Compasso d'Oro on three occasions: in 1981 for his lamp D7, in 1989 for the Lola lamp series produced for Luceplan and in 1995 for the Metropoli lamp series, again for Luceplan. Rizzatto has taught at various university institutes including Columbia University in New York, Milan Polytechnic, Washington University in Saint Louis and the Cranbrook Academy of Art in Michigan. **45, 68**

Hannes Rohringer was born in Austria. He lives and works as a designer/artist in Seewalchen and Vienna, where he graduated with an MA in Fine Art from the Hochschule für Angewandte Kunst. In 1989 he founded the Atrium studio which specializes in architecture, product design and applied art. His work is in the collections of various museums and his client list includes Duravit, Miele, Porsche Design, Molto Luce, Streitner and DCW Software. **77**

Marco Romanelli see Marta Laudani

Heinz Röntgen worked as a freelance designer and consultant for textile companies during the 1950s. Since 1964 he has been marketing his work through his company Nya Nordiska. Recently he has focused on design and product development of interior fabrics. He has won many awards, including the Red Dot Award from Westfalen for the last decade, and the IF Product Design Award (1997, 1998, 2000). His work is held by the Chicago Athenaeum. **172, 173**

Designer Biografien und Register

Ely Rozenberg was born in the Soviet Union in 1967 and emigrated to Israel in 1977. Rozenberg studied industrial design at the Bezalel Academy of Art and Design, Jerusalem. He is the design correspondent on the Biniyan ve Diur (an interior design magazine) and in 1996 was awarded first prize by 'Radad' – the Israeli Cutlery Industry. **25, 136**

Petra Runge is a graphic artist and designer who lives and works in Cologne. She was born in 1957 in Hannover and studied art and psychology. From 1987 to 1993 she worked mostly in France, on multidisciplinary cooperative projects. From 1994 she has worked as a graphic artist and designer for companies such as De Padova srl. **82**

Joan Gaspar Ruiz is an industrial designer who lives and works in Barcelona. He was born in 1966 and studied at the Escuela de Artes y Oficios Artisticos in his native city. He developed his first lighting products for Vapor and since 1991 has worked for Disform, Santa & Cole, Sellex, Eurast and B-Lux. In 1996 he began working for Marset Illuminacion as the development and design director and also teaches at the Industrial Design School in Barcelona. **124**

Junichi Saitou was born in Japan in 1965. He studied industrial design and joined Sharp Corporation in 1985, where he has designed video products. **183**

Kasper Salto was born in Denmark in 1967 and qualified as a cabinetmaker in 1988. In 1994 he graduated from the Danish Design School. Since 1996 he has taught at the Royal Academy of Fine Art in Copenhagen while his furniture designs have won several awards including the ID prize in 1999. **33, 42**

Thomas Sandell was born in 1959 in Finland. In 1981, after National Service, he studied architecture in Stockholm and in 1989 set up his own practice. He has worked on many prestigious interior and product design projects for clients such as Cappellini, IKEA, KLM, Swiss Air, Kallemo, B&B Italia, the Modern Museum in Stockholm and Ericsson. He has taught widely and as a winner of many awards is represented in both British and Swedish museums. **174**

Santos and Adolfsdóttir was founded by Margaret Adolfsdóttir and Leo Santos-Shaw who met while studying at Middlesex Polytechnic, UK. Before forming their practice, Adolfsdóttir worked as a freelance fashion textile designer selling through agents in the USA to Calvin Klein and Perry Ellis. Santos-Shaw worked as a full-time assistant jeweller to Pete Change and then worked on a freelance basis selling to the USA, Europe and Japan. He was an in-house designer for Thierry Mugler in Paris. Santos and Adolfsdóttir produce interior textiles and surface design. Clients include Barneys, New York and Japan, and Whistles, London. They produce and market a range of scarfs which sell in Germany, Austria and at selected outlets in London. **174**

Patrizia Scarzella is an architect and journalist. She was on the editorial staff of Domus from 1980 to 1986 and worked with leading design firms. The author of several books, she was Zanotta's corporate image and communications consultant from 1985 to 1996. **56**

Jürgen Schmidt was born in 1956. He established Design Tech in 1983 and is the author of several books. He has won the Braun Award for technical design and the VDID award of design for the disabled. He is a member of the iF Hannover 2001 design jury. **205**

Henrik Schulz is a member of the Copenhagen-based group -ing. He studied architecture in Gothenburg, design in Copenhagen and architecture at the Royal Danish Academy of Fine Arts, graduating in 2000. Schulz has exhibited in Stockholm, Copenhagen, London and Milan. **24**

Iwan Seiko was born in 1951 in Croatia and studied philosophy in Zagreb. He now lives in Munich and works as a painter, artist and sculptor. **94**

Kazuyo Sejima is an internationally-known architect. She was born in Japan in 1956 and graduated in 1981 in architecture from the Japan Women's University. She joined Toyo Ito and Associates but set up her own practice, Kazuyo Sejima and Associates, in 1987. Her work is characterized by its poetic tone combined with modern architecture and the use of materials like glass, aluminium, metallic grilles and plastics. She has won many international awards and famous works include the Platform House series, the N-House, the Y-House and the Villa in the Forest. Recent projects include the O-Museum, Usika New Station Building, the Museum of Contemporary Art of Sydney Extension and the restoration of the historic centre of Salerno, Italy, for which she won a prize in 1999. **51**

Richard Shemtov graduated from Parsons School of Design in 1990. A native of New York, he founded the International Design Supply Corporation (IDS) in 1991 to showcase his work in interior and furniture design. His interior design work has included a spa, a restaurant and the Madison Avenue branch of Dolce & Gabbana. In 1996 he founded Dune, designing furniture and prototypes for retail and individual designers and in 1998 launched his own furniture line at the ICFF. In 1999 he formed a collaboration with other American designers, Nick Dine, Jeffrey Bernett and Harry Allen and is expanding Dune. **61**

Asahara Sigeaki was born in Tokyo in 1948 and studied in Torino, Italy. Since 1973 he has worked as a freelance industrial designer and in 1992 received the 'I.F. Best of Category' prize at the Hannover Exhibition. He is active between Italy and Japan and is permanently represented in the Brooklyn Museum of New York. **121**

Tuttu Sillanpää was born in Finland in 1967 and graduated with an MA from the University of Art and Design, Helsinki. In addition to teaching art and textile design at Helsinki Secondary School of Visual Arts, she has worked as a designer for the Italian company Ratti SpA. and since 1998 the Finnish company Verso Design. Her work has been exhibited in Italy, France, the UK and Scandinavia. **174**

Claudio Silvestrin was born in 1954 and trained in Milan at AG Fronzoni. He completed his studies at the Architectural Association in London where he now lives and works. He teaches at the Bartlett School of Architecture in London and at the Ecole Supérieure d'Art Visuels in Lausanne. Some of his most important works include shops for Giorgio Armani (Paris), the offices, shops and home for Calvin Klein (Paris, Milan and New York) and works for museums and art galleries. **40, 214, 215**

Borek Sipek was born in Prague in 1948. He studied architecture in Hamburg, philosophy in Stuttgart and architecture in Delft. In 1983 he moved to Amsterdam and started his own studio. Projects include the Tsjeck Pavilion for the World Exhibition 2000 in Hannover, objects for Driade, Scarabas and Vitra. He received La Croix Chevalier dans l'Ordre des Arts et des Lettres from the French government in 1992 and in the same year was appointed Court Architect in Prague. He is currently engaged on projects in Prague. **130, 142, 149**

Barbora Skorpilova was born in 1972 and studied architecture in Prague, under Borek Sipek. Since graduating in 1997 she has worked with Jiri Pelcl. From 1994 she has worked with Elle Décor, Esquire and Harper's Bazaar and, since 1996, with Jan Nedved (b.1973) who also studied under Borek Sipek. In 1999 they founded Studio Mimolimit together. **140**

Smart Design's Director of Design Engineering is Clay Burns. He graduated from Dartmouth College in 1987, and took an MA at Tufts University in 1989. He began his career with Product Genesis, Massachusetts and then moved to New York where he worked as an independent consultant for some time, specializing in product engineering and ergonomics. Recent projects include development of technologies for athletic footwear, cushioning, research and testing of new household firesafes and improvement of grip and vibration attenuation for hammer handles. **210**

Snowcrash design team is based in Stockhom and has emerged as one of the most innovative design companies of recent years. It has explored new material and technologies to great effect in conjunction with the information and communications boom and regularly exhibit in Milan. **100**

Michael Sodeau studied product design at Central Saint Martin's College of Art and Design. He was a founder partner of Inflate in 1995 but left in 1997 to set up a new partnership with Lisa Giuliani. He launched his first collection of furniture and homeware, Comfortable Living, in 1997. **169**

Michael Solis was born in Dallas, Texas, but now lives and works in New York where he runs his own furniture/product studio, WORX. He graduated from Parsons School of Design in 1991. In 1995 he launched his first line of furniture and home accessories at the New York International Contemporary Furniture Fair and in 1996 won the Editor's Award for Best New Designer. Recently he has been working with Nick Dine and also shows at Totem, New York. His work has been included in publications worldwide. **61**

Peter Solomon graduated from Pratt Institute, New York in 1988. Until 1993 he lived in California, designing museums, computers, furniture, lighting, toys and interiors. He then moved to Milan to obtain an MA at the Domus Academy and subsequently established a studio. For over six years he has collaborated with Isao Hosoe and designs a range of products from telephones to furniture, lighting and sporting equipment to interiors. **93**

Ettore Sottsass was born in Innsbruck, Austria, in 1917, and graduated in architecture from Turin University in 1939. In 1947 he opened an architecture and design studio in Milan. In 1958 he began working with Olivetti as a consultant, designing the first Italian computer in 1959. In 1981 he and various colleagues formed Memphis. The following year he founded Sottsass Associati, where he still works as an architect and designer. Sottsass holds honorary degrees from the Royal College of Art, London and the Rhode Island School of Design while the Centre George Pompidou, Paris held a major retrospective of his life and works in 1994. His works form part of the collection of major museums worldwide and he is internationally recognized as a giant of innovative design. **79, 154**

Hanspeter Steiger was born in Switzerland in 1970. He served an apprenticeship as a furniture-maker before undertaking study at the Schule fur Gestaltung, Basel, the National College of Art and Design, Oslo and the Danish Design School in Copenhagen. He has exhibited in Milan and Copenhagen and won several prizes for his work. Steiger is also a member if the -ing group. **24**

Philippe Starck was born in Paris in 1949 and trained at the Ecole Camondo in Paris. After a spell in New York he returned to France where he has built up an international reputation. He has been responsible for interior design schemes for François Mitterrand's apartment at the Elysée Palace, the Café Costes, and the Royalton and Paramount Hotels in New York. He has also created domestic and public multi-purpose buildings such as the headquarters of Asahi Beer in Tokyo, the Ecole Nationale Supérieure des Arts Décoratifs in Paris, and the air traffic control tower for Bordeaux Airport. As a product designer he collaborates with Alessi, Baleri, Baum, Disform, Driade, Flos, Kartell, Rapsel, Up & Up, Vitra and Vuitton. From 1993 to 1996 he was worldwide artistic director for the Thomson Consumer Electronics Group. Awards include the Grand Prix National de la Création Industrielle and his work can be seen in the permanent collections of all the major design museums. In 1997 he completed hotels in Miami and Los Angeles, and in 1998 the Canary Riverside Hotel in London, a hotel in Bali, the restaurant in the Hilton Hotel in Singapore and an incineration plant in Paris/Vitry. In 1999/2000 he finished two central London hotels for the Ian Schrager group and is now working on hotels in New York, San Francisco and Santa Barbara. **32, 101**

Norma Starszakowna is Director of Research at the London College of Fashion. She has taught widely and sat on many advisory boards, including those of the Design Council and the British Academy. She has been closely involved in the production of textiles for public and commercial bodies including Issey Miyake; Nuno Co, Tokyo; Fitch and Co; General Accident Assurance Co; and the Scottish Arts Council. Her work has been exhibited widely in the UK and abroad, is held in many private collections and she has been the recipient of various awards. **165**

Asher Stern was born in Jerusalem in 1972. After completing a diploma in jewellery making he studied at Bezalel Academy of Art and Design, Jerusalem, graduating in 2000. In the same year he exhibited in Milan. **205**

Stile Bertone SpA was founded in 1971 by the Nuccio Bertone. Bertone itself was founded in 1912. In 2000 Stile Berone and Tecno design formed the Bertone Design Machine, a team of specialists utilizing states of the art technologies. They are involved in vehicle design and industrial design, from fork lift trucks to dental chairs, aircraft interiors to mountain bikes. **223**

Reiko Sudo was born in Ibaraki Prefecture, Japan, and educated at the Musashino University of Art. From 1975 to 1977 she assisted Professor Tanaka in the textile department. Before co-founding Nuno Corporation in 1984, she worked as a freelance textile designer and has since designed for the International Wool Secretariat, Paris and Threads, Tokyo. She is the director of Nuno Corporation and a lecturer at the Musashino University of Art. Her work can be seen in the permanent collections of MoMA, New York; the Cooper-Hewitt National Design Museum, New York; the Museum of Art, Rhode Island School of Design; the Philadelphia Museum of Art; the Museum of Applied Arts, Helsinki; and the Musée des Arts Décoratifs, Montreal. Recent exhibitions include the 'Tokyo Creation Festival', Tokyo, 'The Textile Magician' show at the Israel Museum of Modern Art; 'Japanese Textile Design' at the Indira National Centre for Arts in India and 'Structure and Surface: Contemporary Japanese Textiles' at MoMA, New York. She has received many prizes for her work, including the Roscoe Award in 1993 and 1994. **176–7**

Shinichi Sumikawa was born in Tokyo in 1962. After graduating from Cdhiba University's Industrial Design Department in 1984, he joined Sony as a product designer working on Walkmans, radios, headphones and TV. In 1992 he established Sumikawa Design in Tokyo and has been designing communication tools, cars, medical equipment and sports gear. **207**

Marco Susani and Mario Trimarchi are architects and industrial designers and have been working together since 1986, developing various projects including house appliances, kitchen tools, lamps, furniture and corporate identity. They are responsible for the art direction fro Serafino Zani, also developing its new corporate identity. **143**

Martin Szekely is one of France's best-known designers. He has exhibited in Europe, the US and Japan and clients include: Swarovski, Cassina, Hermès, Perrier and Montina. He is working for Hermès, SNCF and Dom Pérignon. Szekely's work is in the collections of major museums in the US, Germany, France and Israel; in 1998 he was included in 'Premises', an exhibition of the four most famous French designers at the Guggenheim Museum, New York. He was awarded the title of Chevalier of Arts and Letters in 1999. **83, 220**

Tomoki Taira was born in Japan in 1971. He studied industrial design in Osaka, graduating in 1991. He then joined Sharp and is in charge of product design development at the Corporate Design Centre and Appliances Design Centre. **199**

Yumiko Takeshita was born in Japan in 1962. In 1985 she graduated in Industrial Design from the Women's University of Art and joined Sharp Corporation. Her preferred field is home appliances and since 1995 she has worked at the corporate design centre in charge of advance design and special projects. **183**

Carlo Tamborini was born in Milan in 1958 and studied there at the European Institute of Design. After graduation in 1993 he worked freelance on interior design projects. From 1997 to 2000 he worked with Lissoni Associati and in 1998 became a member of Codice 31, concentrating on product design. Recent projects have included product design for Palluco Italia and lighting for Fontane Arte. **82**

Pepe Tanzi was born in Monza, Italy, in 1945. He graduated from Milan Polytechnic and today works for Album as industrial designer on their range of lighting products. He also works on a freelance basis for numerous leading lighting manufacturers. **69**

Pascal Tarabay was born in Beirut in 1970. In 1998 he did an MA in design at the Domus Academy, Milan, under Andrea Branzi. The following year he worked as Andrea Branzi's project assistant and also for Donegani & Lauda and Aldo Cibic. Since 1993 he has been a freelance designer, numbering Salvatore Ferragamo, Radice, Driade and Beirut Municipality among his clients. He has won several prizes for his work and has exhibited in Milan and Cologne. **32, 42, 44**

Matteo Thun was born in Germany in 1952 and studied in Salzburg, then Florence where he received his PhD. In 1981, together with Ettore Sottsass, he founded Sottsass Associati and the Memphis design group. From 1983 to 1986 he was professor of design at the University of Applied Arts in Vienna and since 1984 has lived and worked in Milan. **98**

Jacob Timpe was born in Wurzburg, Germany in 1967. He studied architecture in Berlin and Darmstadt and worked as a freelance architect for various studios, winning several prizes. In 1999 he designed 'Tishbocktisch' for Nils Holger Moorman and is currently working as an assistant in the architectural department of the Technical University of Darmstadt. **60**

Pekka Tiovola was born in Finland in 1955 and studied at the University of Industrial Arts in Helsinki. Since 1986 he has worked for Martela and is a leading figure in office furniture design. He has won several awards, including the Gold Clip at the International Fair in Prague, 1997. **66**

Stephan Titz was born in Germany in 1971 and studied mechanical engineering before training as a cabinetmaker. From 1995 to 1997 he worked for MANUFORM Barbin and in 1998 completed an MA in Furniture design at the Savannah College of Art and Design. He currently works as a freelance designer for Natural Living of Austria and Team 7, while his work has been exhibited in New York, Cologne and Paris. **78**

Frank Tjepkema was born in Geneva in 1970. He studied industrial design at Delft University and went to the Design Academy, Eindhoven where his course included some study at the Royal College of Art, London. In 1998 he completed an MA at the Sandberg Institute, Amsterdam. From 1996 to 1998 he worked as an independent designer for Ollily and Pirelli among others. From 1998 to 1999 he worked as a junior art director for Bruggenwurth Maas en Boswinkel in Amsterdam whose clients include Adidas and Heineken. Since 1999 he has been working independently for several advertising, marketing and communication agencies in Amsterdam, the Switzerland-based Swatch group and Droog Design. **85**

TKO Product Design was founded by Andy Davey in 1990. He graduated from the Royal College of Art and has since designed for NEC, Canon and Sony among others, as well as creating eyewear for Seiko, lights for Daiko and toys for Hasbro. Davey was one of the first British designers to establish successful business links with Japanese manufacturers. TKO also works for major companies in the USA and Europe. Davey and his team have won many design prizes including the 1996 BBC Design Award for Best Product, the BBC Designer of the Year and Best of Category in the consumer products section of ID's Annual design review for the Freeplay clockwork radio. **186, 211**

Kazuhiko Tomita was born in Nagasaki, Japan, in 1965. He gained a B.Eng. in industrial design at Chiba University and in 1990 won a Cassina scholarship to study furniture design at the Royal College of Art, London. He was awarded first prize in the 'Architectural Future of Stainless Steel' competition and the MA RCA Marchette Award for his degree work 'Hadaka-no Piano, aria'. He has exhibited frequently at the Milan Furniture Fair as well as Abitare il Tempo. **200**

Luigi Trenti was born in Florence in 1965 and graduated from the Architecture University of Florence with a published and SMAU-awarded thesis on industrial design. He has worked as a product designer since 1989, specializing in lighting and instrumentation design. Clients include Targetti Sankey, Osram, General Electric, Martini, Radim Group and Pineider. In 1993 he was appointed chief of Industrial Design at Targetti Sankey who won the Compasso d'Oro in 1998. In 2000 he won the Young & Design Award. **208**

Oscar Tusquets Blanca is an architect, painter and designer. His works are in various permanent collections around the world. He has received numerous prizes and awards for architecture and design projects including the Chevalier de l'Ordre des Arts et des Lettres. In 1994 he published his first book as an essayist and has since written a second book. **154**

Shigeru Uchida was born in Japan in 1943 and graduated from the Kuwasawa Design School in Tokyo. In 1970 he established the Uchida Design Studio and since then has lectured worldwide. Commercial work has included a Seibu department store, the Wave Building, Roppongi, a shelf component system for Esprit, boutiques for Yohji Yamomoto and a clock for Alessi. Recent projects include the Kobe Fashion Museum, a hotel and an eyewear shop in Japan as well as design for Abet Laminati. He has exhibited widely and his work is held in many major design collections, including MoMA, New York. **55, 79**

Paolo Ulian (b. 1961) studied painting in Carrara followed by industrial design in Florence. From 1990 to 1992 he worked as an assistant at Enzo Mari's studio, then founded Paolo Ulian Industrial Design. He has exhibited widely and collaborates with international companies such as Driade, Segno, Progetti and Zani & Zani. **60, 103, 204**

Patricia Urquiola was born in Oviedo, Spain, in 1961. She studied architecture in Madrid and then at Milan Polytechnic, graduating in 1989. From 1990 to 1996 she worked with Vico Magistretti as a consultant for De Padova and from 1993 to 1996 she developed franchise projects with the architects Marta de Renzio and Emanuela Ramerino. In 1998 she became the design manager for Lissoni Associates, working with Cappellini, Porro and Cassina. Recent projects have included lighting, furniture and product designs for Moroso, Fasem, Bosa and Tronconi. **46**

Jaap van Aarkel was born in The Netherlands in 1967. He studied at the Industrial Design Academy, Eindhoven and since graduating in 1996 has exhibited in Milan, Rotterdam and Paris with Droog Design. **104**

Dick van Hoff was born in Amsterdam in 1971. He trained as a building worker and window dresser before studying three-dimensional design at the Hogeschool voor de Kunsten in Arnhem. In 1995 his tap Stop Kraan was taken up by Droog Design and he has since had several other pieces developed by them and DMD as well as Rosenthal and United Colors of Benetton. **221**

Christine van der Hurd studied textiles at Winchester College of Art, UK. After graduation she designed fabrics and home furnishings for clients such as Kenzo, Mary Quant, Biba, Cacharel, Liberty, Osborne & Little and Courtaulds. In 1976 she moved to New York and in 1980 began to specialize in carpeting. In 1981 she established the contemporary furniture store 'Modern Age' with her husband and in 1990 set up Christine van der Hurd Inc. She returned to the UK in 1997 and in 1998 Modern Age was relaunched as 'Cappellini-Modern Age', a flagship store for the Italian company. As well as being president of this venture, van der Hurd designed an exclusive range of rugs for Cappellini, launched at the 1999 Milan Furniture Fair. Christine van der Hurd Inc. is now based in London. **176**

Peter van der Jagt was born in The Netherlands in 1971 and studied 3D design in Arnhem. In 1996 he set up his own studio and has completed several projects for Droog Design and Authentics. His work has been displayed at exhibitions in Rotterdam, San Francisco, Berlin, Milan, Frankfurt, Cologne and London. In 1999 he won the Rotterdamse Designprijs and he currently works as a freelance industrial designer and creative consultant for several companies. **85**

Marijn van der Poll was born in The Netherlands in 1973. After moving around the Middle and Far East his family moved back to The Netherlands in 1993. He studied fine arts and interior design/architecture and is currently studying under Gijs Bakker at the Design Academy, Eindhoven. **85**

Jan van Lierde was born in The Netherlands in 1954. He studied architecture in Ghent and in 1978 set up his own practice, undertaking domestic and commercial projects in Belgium, Algeria, Egypt and Scotland. In 1983 he established Kreon in Beveren-waas, a company which offered advice and distributive trade in light fixtures and interior design. In 1984 Kreon moved to Antwerp and in 1986 exhibited the 'Metis' collection in Milan. **113, 133**

Maarten Van Severen is an interior and furniture designer. He is mainly active in the design of small-scale domestic and retail schemes and has recently completed the Maison à Floirac with the architect Rem Koolhaas and the interior entrance hall of the City Hall in Ghent. His furniture and lighting designs have been in production since 1997 and he now works for clients such as Vitra, Switzerland, U-line Lighting and Target Lighting in Belgium. He has exhibited his work in group shows throughout Europe. In 1998 he received the IF Design Award, Hanover for U-line and the Flemish government's design prize. He is a visiting professor at the Academy of Fine Arts in Maastricht. **44, 80**

Luc Vincent was born in 1952. After graduating in both Interior Architecture and Journalism, he worked on product development for companies such as Habitat, Casa and La Maison. From 1987 to 1992 he helped develop Barcelona Airport, the Swift Building, J.C Decaux Building, and the Rochas building as well as products for Cassina, Alessi and Cartier. For the past ten years he has owned an interior architecture bureau in Brussels which participated in the building of the European Parliament and has developed products for Modular Lighting Instruments, Obumex and Totem. **114–5**

Roderick Vos was born in 1965 in The Netherlands and studied industrial design in Eindhoven. He worked for Kenji Ekuans GK in Tokyo and then for Ingo Maurer in Munich before founding his own studio, Studio Masaupertuus, with Claire Vos-Teeuwen. The client portfolio includes Espaces et Lignes, Driade, Authentics and Alessi while work has been shown at the Milan, Cologne and New York furniture fairs. **16, 17, 220**

Norbert Wangen was born in 1962 in Prum, Germany, and served a carpenter's apprenticeship before studying sculpture and architecture in Dusseldorf, Aachen and Munich. In 1991 he graduated in architecture from the Technical University in Munich and worked as a set designer. In 1995 the folding armchair Atilla became part of the 'Die Neue Sammlung Munchen' and in 1997 became part of the Vitras Design Museum collection. The kitchen was presented at the Milan Furniture Fair in 2000. **216**

Carol Westfall graduated from the Rhode Island School of Design in 1960 and Maryland Institute College of Art in 1972 after which she undertook diverse postgraduate study in the USA, Mexico, India and Japan. Currently a Professor at Montclair State University, New Jersey, her work has been exhibited worldwide, awarded various prizes and is held in many collections. **175**

Hannes Wettstein works in product design, corporate design, interior design and architecture. He was born in Switzerland in 1958 and started off doing freelance work. He then joined the Eclat Design Agency as a partner. In 1993 he co-founded 9D Design and he also teaches, having held a professorial chair at the Academy of Design in Karlshule since 1994. He has won many awards and notable projects include the Swiss Embassy in Tehran and the Grand Hyatt Hotel in Berlin. His varied list of clients has recently numbered Cassina, UMS Pastoe, Shimano, Baleri Italia and Artemide. **26, 45, 72, 187**

Peter Wheeler is a partner in the design studio Bius. His background is in designing furniture for manufacture while Mary Little designs one-offs. Bius design unique furniture to commission for public art, corporate and private clients. Its work is in many public collections, including Manchester City Art Galleries and Museums, UK and Museo de las artes decoratives, Barcelona, Spain. **27**

Sachio Yamamoto was born in Japan in 1950 and graduated in industrial design from Musashino Art University in Tokyo in 1975. He then joined Sharp Corporation where he has been in charge of product design development in the field of home appliances, audio and communication products. Since 1999 he has been a chief designer in charge of advance design development. **183**

Kazuhiro Yamanaka was born in 1971 and studied furniture design in Tokyo, then interior design at the Royal College of Art, London. In 1999 he won the 100% Design/Crafts Council Bursary Award. **112**

Paolo Zani was born in Italy in 1960. He studied Industrial Design in Faenza and then took an MA at the Domus Academy, Milan, finishing in 1987. As an independent designer he has worked in many areas for many companies such as Ross El, Winterling and Bareuther, Optly Holding, Schopenhauer, Fontanaarte, Moroso and Mont Blanc. Since 1991 he has been a member of the Domus Design Agency and exhibits frequently in Europe and Japan. **155**

Hersteller

Abet Laminati spa.
Viale Industriale 21, 12042 BRA, Italy.
T. (+39)0172 419 111 F. (+39)0172 431 571
E. abet@abet-laminati.it **79, 80**

Acerbis International S.p.A
Via Brusaporto 31, 24068 Seriate (BG), Italy.
T. (+39)035 294 222 F. (+39)035 291 454
E. info@acerbisinternational.com **49**

Agape srl
Via Ploner 2, 46038 Mantova, Italy.
T. (+39)0376 371 738 F. (+39)0376 374 213
E. agape@interbusiness.it **218**

Agora e Moda
R. Alvaro Annes 79, 05421-010 Sao Paulo, Brazil.
T. (+55)11 2123168 F. (+55)11 69124841 **103**

Album s.r.l
Via Leoncavallo 7, 200052 Monza (MI), Italy.
T. (+39)039 389745 F. (+39)039 230 2433
E. album@album.it **69**

Alcatel Telecom
32 Avenue Kleber, 92707 Colombes, Cedex, France.
T. (+33)1 55 66 7961 F. (+33)1 55 66 7495
E. Anne.Bigand@alcatel.fr **186**

Aliantedizione snc
Via G. Foschiani 7, 33044 Manzano (UD), Italy.
T./F. (+39)0432 75 12 76
E. aliantedizioni@libero.it **93**

Alias srl
Via dei Videtti 2, 24064 Grumello del Monte, Bergamo, Italy.
T. (+39)035 44 22 511 F. (+39)035 44 22 50
E. info@aliasdesign.it **26, 36, 45, 81**

Alessi SpA
Via Privata Alessi 6, Crusinallo, Verbania (VB), Italy.
T. (+39)323 86 86 11 F. (+39)323 86 61 32
E. pub@alessi.it **138, 139, 200, 218, 219**

Antonangeli illuminazione srl
Via Volterra 10, 20052 Monza (MI), Italy.
T. (+39)039 2720552 F. (+39)039 2720796
E. antoill@tin.it **104**

Anthologie Quartett
Schloss Hünefeld, 49152 Bad Essen, Germany.
T. (+49)5472 940 90 F. (+49)5472 940 940 **149**

Apple Computer Inc.
20730 Valley Green Drive
Cupertino 95014, California, USA.
T. (+1)650 728 0530 F. (+1)415 495 0251 **188, 189**

Ron Arad Associates Ltd
62 Chalk Farm Road, London NW1 8AN, UK.
T. (+44)207 284 4963/5 F. (+44)207 279 0499
E. ronarad@mail.pro-net.co.uk **141**

Arflex International SpA
Via Don R. Bereta 12, 20034 Guissano, Italy.
T. (+39)0362 85343 F. (+39)0362 853080
E. info@arflex.it **45**

Arnolfi di Cambio, Compagnia Italiana del Cristallo srl
53034 Colle di Val d'Elsa, Siena Loc. Pian dell'Olmino, Italy
T. (+39)577 9282 79 F. (+39)577 92 96 47
E. dicambo@cyber.dada.it **132, 148, 154**

Artelano
4 Rue Schoelcher, 75014 Paris, France.
T. (+33)1 43 22 74 91 F. (+33)1 43 22 84 49
E. artelano@aol.com **60**

Artemide SpA
Via Canova 34, 20145 Milan, Italy.
T. (+39)2 34 96 11 1 F. (+39)2 34 53 82 11
E. pr@artemide.com **88, 116, 118**

Arzenal, Valentinska
1100 Prague 1, Czech Republic.
T. (+42)2 248 14099 F. (+42)2 2481 0722
E. galerie@arzenal.cz **130, 142, 149**

Asplund
31 Sibyllegatan, Stockholm 11442, Sweden.
T. (+46)8 662 52 84 F. (+46)8 662 38 35 **161, 174**

Atelier Pelcl
Farskeho 8, 17000 Prague, Czech Republic.
T. (+42)02 878869
E. atelier@pelcl.cz **80**

Atrox GmbH
Seeblick 1, Cham, 6330, Switzerland.
T. (+41)41 785 0410 F. (+41)41 785 0419
E. atrox@datazug.ch **162, 163**

Bahnsen Collection
Holmevej 10, 5683 Haarby, Denmark.
T. (+45)6 473 1188 F. (+45)6 473 1178 **74, 75**

Baleri Italia
Via F. Cavalotti 8, 20122 Milan, Italy.
T. (+39)2 76 01 46 72 F. (+39)2 76 01 44 19
E. info@baleri-italia.com **27, 105**

B&B Italia SpA
Strada Provinciale, 3222060 Novedrate (CO , Italy.
T. (+39)031 795 111 F. (+39)031 791 592
E. beb@bebitalia.it **47, 72**

Bellato Italia spa
Via Azzi 36, 31040 Castagnole di Paese - Treviso , Italy.
T. (+39)0422 4438800 F. (+39)0422 443 8555 **66**

Belux AG
Bremgarterstrasse 109, 5610 Wohlen, Switzerland.
T. (+41)56 618 73 73 F. (+41)56 618 73 27
E. belux@belux.ch **89, 123**

Bent Krogh A/S
Gronlandsvej 5, Postboks 520, 8660 Skanderborg, Denmark.
T. (+45)86 52 09 22 F. (+45)86 52 36 98
E. bk@bent-krogh.dk **71**

Bius-Mary Little and Peter Wheeler
120 Battersea Business Design Centre, 103 Lavender Hill
London SW11 5AL, UK.
T. (+44)207 924 7724 F. (+44)207 924 6524 **27**

BMW AG
Knorrstraße 147, 80937 Munich, Germany.
T. (+49)89 3824 3448 F. (+49)89 3824 5412 **222**

Bodum AG
Kantonstrasse 100, 6234 Triengen, Switzerland.
T. (+41)41 935 45 00 F. (+41)41 935 45 80 **156, 200**

Boffi SpA
Via Oberdan 70, 20030 Lentate sul Seveso, Milan, Italy.
T. (+39)362 5341 F. (+39)362 56 50 05
E. boffimarket@boffi.it **213, 214, 215**

Bosch Telecom GmbH
John F. Kennedy Strasse 43–53, 38228 Salzgitter, Germany. **186**

Botium
Bella Center, Center, Blv. 5, 2300 CPH, Denmark.
T. (+45)32 51 69 65 F. (+45)32 51 33 45 **33**

Boum Design
527 East 6th Street 5w, New York, NY 10009, USA.
T. (+1)212 254 1070 F. (+1)212 431 6121 **58, 59**

Böwer GmbH
Mettinger Strasse, 49586 Neuenkirchen, Germany.
T. (+49)5465 9292 0 F. (+49)5464 9292 15 **64**

Box Design AB
Repslagargatan 17b, 11846 Stockholm, Sweden.
T. (+46)46 6 6401212 F. (+46)46 6 6401216 **200**

Britefuture
Via longhi 6, 20137 Milan, Italy.
T./F. (+39)273 80327
E. britefuture@tiscalnet.it **134**

Build
4-2-11 Jingu Mae, Shibuya-Ku, 150 0001 Tokyo, Japan.
T. (+81)81 3 3405 1211 F. (+81)81 3 3401 9798 **55**

Bulthaup GmbH & Co
84153 Aich, Germany.
T. (+49)1802 212534 **217**

Bute, c/o Caro Communications
1st Floor, 49–59 Old Street, London EC1V 9HX, UK.
T. (+44)207 251 9112 F. (+44)171 490 5757
E. pr@carocom.demon.co.uk **171**

Byra Interior Objects
Lessingstrasse 12, 65189 Wiesbaden, Germany.
T. (+49)611 37 32 46 F. (+49)611 37 51 31 **149**

Canon Inc
30–2 Shimaruko 3-chome, 146-8501, Ohta-ku, Japan.
T. (+81)37 58 2111 F. (+81)3 5482 9711
E. richard@cpur.canon.co.jp **181, 193**

Casas M. sl
Polignono Santa Rita, P.O. Box 1.333,
08755 Castellbisbal, Barcelona, Spain.
T. (+34)93772.4600 F. (+34)93772 2130
E. casas@casas.net **54**

Cappellini SpA/Units srl
Via Marconi 35, 22060 Arosio (Como), Italy.
T. (+39)31 75 91 11 F. (+39)31 76 33 22 **38, 39, 40, 41, 82**

Cassina SpA
Via L Bisnelli 1, Meda/Milan, Italy.
T. (+39)362 372 1 F. (+39)362 34 22 46/34 09 59
E. info@cassina.it **72**

Ciatta a Tavola
50010 Badia a Settimo, Firenze, Italy.
T. (+39)55 7310817 F. (–39)55 73310827
E. maciatti@tin.it **212**

Cibic & Partners
Via Varese 18, Ingresso Viale F. Crispi 5
20121 Milan, Italy.
T.(+39)2 657 1122 F. (+39)2 290 601 41
E. cibic@tin.it **150**

ClassiCon GmbH
Perchtinger Strasse 8. 81379 Munich, Germany.
T. (+49)89 7 89 99 96 F. (+49)89 7 80 99 96 **64, 124**

Codice 31
Via le Regina Giovanna 26, 20129 Milan, Italy.
T. (+39)2 29 51 77 22 F. (+39)2 66 98 33 87 **102**

Covo srl
Via Degu Olmetti 3/b, 00060 Formello (Rome), Italy.
T. (+39)06 90400311 F. (+39)06 90409175
E. mail@covo.it **153, 200**

De Padova srl
Corso Venezia 14, 20121 Milan, Italy.
T (+39)2 77 720 1 F. (+39)02 78 40 82 **82, 171**

D4 Industrial Design
Nieuevaart 128, 1018 ZM Amsterdam, The Netherlands.
T. (+31)20 7760018 F. (+31)20 7760019 **145**

Daiko Electronic
Nakamichi 3-15-16, Higashinari-ku, Osaka, Japan 537 - 0025.
E. info@lighting-daiko.co.jp **107**

Design Gallery Milano
Via Manzoni 46, 20121 Milan, Italy.
T. (+39)02 798955 F. (+39)02 784082 **102, 122**

Desso
Molenweg 81, 9349 AC Oss, The Netherlands.
T. (+31)412 667911 F. (+31)412 635 165 **168**

Disegni
Via Gaudenzio Ferrari 5, 20123 Milan, Italy.
T. (+39)02 58114412 F. (+39)02 58114412
E. disegni@disegni.com **83**

dix heures dix
127 Avenue Daumesnil, 75012 Paris, France.
T. (+33)1 43 40 74 60 F. (+33)1 43 40 74 85
E. Dixheuresdix@wanadoo.fr **95**

Driade Spa
Via Padana Inferiore 12A,
29012 Fossadello di Caorso (PC), Italy.
T. (+39)0523 818 660 F. (+39)0523 8922 360 **16, 51, 54, 130, 132, 220**

Domeau & Peres
21 Rue Voltaire, La Garenne-Colombes, France.
T. (+33)1 4760 9386
E. domeau-peres@domeau.peres.fr **45**

Droog Design
Sarphatikade 11, 1017 WV Amsterdam, The Netherlands.
T. (+31)20 62 69 809 F. (+31)20 63 88 828
E. droog@euronet.nl **84, 85, 104**

Dune
50 East Houston Street, New York, NY 10012, USA.
T. (+1)212 925 6171 F. (+1)212 925 2273 **61**

Dumoffice
Tollenstraat 60, 1053 RW Amsterdam, The Netherlands.
T. (+31)020 489 0104 F. (+31)020 489 0104
E. d.umoffice@planet.nl **89**

Eastman Kodak Company
343 State Street, Rochester NY 14650, USA. **181**

Edra SpA
Via Livornese Est 106, 56030 Perignano, Italy.
T. (+39)587 61 66 60 F. (+39)587 61 75 00 **30, 45**

EMECO
805 Elm Avenue, PO Box 233, Hanover, PA 17331, USA.
T. (+1)717 637 595 F. (+1)717 633 6018
E. info@emeco.net **32**

Espaces et Lignes
Rue Ulens 55, 1080 Brussels, Belgium.
T. (+32)2 427 4343 F. (+32)2 427 6100 **16**

Eva Denmark A/S
59 Højnæsvej, Rodovre, 2610, Denmark.
T. (+45)36 73 20 60 F. (+45)36 70 74 11
E. mail@evadenmark.com **131, 201**

David Hockney, Maler, auf Persona. Design: Mario Bellini mit Dieter Thiel. Stühle, Sessel, Tische und Einrichtungs-Systeme von Vitra, D-79576 Weil am Rhein, Telefon 0 76 21/702 17 33, Telefax 0 76 21/702 17 20. CH-Basel-Birsfelden, Telefon 061/377 15 18. A-Wien, Telefon 01/405 75 14. www.vitra.com, info@vitra.com

vitra.

Hersteller

Christopher Farr
212 Westbourne Grove, London W11 2RH, UK.
T. (+44)20 7792 5761 F. (+44)20 7792 5763 **169**

Flos
Via Angelo Faini 2, 25073 Bovezzo (BS), Italy.
T. (+39)0302 4381 F. (+39)0302 711578 **101, 120**

Flou SpA
Via Cadorna 12, 20036 Meda, Italy.
T. (+39)0362 37 31 F. (+39)0362 748801
E. infoflou@flou.it **56**

Fontana Arte
Alzaia Trieste 49, 20094 Corsico, Milan, Italy.
T. (+39)2 45 12 330 **110, 122, 155**

Frederica Furniture AS
Treldevej 183, 7000 Frederica, Denmark.
T. (+45)7592 3344 F. (+45)7592 3876 **57**

Galerie Kreo
11 Louise Weiss, 75013 Paris, France.
T. (+33)53601842 F. (+33)153601758
E. kreogal@club-internet.fr **83, 220**

Garcia Garay Illuminación Diseño
San Antonio 13, Sta Coloma. De Gramenet
08923, Barcelona, Spain.
F. (+34)93 386 23 72 **111, 112**

Gervasoni SpA
33050 Pavia di Udine, Italy.
T. (+39)0432 656611 F. (+39)0432 656612 **20**

Giga
23 Vinohradska, 12000 Prague 2, Czech Republic.
T. (+42)02 22250662 F. (+42)02 2225 4436
E. gigaline@giga.cz **140**

Natanel Gluska
Rengerstrasse 85, 8038 Zürich, Switzerland.
T (+41)1 48 30 366 **21**

Tobias Grau KG GmbH & Co
Siemensstrasse 35b, 25462 Rellingen, Germany.
T. (+49)4101 37 00 F. (+49)4101 370 1000
E. info@tobiasgrau.com **90, 124**

Heller Inc., USA
41 Madison Avenue, New York, NY 10010, USA.
T. (+1)212 685 4204 F. (+1)212 685 4204 **32**

Hewlett Packard Company
10500 Ridgeview Ct., Cupertino, CA 95014, USA.
T. (+1)408 343 5260 F. (+1)408 343 6526 **190**

Horm
Via Crocera di Corva 25, 33082 Azzano Decimo, Italy.
T. (+39)0434 640733 F. (+39)04334 640735 **81**

IGuzzini Illuminazione S.r.l
SS77, km 102, 62019 Recanati, Italy.
T. (+39)071 75881
E. iguzzini@iguzzini.it **117**

IKEA of Sweden
Box 702, Almhult 34381, Smaland, Sweden.
T. (+46)47681012 F. (+46)476 15123 **94**

-ing Design, c/o Todd Bracher
110 Utterby Road, Melverne, NY 11565, USA.
T./F. (+1)516 887 1269 **24**

Interlübke Gebr. Lübke GmbH & Co KG
Ringstrasse 145, 33378 Rheda-Wiedenbrück, Germany.
T. (+49)05242 12 232 F. (+49)05242 12 311 **72**

Iridium
709 Hyundaigolden tel 102
Kwang Jang Dong, Seoul, Korea.
T. (+82)82 2 34376525 F. (+82)82 2 3437 6524 **206**

Dakota Jackson Inc.
42–24 Orchard Street, Fifth Floor, LIC
New York, NY 11101, USA.
T. (+1)718 7886 8600 F. (+1)718 706 7718 **81**

Jam design & communications Ltd
2nd floor, 1 Goodsway, London NW1 1UR, UK.
T. (+44)20 7278 5567 F. (+44)20 7278 3263
E. all@jamdesign.co.uk **212**

Karim Rashid Inc.
357 W 17 Street, New York, NY 10011, USA.
T. (+1)212 929 8657 F. (+1)212 929 0247
E. karim.rashid@mciworld.com **98/99**

Kartell SpA
Via della Industrie 1, 20082 Noviglio (MI), Italy.
T. (+39)2 90 01 21 F. (+39)2 90 53 316 **68**

Komplot Design
Ameger Strandvej 50, 2300 København S, Denmark.
T. (+45)3296 3255 F. (+45)3296 3277
E. komplot@get2net.dk **22**

Kreon NV
Frankrijklei 112, 2000 Antwerpen, Belgium.
T. (+32)2 231 24 22 F. (+32)3 231 88 96
E. mailbox@kreon.be **115**

Lapalma
Via Belladoro 25, 35010 Cadoneghe, Padova, Italy.
T. (+39)049 702788 F. (+39)049 700889
E. info@lapalma.it **28**

Lammhults Möbel AB
PO Box 26, Lammhult 360 30, Sweden.
T. (+46)472 2695 00 F. (+46)472 2605 70
E. info@lammhults.se **33**

lemongras design studio
Thalkirchner Strasse 59, 80337 Munich, Germany.
T. (+49)89 7205 9911 F. (+49)89 7205 9912
E. people@lemongras.it **140**

Leonardo Glas
Industriegebiet Herste, 33014 Bad Driburg, Germany.
T. (+49)5253/86 0 F. (+49)5253/ 86 325 **152**

Lerche
42653 Solingen, Germany.
T. (+49)212 5 97 97 F. (+49)212 59 25 06
E. info@lerche-solingen.de **205**

Leucos SpA
Via Treviso 77, 30037 Scorze (VE), Italy.
T. (+39)041 5859111 F. (+39)041 447598 **98**

Ligne Roset
Serrieres de Briord 01470, Briord, France.
T. (+33)4 74 36 17 00 F. (+33)4 74 36 16 95 **26, 60, 94, 151, 168, 169**

Living Divani
Strada del Cavolto, 22040 Anzano del Parco, Como Italia, Italy.
T. (+39)031 630 954 F. (+39)031 632 590
E. info@livingdivani.it **47**

Loom, Goodbert Reisenthal
Justus-von-Liebig-Strasse, 3, 86899 Landsberg, Germany.
T. (+49)81 91/91 94 260 F. (+49)81 91 94 129
E. info@lloydloom.de **18**

Luceplan Spa.
via E.T Moneta 46, 20161 Milan, Italy.
T. (+39)02 66242 1 F. (+39)02 662 03 400
E. luceplan@luceplan.com **121, 122**

Lucitalia S.p.a
Via Pelizza da Volpedo 50, 20092 Cinisello B. (MI), Italy.
T. (+39)02 612 6651 F. (+39)02 660 0707
E. lucital@tin.it **121**

Lumina Italia srl
Via Casorezzo 63, 20010 Milan, Italy.
T. (+39)02 9037521 F. (+39)02 90376655
E. Market@lumina.it **124**

W. Lusty & Sons Ltd, Lloyd Loom Furniture
Hoo Lane, Chipping Campden, Glos., GL55 6AU, UK.
T. (+44)1386 841333 F. (+44)1386 841322 **19**

Luxo Italiana SpA
1 Via Delle More, 24030 Presezzo (BG), Italy.
T. (+39)035 603511 F. (+39)035 464817
E. office@luxo.it **93**

Maarten Van Severen Meubelen
Couthoflaan 20b, 8972 Proven, Belgium.
T. (+32)9 225 2955 F. (+32)9 233 1142 **80**

Magis srl
Via Magnadola 15, 31045 Motta di Livenza (Treviso), Italy.
T. (+39)42276 87 42/3 F. (+39)422 76 63 95 **223**

Mandarina Duck Plastimoda
13 Via Minghetti, 40057 Cadriano Di Granorola, Italy.
T. (+39)51 764 506 F. (+39)51 602 0508
E. pcstile@mandarinaduck.it **210**

Maplestead Pottery Services, the Warehouse
Sudbury Road, Little Maplestead, Essex CO9 2SE, UK.
T. (+44)01787 477252 **142**

Marset Illuminacion SA
Alfonso XII 429, 08918 Badalona, Spain.
T. (+34)93 4600107 F. (+34)93 4601089 **124**

Martela OYJ, Strombereinte
11380 Helsinki, Finland.
T. (+358)10 37550 F. (+358)10 345 5744 **66**

Massimo Lunardon
Via Mottarello 6, 36060 Molvena (VI), Italy.
T. (+39)0424 708329 F. (+39)0424 708329 **146, 147**

Matsushita Electric Industrial Co Ltd
2-1-61 Shiromi, 540-6214 Chuo-ku, Osaka, Japan.
T. (+81)6 6949 2043 F. (+81)6 6947 5606 **197, 202, 203, 206**

Ingo Maurer GmbH.
Kaiserstrasse 47, 80801 Munich, Germany.
T. (+49)89 381 6060 F. (+49)381 60 620 **96, 97**

Mauser Office GmbH
34513 Waldeck, Germany.
T. (+49)5623 / 581-0 F. (+49)5623 581 208 **63**

Meccano
Domein 4, 1261 JP Blaricum, The Netherlands
T. (+31)355395450 F. (+31)355395456
E. info@meccano.nl **133**

Memphis srl
Via Olivetti 9, 20010 Milan, Italy.
T (+39)2 93 29 06 83 F. (+39)2 93 59 12 02
E. memphis.milano@tiscalinet.it **79, 112**

Metabowerke GmBH & Co.
Metabo-Alee 1, 72622 Nürtingen, Germany.
T. (+49)7022 720 F. (+49)7022 272595
E. metabo@metabo.de **205**

Metalarte SA
Avenida de Barcelona 4, Sant Joan Despi,
Barcelona 08790, Spain.
T. (+34)934 770 069 F. (+34)934 770 086 **118**

Mexx Time
Noalsgade 23, 2300 Copenhagen S, Denmark. **187**

Herman Miller USA
855 East Main Avenue, Zeeland, Michigan, USA.
T. (+1)888 443 4357
E. answers@hermanmiller.com **67**

Mobileffe
Via Ozanam 4, 20031 Cesano Maderno, (MI), Italy.
T. (+39)0362 52941 F. (+39)0362 502212
E. mobileeffe@uli.it **64**

Modular Lighting Instruments
Rumbeeksesteenweg 258, 8800 Roeslare, Belgium.
T. (+32)51 25 27 25 F. (+32)51 25 27 88
E. edouard@supermodular.com **114, 115**

Molteni SpA
Via Rossini 50, 20034 Ginssano, Italy.
T. (+39)0362 851 334 F. (+39)0362 35 51 70 **26, 48**

Monotub Industries
90 Long Acre, London, WC2E 9RZ, UK.
T. (+44)20 7917 1863 F. (+44)20 7917 1883
E. brian.austin@monotub.co.uk **211**

Montina International srl
Via Communale del Rovere 13/15
33048 S. Giovanni al Natisone, Udine, Italy.
T. (+39)0432 75 60 81 F. (+39)0432 75 60 36 **26**

Moormann Möbel GmbH
An der Festhalle 2, 83229 Aschau, Germany.
T. (+49)8052 4001 F. (+49)8052 4393
E. info@moormann.de **60**

Moroso SpA
Via Nazionale 60, Cavalicco do Tavagnacco
33010 Udine, Italy.
T. (+39)432 577 11 F. (+39)432 570 761
E. info@moroso.it **31, 46**

Murano Due
Via delle Industrie 16, 30030 Salzano, Italy.
T. (+39)041 5740292 F. (+39)041 5744070
E. m2export@muranodue.com **90**

NAC Sound srl
Via Boncompagni, 7900187 Rome, Italy.
T. (+39)6 44 55 730 **196**

Nava Design SpA
Martin Lutero 5, 20126 Milan, Italy.
T. (+39)2 25 70 251 F. (+39)2 26 30 05 18 **187, 209**

Nicehouse, the Italian Centre Courtyard
Ingram Street, Glasgow, G1 1DN. UK.
T. (+44)141 553 1377 F. (+44)141 552 5665
E. nicehouse@dial.pipex.com **30**

Not tom dick & harry
Openhartsteeg 1, 1017 BD Amsterdam, the Netherlands.
T. (+31)20 42 230 F. (+31)20 62 09673
E. ntdh@wxs.nl **164**

(Leben Sie Ihren Stil.)

LE STYLE

DE VIE.

SMALA. Design: Pascal Mourgue. Vielfältige Möbelfamilie mit Sofa, Meridienne, Hocker, Tischen, Stühlen und Accessoires. Schaukelleuchte Cloud. Design: Arik Levy © design. Mehr aus der Welt von ligne roset erhalten Sie in unserem kostenlosen Gesamtkatalog mit Händlernachweis. Roset Möbel GmbH, Postfach 12 30, D-79191 Gundelfingen. Internet: www.ligne-roset.de. Hotline: (D) 0180-2244555, (A) 0662-8070170. Aus anderen Ländern bitte per Fax anfordern: +49 (0) 761-581518.

Hersteller

Nuno Corporation
Axis B1F 5-17-1 Roppongi, Minato-ku, Tokyo, 106-0032, Japan.
T. (+81)3 3582 7997 F. (+81)3 3589 3439 **176, 177**

Nya Nordiska Textiles GmbH
An den Ratweisen, 29451 Dannenberg, Germany.
T. (+49)5861 809 43 F. (+49)5861 809 12
E. nya@nya.de **172, 173**

Nucleo Global Design Factory
Via Piossasco 29/b, 10152 Torino, Italy.
T. (+39)011 249 0013 F. (+39)011 247 5066
E. nucleo@nucleo.to **144**

oLuce s.r.l
Via Cavour 52, 20098 San Guiliano Milanese, Milan, Italy.
T. (+39)02 98 49 14 35 F. (+39)02 98 49 07 79
E. info@oluce.com **106**

OXO International
75 Ninth Avenue, 5th Floor, 10011 New York, USA.
T. (+1)212 242 3333 **210, 218**

OZ
Via Romanello da Forli 25, 00176 Rome, Italy.
T./F. (+39)06 272057 **25, 136, 137**

Atelier Satyendra Pakhalé
70 R.J.H Fortuynplein, 1019 WL Amsterdam, The Netherlands.
T. (+31)20 419 72 30 F.(+31)20 419 72 31
E. satyen@euronet.nl **157**

Pallucco Italia SpA
Via Azzi 36, 31040 Castagnole do Paese, Treviso, Italy.
T. (+39)0422 4438800 F. (+39)0422 4438555
E. infopallucco@palluccobellato.it **82, 123**

Philips Electronics BV
24 Emmasingel, Eindhoven, 5611 AZ, The Netherlands.
T. (+31)40 27 59 006 F. (+31)40 27 59 091 **170, 184, 185, 189, 190, 194, 200, 206**

Francesco Pineider SpA
Via del Roseto 54, 50144 Firenze, Italy.
T. (+39)055 62311 F. (+39)055 696 390 **208**

Privatbank IHAG Zürich AG
Bleicherweg 18, 8022 Zurich, Switzerland.
T. (+41)1 205 11 11 F. (+41)1 205 12 85
E. info@pbihag.ch **208**

Radice SNC
Via Kennedy 22, 22060 Figino Serenza, Como, Italy.
T. (+39)031 780146 F. (+39)031 780289
E. info@radice.it **68, 69**

Regent Beleuchtungskörper AG
Dornacherstrasse 390, 4018 Basel, Switzerland.
T. (+41)61 335 54 83 F. (+41)61 335 55 96
E. export.bs@regent.ch **117**

Rhoss SpA
Viale Aquileia 75, 33170 Pordenone, Italy.
T (+39)0434 549111 F. (+39)0434 43575
E. rhoss@rhoss.it **198**

Roncato SpA
Via Della Pioga 3, 35011 Campodarsego (PD), Italy.
T. (+39)049 9200311 F. (+39)049 5555570
E. ufficio.tecnico@vroncato.it **210**

Rosenthal AG
Wittelbacherstrasse 43, 95100 Selb, Germany.
T (+49)9287 72586 F. (+49)9287 72271 **135**

Lorenzo Rubelli SpA
San Marco 3877, 30124 Venice (VE), Italy.
T. (+39)041 521 6411 F. (+39)41 5225557
E. info@rubelli.it **166, 167**

Sawaya & Moroni SpA
Via Andegari 18, 20121 Milan, Italy.
T. (+39)2 86 39 51 F. (+39)2 86.46 48 31 **52**

sdb Industries BV
De Beverspijken 20, 5221 ED Den Bosch, The Netherlands.
T. (+31)736339133 F. (+31)736312422
E. info@sdb-industries.nl **34, 35**

de Sede AG
Oberes Zelgi 2, 5313 Klingnau, Switzerland.
T. (+41)56 2680 226 F. (+41)56 2680 126
E. info@desede.ch **46**

Serafino Zani srl
Via Bosca 24/26, 25066 Lumezzane Gazzolo (BS), Italy.
T. (+39)30 871861 F. (+39)30 89 70 620
E. info@serafinozani.it **143**

Sele 2
Gustav Maurer Strasse 8, 87702 Zollikon, Switzerland.
T. (+41)41 1 396 70 12 F. (+41)411 1 396 70 11
E. sele2@sele2.ch **65**

Sharp Corporation
Corporate Design Centre, 22-22 Nigaike–cho, Abeno-ku
Osaka, 545 8522, Japan.
T. (+81)6 6621 3637 F. (+81)6 6629 1162 **182, 183, 192, 194, 198, 199**

Siemens AG
c/o designafairs
Tölzer Strasse 2c, 81379 Munich, Germany.
T. (+49)89 6368 3604 F. (+49)89 6368 1836
E. info@designafairs.com **186, 191**

André Skrive
Wilhelm Bergsøvej 61, 8201 Aarhus V, Denmark.
T. (+45)40 98 49 55 **23**

Snowcrash
Linnegaten 23, Box 483, 35 06 Vaxjo, Sweden.
T./F. (+46)470 74 24 00
E. info@snowcrash.se **70, 100**

Michael Sodeau
26 Rosebery Avenue, London EC1R 4SX, UK.
T. (+44)20 7833 5020 F. (+44)20 7833 5021
E. michael@msp.uk.com **169**

Sony Corporation
6-7-35 Kitashinagawa, Shinagawa –ku
Tokyo 141-0001, Japan.
T. (+81)3 5445 6780 F. (+81)3 5448 7823 **181, 189**

Sony Television Europe
The Heights, Brooklands, Weybridge, Surrey KT13 0XW, UK.
T (+44)1932 816190 F. (+44)1932 817003 **192, 193**

Spatial Interference
63 Cross Street, London N1 2BB, UK.
T. (+44)20 7704 6003 F. (+44)20 7688 0478 **79**

Spirix Lexon
98 Boulevard Eloise, 95100 Argenteuil, France.
T. (+33)39 47 04 00 F. (+33)39 47 07 59
E. spirix@lexon-design.com **180, 186**

Stile Bertone SpA
Via Roma 1, 10040 Capri (Torino), Italy.
T. (+39)011 9638 322 F. (+39)011 9632 003 **223**

Streitner GmbH
Ipftal 1, 4491 Niederneukirchen, Austria.
T. (+43)07224 7385 0 F. (+43)07224 7404 **77**

Team 7, Natürlich Wohnen GmbH
Postfach 228, 4910 Ried, Austria.
T. (+43)7752 977 169 F. (+43)7752 977 222 **78**

Gebrüder Thonet GmbH
Postfach 1520, Michael Thonet Straße 1
35066 Frankenberg, Germany.
T. (+49)6451 508 0 F. (+49)6451 508 108
E. info@thonet.de **53**

Tronconi srl
Via Bernini 5/7, 20094 Corsico (MI), Italy.
T. (+39)02 45867089 F. (+39)02 4585011
E. tronconi@tronconi.com **109, 119**

Tuttoespresso
23/25 Via Per Caronna, 21040 Origgio (VA), Italy.
T. (+39)02 96730600 F. (+39)02 96731856 **200**

Umbra
2358 Midland Avenue, Scarborough
M1S 1P8, Ontario, Canada.
T. (+1)800 387 5122 F. (+1)416 299 1706 **32**

Val Cucine SpA
Via Malignani 5, 33170 Pordenone, Italy.
T. (+39)434 517911 F. (+39)434 572344 **215**

Venini SpA
Fondamenta Vetrai 50, 30142 Murano Venezia, Italy.
T. (+39)417 39955 F. (+39)04 17 39 369 **144**

Ventura Design, OL Time SA
8064 Volkeswit, Switzerland.
T. (+41)1 908 55 99 F. (+41)1 908 55 22 **187**

Verso Design OY
Mantypaadentie 7 B, 00830 Helsinki, Finland.
T./F. (+358)358 9 755 47 40
E. verso.design@versodesign.fi **174**

V.I.A.
29-35 Avenue Daumesnil, 75012 Paris, France.
T. (+33)1 46 28 11 11 F. (+33)1 46 28 13 13
E. via.ifa@mobilier.com **29**

Vitra (International) AG
Klünenfeldstrasse 22, 127 Birsfelden, Switzerland.
T. (+41)61 377 15 09 F. (+41)61 377 15 10
E. info@vitra.com **29, 33, 62**

VS Vereinigte Spezialmöbelfabriken GmbH & Co.
Hochhäuser Strasse 8, 97941 Tauberbischofsheim, Germany.
T. (+49)9341/880 **37**

Norbert Wangen
Grafinger Strasse 6, 81671 Munich, Germany.
T. (+49)89 49 001 572 F. (+49)89 49 001 573 **216**

Wogg AG
Im Grund 16, 5405 Baden, Dättwil, Switzerland.
T. (+41)56 483 37 00 F. (+41)56 483 37 19 **76**

WMF
Eberhardstrasse 1, 73312 Geislingen, Germany.
T. (+49)7331 258231 F. (+49)7331 258997 **136**

XO
RN 19, Servon, 77170 Paris, France.
T. (+33)1 60 62 60 60 F. (+33)1 60 62 60 62 **151**

Yamaha Corporation
10-1 Nakazawa-cho, Hamamatsu
Shizuoka Prefecture, 430 8650, Japan.
T. (+81)53 460 2883 F. (+81)53 4673 4992 **195**

Zanotta SpA
Via Vittorio Veneto 57, 20054 Nova Milanese (MI), Italy.
T. (+39)362 36 83 30 F. (+39)362 45 10 38
E. zanottaspa@zanotta.it **43, 48, 49**

Zeritalia
Via Dell' Industriale 10,
61022 Bottega do Colbordola (PU), Italy.
T. (+39)0721 49441 F. (+39)0721 49946
E. zeritalia@zeritalia.it **66**

Zeus, c/o Noto srl C
San Gottardo 21/9, Milan 21036, Italy.
T. (+39)2 89 40 11 42 F. (+39)2 89 40 11 98
E. zeusnoto@tini.it **111**

Zumtobel Staff GmbH
Schweizer Strasse 30, Postfach 72, 6851 Dornbirn, Austria.
T. (+43)5572 390 0 F. (+43)5572 20 721
E. info@zumtobelstaff.co.at **125**

SAWAYA & MORONI

moraine - design zaha hadid
SAWAYA & MORONI SPA - 20121 MILANO - VIA MANZONI, 11 - TEL. 02 86395.212/200 - FAX 02 86464831
e-mail: sawaya-moroni@apm.it

Fotonachweis

Riccardo Abbondanca (200 top centre)
Maos Armgaard (187 bottom right)
Toshi Asakawa (55)
Clive Bartlett (153 bottom)
Rien Bazen (133)
Jan Benatsson (200 bottom right)
Joachim Bergamin (79 top)
Fabrizio Bergamo (47 top)
Francesco Bighin (90 top left)
Bitetto-Chimenti (101 left, 102 left, 111 left)
Bius (27 bottom)
BMW GB Ltd (222)
Allessandro Bon (198 top right, bottom right)
Todd Bracher (24 bottom left)
Erik Brahl (22–3)
Brahl Fotografi (57)
Bruno Bruchi (132 top, 148, 154)
Bulthaup (217)
Santi Caleca (112 top right, 143, 153 top left, top right)
Cinzia Camela, Sara de Bernardinis (25 bottom)
Pietro Carrieri (32 bottom)
Giampetro Casadei (36 top left, top centre, top right)
Armen Casnati (83 top left, bottom left)
Scott Chaney (176 top left, bottom)
Corado Maria Crisciani (105)
Geoff Crowther (141)
Karsten Damstadt (131, 201)
Design 3 (186 bottom right)
D. James Dee (175)
Hans Doering (124 top right)
Eastman Kodak Company (181 bottom left)
Claus-Christian Eckhardt (186 top right, centre right)
Rick English (189 bottom centre, 190 top right, bottom right, 210 top left, centre left, middle left, middle centre, borrom left)
EOS (78)
Estudycolor (112 bottom)
Fabrice für Fotografi (200 top left)
Ramak Fazel (79 bottom left, bottom right, 80 bottom left, 120)
D. Feintrenie (29 right)
Frans Feijen (157)
Christophe Fillioux (43 top right, bottom right)
Facchinetti Foriani (92, 93 top left)
Friedrich Forssmann (60 top left)
Lyn Gardiner (98 right, 99)
Hynek Glos (149 top right, bottom right)
Enrico Graglia (168 top left)
© Tobias Grau/Michael Wurzbach (90 right, bottom left, 124 top left, centre left)
Rolando Paolo Guerzoni (210 bottom right)
Walter Gumiero (38 top left, top right, bottom left, bottom right, 39–41)
Hans Hansen (33 bottom, top right)
Patrick Hanssens (114–5)
Hiroki Hayashi (193 top left, top right, bottom left)
Hayo Heye/Stefan Thurmann (63)
Claudy Jongstra (164)
Bernd Kammerer (18 top right, bottom right)
Lasse Keitto (174 top right)
Malcolm Kennard (221 top left, bottom left)
Jutta Kennepohl (64 top right, bottom right)
Tobias Koeppe (205 right)
Iveta Kopicova (80 top left, top right)
Rene Koster (35 bottom left)
Richard Learoyd (171 top left, bottom left)
Bernhard Lehn (94 left)
K.C. Lo (129)
Lars Mardahl (71)
Ramazzotti Marino (49 top right, bottom right, bottom left)
Kenny McCracken (142 top left, top right)
Ian McKinnell (186 bottom left, 211)
Jaime Miró (111 top right, bottom right)

Ricardo Moncada (25 top, 137)
Carlo Monzio/Gianmarco Bassi (110 top right, bottom right)
O. Moritz (180, 186 top left)
Daniel Nicolas (34 top centre, centre right, 35 top, bottom right)
Søren Nielsen (33 top centre, 42 top left, bottom left)
Yoshi Nishima (155)
Manuel Nunes (34 top right)
Oxo International (218 top right)
A. Paderni (46 top right)
Pallucco Italia SpA (123 top left)
Keith Parry (30 bottom left)
Paterno (77)
Antje Peters (221 right)
Bianca Pilet (84–5)
Pink Moon (26 top centre, 45 top left, 72 bottom left)
Carlos Piratininga (103)
Walter Posern (93 top right)
Amiel Pretsch/AS (48 left)
Miguel Ribot (124 bottom left)
Francesco Riva/Smoky Minds (134)
Romano Fotografie (122 top right)
Jonathan Rose (18 bottom left)
Finn Rosted (136 bottom)
Ilan Rubin (18 top left)
Hideto Sasaki (207)
Pietro Savorelli/Studio 33 (212 top right, bottom right)
R. Schmutz (72 bottom centre, bottom right)
Frank Schwarzbach (208)
Jurgen Schwopp (140 bottom right)
Luigi Sciuccati (194 top left, bottom left)
Altin Sezer (162–3)
Filip Slapal (27 top right, 28 top right, bottom right, 74 top left, bottom, 130 bottom right, 142 bottom, 149 left)
Sharp Corporation Advertising Division (182–3, 192 top right, 198 left, 199)
Luciano Soave (82 top right)
David Spero (94 centre right)
David Steets (104 top right)
Thomas Stewart (19 bottom left)
Studio Bitetto-Chimenti (47 bottom left, bottom right, 214, 215 bottom
Studio Bertone SpA (223 bottom)
Studio Feruglio (26 top right, bottom right)
Studio Fuoco (98 left)
Studio Haas (218 top left)
Studio Reflex (44 top left)
Studio Synthesis (28 top left)
Studio Leo Torri (218 bottom left, bottom centre)
Studio Uno (68 top left, centre left, bottom left)
Peter Tahl (16–17)
Kozo Takayama (107)
Luca Tamburlini (26 top left, centre left, bottom left, 36 bottom left, bottom right, 187 bottom left)
Andy Taylor (165)
Alexander Tsoehler (65)
Paolo Ulian (204)
Tom Vack (51, 96–7)
© Patricia von Ah (14–15, 21)
Reinout van den Bergh (34 bottom left, bottom centre, right, top left)
Toine van den Nieuwendijk (14 bottom left)
Camille Vivier (220)
Pelle Wahlgren (33 top left)
Felix Wey (76, 89, 123 top right, bottom right)
Gianluca Widmer (145 top right, bottom right, 93 bottom left)
Jonata Xerra (106)
Miro Zagnoli (88 right, 116, 121 left)
Max Zambelli (104 top left)
David Zanardi (210 bottom middle)